Civil Resistance in Kosovo

Civil Resistance in Kosovo

Howard Clark

Pluto Press
LONDON • STERLING, VIRGINIA

First published 2000 by Pluto Press
345 Archway Road, London N6 5AA
and 22883 Quicksilver Drive,
Sterling, VA 20166–2012, USA

www.plutobooks.com

British Library Cataloguing in Publication Data
A catalogue record for this book is available from
the British Library

Library of Congress Cataloging in Publication Data
Clark, Howard.
  Civil resistance in Kosovo / Howard Clark.
      p. cm.
Includes bibliographical references and index.
  ISBN 0–7453–1574–7
  1. Kosovo (Serbia)—History—1980– 2. Albanians—Yugoslavia—Kosovo
(Serbia)—History. 3. Passive resistance—Yugoslavia—Kosovo (Serbia)
4. Kosovo (Serbia)—History—Civil War, 1998– I. Title.
  DR2086 .C58 2000
  949.71—dc21
                                                           00–008501

ISBN 0 7453 1574 7 hardback
ISBN 0 7453 1569 0 paperback

09   08   07   06   05   04   03   02   01   00
10   9   8   7   6   5   4   3   2   1

Designed and produced for Pluto Press by Chase Production Services
Typeset from disk by Stanford DTP Services, Northampton
Printed in the European Union by TJ International, Padstow

To those who work for peaceful co-existence in Kosovo

'If I were free, I would have much work, I would help those that are suffering more now. Now it is not Albanians that are suffering the most, now it is others, and I would work with all my strength in order to help them. ... I would do anything so that the Serbian community and the Albanians reconcile.'

From the final statement of Flora Brovina, Kosovo Albanian doctor and founder of the League of Albanian Women, to the court in Niš on 9 December 1999. She was sentenced to 12 years in prison.

Contents

MAPS

Acknowledgements

There are some people who do not wish to be thanked by name for the help they have given me in bringing this book to publication, both in Kosovo and in Madrid. Almost every chapter in the book shows my debt to the writings of Shkëlzen Maliqi, who I have managed to visit on most of my trips to Kosovo. I would also like to thank Afërdita Saraçini-Kelmendi, her family and colleagues in the Women's Media Project/Radio 21; Albin Kurti and others in the Students' Union, UPSUP, especially the woman on whose organising they all relied (she and they know who I mean); Burim, Jetish, Vallon and their generation of LDK Youth; Fadil Bajraj and Ylber Hysa were also repeated points of reference; and in the diaspora Isa Zymberi and colleagues at the London Kosova Information Centre.

From other parts of former Yugoslavia, I should acknowledge the encouragement I received to get involved with Kosovo from friends in Ljubljana, especially Marko Hren, and in Belgrade, especially Vuk Stambolović and Staša Zajović, plus the continued help and encouragement of others in Women in Black in Belgrade, especially Indira Kajošević who accompanied the Balkan Peace Team's April 1994 exploratory visit to Kosovo.

This book has grown out of political work that began when I was Coordinator of War Resisters' International and which I have subsequently carried on through the Balkan Peace Team. I have greatly benefited from my involvement with both these bodies. I should thank my friends throughout the WRI network for the opportunities they gave me. The Balkan Peace Team has a policy of 'non-partisanship' and in no way can be associated with the opinions I express in this book. Nevertheless, as a member of its Coordinating Committee and through my frequent contact with volunteers, I am grateful for many insights.

I would like to thank Ken Simons for the maps and the following individuals for other types of help: Alberto L'Abate, Denisa Kostovičová, Martyn Lowe, Mary Motes, Bob Overy, Michael Randle, Mark Salter, Antonia Young and especially Andrew Rigby.

This book would not have been possible without a grant from the Albert Einstein Institution (Cambridge, Mass) to research nonviolent struggle in Kosovo. This institution is devoted to the development of strategic nonviolence, and I specifically thank Bruce Jenkins, Ron McCarthy and Gene Sharp for their support. Two other groups have provided useful opportunities for discussion: the Committee for Conflict Transformation Support (London) and the Nonviolent Action Research Project (Bradford).

Finally, I must thank everyone at Pluto Press for their understanding about the difficulties of writing a book about an episode of nonviolent struggle in a situation that has turned into war.

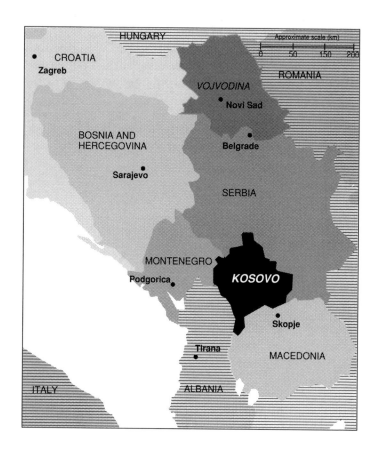

Map 1 Regional Map (Ken Simons)

Map 2 Kosovo – Albanian spellings, except Kosovo Polje (Ken Simons)

Acronyms and Abbreviations

AIM	Alternativna Informativna Mreža (independent journalists' network)
BPT	Balkan Peace Team
BSPK	Independent Union of Trade Unions of Kosova
CDHRF	Council for Defence of Human Rights and Freedoms
CSCE	Conference for Security and Cooperation in Europe
EC	European Community
EU	European Union
FRY	Federal Republic of Yugoslavia
FYROM	Former Yugoslav Republic of Macedonia
ICFY	International Conference on Former Yugoslavia
ICTY	International Criminal Tribunal on Former Yugoslavia
IWPR	Institute for War and Peace Reporting
LDK	Democratic League of Kosova
MTA	Mother Theresa Association
MUP	Serbian Ministry of the Interior police
PPK	Parliamentary Party of Kosova
NATO	North Atlantic Treaty Organisation
SPO	Serbian Renewal Movement
SPS	Socialist Party of Serbia
UÇK	Kosova Liberation Army
Udba	Secret police in the Ranković era
UPSUP	University of Prishtina Students' Union

Brief Chronology

1389	28 June	Battle of Kosovo Polje.
1878		Serbia, backed by Russia, gains independence.
		Albanians form League of Prizren.
1912		Serbia forcibly incorporates Kosovo.
	28 November	Albania declares independence.
1914		Austria-Hungary and Bulgaria occupy Kosovo.
1918		Serbia retakes Kosovo.
1921		Ratification of the Constitution of the Serbs, Croats and Slovenes.
1941		Italy, Germany and Bulgaria occupy Kosovo.
1944	January	Kosovo Partisans 'Bujan declaration' envisages right to self-determination including secession.
	December (until February 1945)	Kosovo 'pacified'.
1948		Stalin expels Yugoslavia from Cominform, break with Hoxha's Albania.
1953		Agreement with Turkey for 're-patriation' of Albanians.
1955		Start of wave of Ranković terror in Kosovo.
1966	July	Fall of Ranković.
1968	November	Demonstrations for Kosovo Republic.
	December	Greater self-administration granted.
1969		Further autonomy.
1974		New constitution.
1980	May	Death of Tito.
1981	March–April	Student demonstrations in Kosovo.
1985	May	Djordje Martinović 'rape with bottle' case.
1986	September	Publication of parts of SANU memorandum.

1987	April	Milošević 'Nobody should dare to beat you' speech.
	September	Aziz Kelmendi opens fire on fellow-recruits.
1988		Milošević proposes constitutional amendments limiting autonomy for Kosovo and Vojvodina.
		'Meetings of Truth' begin.
	November	First Trepça miners' march in defence of autonomy.
1989	February	Miners' strike.
	March	Intellectuals 'isolated'; 'Constitution of the Tanks'.
	June	600th anniversary of Battle of Kosovo Polje.
	September	Segregated education imposed.
	December	Foundation of LDK and CDHRF.
1990	February	Campaign to Reconcile Blood Feuds launched.
	March	'Poisoning' of Kosovo schoolchildren.
		Belgrade adopts Programme for Peace, Liberty, Equality, Democracy and Prosperity for Kosovo.
	April	Dismissal of Albanian police begins.
	June	Petition *For Democracy, Against Violence* presented to the UN with 400,000 signatures.
	July	Kosovo parliamentarians declare republic.
		Assembly of Serbia suspends Kosovo Assembly.
		Shut-out at Radio and TV Prishtina.
	August	Sackings at Medical Faculty.
		Rilindja banned.
		Uniform curriculum announced.
	September	Kosovo parliamentarians pass Kaçanik constitution.
		Assembly of Serbia passes new constitution.
	December	Kosovo Albanians boycott Serbian elections.

1991	January	Secondary schoolteachers' salaries stopped.
	April	Armed incidents in Croatia and Bosnia-Herzegovina.
	June	'Quiet burial of violence' demonstration.
	June–July	War in Slovenia.
		Beginning of war in Croatia.
	September–October	Albanian pupils and students refused access to buildings.
	September	Kosovo parliamentarians declare independence.
		Referendum.
	October	Republic of Kosova forms government-in-exile.
1992	January	Croatia and Serbia observe ceasefire with UN blue helmets in contested regions.
		Parallel schools throughout Kosovo.
	February	Parallel university starts.
	March	Sali Berisha elected president of Albania.
	April	War starts in Bosnia.
	May	Parallel elections in Kosovo.
	June	Police prevent Kosovo parliament convening.
	August	London Conference on former Yugoslavia.
	October	Education demonstrations.
		Panić visits Prishtina – beginning of negotiations on education.
		CSCE Mission to Kosovo, Sandžak and Vojvodina agreed.
	December	Kosovo Albanians boycott federal and Serbian elections.
		US president Bush threatens air strikes against FRY if there is crackdown on Kosovo.
1993	May	Demaçi hunger strike for press freedom.
	June	FRY withdraws from education negotiations.

	July	CSCE Mission mandate not renewed.
1994		Mass arrests of former police and other officials accused of forming alternative ministries of the Interior and Defence.
	March	*Koha* weekly launched.
		LDK/government-in-exile split surfaces.
1995		Trials of former police.
	November	Dayton Peace Accords on Bosnia.
1996	April	First attacks claimed by the UÇK.
	May	Rugova extends parliament mandate.
	September	Education Agreement.
	November	Belgrade pro-democracy demonstrations begin.
		First polio immunisation campaign.
1997	Spring	Riots in Albania after collapse of pyramid schemes bring down Berisha government.
	October	Student demonstrations begin.
	28 November	UÇK 'public showing'.
1998	February	Serbian offensive begins in Drenica.
	October	Ceasefire agreed with OSCE Verifiers.
1999	February	Rambouillet talks.
	24 March	NATO bombings begin.
	12 June	Serbian forces withdraw.

Background on Kosovo

Kosovo is an area of 4,200 square miles (10,908 km^2), bordering Macedonia, Albania, Montenegro and 'inner Serbia'. At the beginning of the twentieth century, it was commonly called 'old Serbia', a reference to its place in the medieval kingdom of Serbia. In 1912, after some 500 years under Ottoman rule, the territory was forcibly incorporated into Serbia and hence, at the end of the First World War, into the Kingdom of the Serbs, Croats and Slovenes, the first Yugoslavia. In the Second World War, the Axis powers briefly re-united most of Kosovo with Albania, but with their defeat, Kosovo reverted to Yugoslavia, again as part of Serbia. In 1974, it attained the status of an autonomous province of Serbia, but with equal representation to Serbia on the federal presidency. By the time its autonomy was annulled in 1989, Kosovo had a population of around 2 million people, perhaps 90 per cent Albanian, and more than half the Albanians under 19 years old. The majority of Albanians were Muslim, although there were about 55,000 Catholics.

Kosovo was important to Yugoslavia economically and militarily. Although the population was predominantly rural, Kosovo's industries – mines (lignite, lead, zinc, gold and silver), chemical factories and electric power plants – made a significant contribution to the Yugoslav economy. Militarily, it was valued for its strategic position as a buffer against any threat from the south and for its facilities as a landing zone.

Despite these economic and military interests, during the Second World War the Communist Party of Yugoslavia treated the future status of Kosovo as an open question, while Kosovo Communists expected some kind of unification with Albania, perhaps in the framework of a Balkan federation. In the event, to make sure of Serbian support for the renewed Yugoslavia, Kosovo was again incorporated into Yugoslavia.

Kosovo's primary importance to Serbia – and hence to Yugoslavia – is symbolic. It is impossible to read much about Kosovo without learning that Serbs regard it as 'the cradle of Serbian civilisation', their 'Jerusalem'. It is the seat of the Serbian Orthodox Church and the site of its most sacred places. It provides the setting for stories from Serbian history and legend – dramatised in epic poems handed down orally through the generations – that nineteenth century Serbian nationalists saw as the very essence of their nation. It has also been the home of a Serb and Montenegrin minority who – while their proportion of the population has not risen above 30 per cent since the Second World War – came to be seen as an historic remnant. The manipulation of these symbols has been at the root of Kosovo's recent misfortunes.

Albanians were later than Serbs in developing a national identity having had strong clan structures and being divided between two ethnic groups, the southern Tosks and nothern (including Kosovo) Ghegs. Because of restrictions on Albanian-language education, they were later in developing a written culture than Serbs, and they had no unifying religion. Nevertheless, Albanians have their own myths. They claim descent from the ancient Illyrians, while Slavs did not arrive in Kosovo until the sixth and seventh centuries AD. The claim to be 'autochthonous' has particular importance because Serbian authorities, regarding this as an Austrian-instilled myth, treat Albanians as immigrants and twice in the twentieth century they have sought to 'repatriate' Albanians to Turkey. Whatever their origins, Albanians and Serbs have coexisted in Kosovo for centuries.

Introduction

31 December 1991: Serbian police surround the village of Prekaz and open fire. Villagers return fire. Three villagers and two police are wounded. The next day a delegation from the coordinating board of the Albanian political parties and the Human Rights Council goes to Prekaz to cool out the situation, documenting the police action but more importantly urging the villagers not to be provoked and to return to their homes.

The police commander in Prishtina declines to give written permission for the delegation to visit Prekaz but promises to radio local units. Nevertheless, on their way to the village, the delegation is stopped repeatedly, and twice are thoroughly searched.

When the delegation finally arrives in Prekaz, they find four houses surrounded by eight police armoured cars and patrol cars. Lined up facing the wall are 26 people, standing in the ice and snow, some with no coats, some with no shoes. For nine hours, from 7 a.m. to 4 p.m., they stand exposed to the sub-zero temperatures. Ten kilometres away from this calculated act of cruelty, groups of villagers are being taken into the police station, beaten up and then released.

The local police commander was not available to meet the delegation.[1]

The secretary of the Council for the Defence of Human Rights and Freedoms (CDHRF), Zenun Çelaj, was reporting to his colleague, Flaka Surroi, who in turn was translating for me. I was on my first visit to Kosovo. This was the latest police action against Albanian villages. 'They would prefer to have Kosova as a permanent military zone, but they need a pretext such as armed resistance from Albanians,' Shkëlzen Maliqi had told me the day before.

Back home an image kept returning to my mind – this line of people, some with bare feet, standing for hours in the ice and snow, waiting to be beaten up. And with that image, the questions 'How long could the Albanian population refuse to be provoked?' and 'What could be done to help this nonviolent struggle succeed?'.

If I write now as a researcher, I came to Kosovo as an activist, and I began my research when the civil resistance was not history but a movement in need of reinvigoration. From 1985 to 1997, as

1

coordinator of War Resisters' International (WRI), I had been active in the process of East-West European 'détente from below'. I had worked closely with the Ljubljana Peace Movement Working Group, from whom I began to learn about Kosovo.

In Kosovo several impulses had converged. The defence of autonomy had grown into a movement for independence from Serbia. The desire for a democratic and pluralistic transition from Communism fused with the aspiration to join 'Western civilisation' and shed anachronistic traditions such as the blood feud and restrictions on women. And now came the determination to avoid a war that everyone seemed convinced Milošević wanted. 'Ours is the largest peace movement in Europe' several Kosovo Albanians claimed at that time: it had become one of their sayings.

That first visit was to see if WRI might play a useful role there, perhaps in relation to the nonviolent struggle. With our limited funds, perhaps this was somewhere we could apply ourselves effectively in helping to prevent a war. My subsequent work in Kosovo has focused on four elements.

The most routine part was my office work for WRI, from time to time providing evidence to support asylum claims from draft-age Kosovo Albanians.

Second has been my role in an international volunteer project, the Balkan Peace Team (BPT). In Kosovo and FRY, this has concentrated on promoting contact between Serbs and Albanians and facilitating dialogue. A project that has learned from its mistakes – and in fact uses them in training new volunteers – the BPT made a couple of false starts in Kosovo in 1994 and 1995 before finding its niche. Scrupulously 'non-partisan' in its stance, BPT has in general tried to be low-profile and discreet.

The third element has been looking at the role of third parties in supporting civil society developments or cross-community initiatives, largely carried out in conjunction with the Committee for Conflict Transformation Support (London) or the Life and Peace Institute (Uppsala). With the arrival of war in Kosovo came also – too late – the demand for ideas about post-war peacebuilding.

The fourth element is that largely reflected in this book, the analysis of the potential for civil resistance in Kosovo, recording its achievements as well as acknowledging its limits, and raising issues for discussion among those interested in strategic nonviolent conflict. My initial hope was that through my research I would engage with people trying to revitalise and give new direction to nonviolent struggle in Kosovo. In 1997 Shkëlzen Maliqi was proposing a seminar for this purpose and back in 1992, on behalf of WRI, I had been in discussions with the Council for the Defence of Human Rights about a possible seminar.

For this book, I have preferred the term 'civil resistance' to 'nonviolent struggle', although they are largely interchangeable. The main reason for this is that, although for several years there was a popular consensus on 'nonviolence', nowadays the term tends to be identified primarily with one faction in Kosovo politics, Ibrahim Rugova and the LDK. A secondary reason is that 'civil resistance' is a more analytical term, one less charged with philosophical and ethical assumptions. The simplest definition of 'civil resistance' is 'resistance by the civilian population', although Jacques Semelin offers interesting nuances by suggesting it is the resistance of 'civil society'.[2]

In Kosovo, the main obstacle to war was the self-restraint of the Albanian population, in particular their belief that civil resistance offered an alternative. Almost every Kosovo Albanian family had direct experience that led them to know what to expect from police violence. Yet, traditionally gun-loving, the Kosovo Albanians – with rare exceptions such as Adem Jashari in Prekaz – had shifted towards a stance of nonviolence. They had launched a movement for self-reform, addressing problems in their own society and making it fit to be independent, a movement typified by the campaign to end blood feuds. While strong patriarchal traditions remained in place, at least women were now gaining the opportunity to play a fuller public role. Kosovo Albanians were engaged in constructing a new identity as Kosovars and as what they considered 'Europeans'. At the time of my first visit, January 1992, Kosovo Albanian 'parallel institutions' were not yet fully in place; however, it was clear that the Albanians recognised that their key strength was social solidarity.

What they lacked was an obvious point of leverage. They had just lost their former allies inside the old Yugoslavia – the Slovenes and Croats. Worse, non-cooperation – normally the most powerful pressure in a nonviolent struggle – already seemed a spent force. Albanians had refused to cooperate with Milošević's measures in many ways, especially the miners and teachers. They had some short-lived success, but then the sackings began – by the thousand. The figure I heard on that first visit was already 85,000 and rising. The remaining forms of non-cooperation – such as boycotting the census and elections – were primarily symbolic. Far from requiring

Albanian cooperation, Milošević – as Gazmend Pula explained – 'would quite happily see Kosova as an industrial park for power plants and other polluting industry, serving Serbia.'

A few months later, the war in Bosnia began, a war more vicious even than that in Croatia. The international support for which the Bosnians had appealed before their reluctant declaration of independence was excruciatingly slow in arriving and then carried with it a plan for partition. In 1994 a Bosnian speaker at a demonstration in London said, 'if we had known it would have turned out like this, we would have preferred to sweat it out under Milošević.' In all the debates about military intervention or arming the Bosnians, I desperately hoped that somehow the Kosovo Albanians would demonstrate that there was another way to defeat the Milošević regime. A form of action less self-destructive, less corrosive in its after-effects.

That was not to be. Pinprick armed actions stung the Serbian security forces into mounting offensives – and with them committing atrocities – and in 1998 war came to Kosovo. One of the early massacres happened at Prekaz. I now know that when I had been asking myself 'How long can people stay nonviolent in the face of this police force?', some people were responding to the incident at the turn of 1991–92 by beginning to plan armed resistance. That police raid had been looking for Adem Jashari and his brother. They escaped – helped by a schoolteacher called Jakup Krasniqi, a former political prisoner active in the LDK in Gllogovc – and went to Switzerland. In 1993, Adem Jashari returned and hosted a meeting at the family home to discuss the formation of a Kosova Liberation Army, UÇK.[3] On 22 January 1998, police attacked the Jashari family compound in Prekaz and were repulsed by UÇK fighters. They returned more like an army on 5 March, shelling that quarter of village until Adem Jashari and more than 40 of his family were dead. (See Chapter 7.)

The narrative followed by visiting journalists tends to be that the passivity of the LDK in the face of relentless Serbian repression bred a mounting frustration that ultimately burst out in armed struggle. My analysis is that in the face of enormous adversity the Kosovo Albanians established a base – an educational system involving every family in Kosovo, a parallel medical system, a system of voluntary taxation – but then failed to build on it. The civil resistance movement lost momentum. Some people offered a more active form of nonviolence – the students, for instance, and various mainly small groups described in Chapter 6 – while a much smaller number prepared to take arms. Later, many joined UÇK in a vain effort at self-defence but, ultimately, the whole Albanian population of Kosovo looked less to UÇK than to NATO.

The phase of the story at the beginning of the year 2000 is even more dispiriting. There is an atmosphere of ethnic intimidation in Kosovo, now with complete separation between the dominant Albanians and Serbs, grouped together in protective enclaves surrounded by international troops. British soldiers talk about 'granny-sitting', protecting old Serb women who stay alone in Prishtina, unable to leave their homes even to shop. This week as I write this Preface, three Serbs who thought they could return were beaten to death in the south of Kosovo. I cannot believe that they would have returned if they were in any way war criminals or had anything on their conscience. The monks of Deçan, the most peace-minded group of Serbs in Kosovo, on the eve of Serbian troop withdrawal in June 1999 went down into the city to rescue Albanians from the last police rampage, taking them back for shelter at the monastery. By the end of the week, the monastery itself had to be put under international protection to save it from what was called Albanian 'revenge'.

Perhaps it is a matter of time – a matter of time before the Kosovo Albanian voices appealing against intimidation organise themselves to stop it, a matter of time before the Albanian community regains its own equilibrium and ability to discriminate between Serbian war criminals and innocent neighbours, a matter of time before more Serbs make a genuine choice for peaceful coexistence and express regret for the past, perhaps too a matter of time before the UN administration of Kosovo gets its act together. Always, there are signs of hope and it is with these that peacebuilders work.

It could all have been so different. Civil resistance generated hope – for pluralism and democracy, for the end of their worst traditions, for a new role for women, for demilitarisation, as well as for an end of Serbian rule.

This book now has several purposes. First, to counter the tendency to write nonviolence out of history. The importance of this episode for the Balkans' history is that it demonstrated alternative possibilities to the calamity in Bosnia, averting war for eight years and giving those intergovernmental bodies that claim responsibility for European security time to develop a preventive peace policy.

Second, the episode is likely to be simplified and 'nonviolence' identified solely with Ibrahim Rugova. There is no denying Rugova's supremacy in Kosovo in the 1990s, but all the initiatives that made nonviolence a viable strategy came from elsewhere. Moreover, it is a misrepresentation to call him a pacifist. Above all, he was pragmatic. He followed a peace policy broadly speaking, but at one stage (see Chapter 3) seems to have favoured Kosovo having its own territorial defence system, and later worked for NATO intervention. Neither was he a Gandhian. The Gandhian strategy of nonviolence is active, emphasises self-reliance and a constructive programme as well as civil resistance, while Gandhi's personal philosophy was based on a dialogue for truth.

Third, the potential and limitations of civil resistance in Kosovo can illuminate international discussion on such strategy. At moments writing the later chapters of this book, I have had to step away from my keyboard shaking my head that what I first experienced as 'tangible hopes' for Kosovo are now mere 'what might have beens'. They warrant setting down for what they might contribute in strategic development in other situations. Kosovo was a place where prior analysis would say 'nonviolence cannot work' – the opponent was a notorious 'ethnic cleanser' and the civil resistance movement had no direct form of leverage through 'non-cooperation'. Yet, I argue, nonviolence achieved a great deal.

Fourth, it is hard to disguise my anger against those whose responsibility should have been to develop preventive strategies in Kosovo. Perhaps this is my guilt that the project in which I was involved was so tiny and marginal. I will not argue what NATO or anybody else should have done in 1999, or analyse media manipulation and quick-fix interventions. Rather I want people in struggle, who refuse to take up arms, to get an adequate and timely response.

1
When a Dam Breaks

The Serbian will to Kosovo is not a rational affair. It does not stem from the economic desire to control and exploit the mineral wealth of the territory, nor from the military wish to have a buffer zone in the south of Serbia. Such goals were both put in peril in the Milošević era as the regime rekindled Serbia's will to Kosovo, manipulating emotions and symbols for the purposes of its own power.

The foundation of Tito's Yugoslavia had been *Bratstvo i Jedinstvo* (Brotherhood and Unity), the pretence that under socialism Yugoslavia was free of ethnic conflict. It had tried to construct a new multi-national identity to supplant the old nationalisms. Towards the end of the 1980s, Yugoslavia was in crisis – economically, especially with its soaring inflation, and ideologically as Titoite Communism lost its hold. Over Kosovo, the most powerful nation (*narod*) – Serbia – found itself confronted by the least integrated and most numerous nationality (*narodnost*) – the Albanians. In this situation, an alternative form of authoritarian populism arose to supplant the previous ruling ideology – nationalism. What began with isolated voices marginal to the mainstream of political life grew into a mass crusade orchestrated by the Party leadership. Its symbolic centre – as in the first era of Serbian nationalism, in the nineteenth century – was Kosovo. The old myth, constructed in the struggle for Serbian independence, was re-activated.

The wars in Yugoslavia should be seen less as an eruption of ancient ethnic enmities than as the consequence of specific policies. History provided plenty of fuel for the conflict, but its engine was to be found in the close-at-hand and immediate. Serbian nationalism exploited the now perceived but previously denied maltreatment of Serbs in parts of Yugoslavia where they were a minority, particularly – but not only – in Kosovo where they were outnumbered and ruled mainly by Albanians. After 1987, while Slobodan Milošević seized the opportunity to manipulate political events, his allies in the media fomented hatred against the Kosovo Albanians and lionised him as the new Serbian hero.

This chapter sets the context for what the Kosovo Albanian civil resistance had to withstand. It analyses the role of the Kosovo issue in propelling the revival of Serbian nationalism, discussing current experiences, recent history and national traditions. Rather than try to disentangle historical truth from legend, I focus on what people believed about what happened, what they were prepared to believe and what certain political projects aimed to make them believe.

I use the image of a dam erected by the League of Communists of Yugoslavia (LCY) and the Titoite ideology that was flawed in its construction, particularly in expecting to control ethnic feeling simply by denying its existence or attributing it to 'counter-revolutionary agitation'. In the late 1980s this 'dam' was swept away. Such a metaphor should not be taken too far. I would not suggest that the torrents of the late 1980s were forces of nature.[1] Rather, this was a case of 'the repressed returns'. Traditions, beliefs, forms of interpretation and experiences that had been submerged came to the surface. Selected 'hidden transcripts'[2] previously confined to the private sphere not only became public but became the dominant script shaping 'reality'.

The awakening of Kosovo Albanian consciousness, specific features of Serbian rule and legislation in Kosovo, and Serbian opposition attitudes will feature in later chapters.

THE DEMOGRAPHIC BATTLEFIELD: 1912–66

The central problem for Serbian policy over Kosovo was that, while it claimed Kosovo as Serbian, too few Serbs wanted to live there. Serbia lost the demographic battle. Already by 1981, Serbs and Montenegrins in Kosovo were outnumbered by Albanians five to one, twice as high as the 1961 ratio and still rising – perhaps to nine to one by 1990. This battle, however, did not begin in the 1960s, but was actually a feature of the history of Serbia and Kosovo, since Serbia's independence in 1878 and its annexation of Kosovo in 1912. Indeed, were it not for the previous 'repatriation' of Albanians to Albania or Turkey and the settling of Serbs and Montenegrins in Kosovo, the proportions would have changed much earlier. Some of this history is worth discussing in detail because of its emotive power and because it illustrates the repertoire of methods to 'deal' with the numerical preponderance of Albanians in Kosovo. The quantity and detail of the footnotes provide further evidence of how fraught certain issues remain.

Whatever the ethnic composition of the territory in 1389, when Kosovo returned to Serbian rule in 1912 it was largely inhabited by Albanians.[3] Indeed, the visiting Englishwoman Edith Durham surmised, 'were it not for the support and instruction that has for long been supplied from without, it is probable the Serb element would have been almost, if not quite, absorbed or suppressed by this time.'[4] Ethnic relations in the territory had worsened after the winter of 1877–78 when Serbian forces had 'ethnically cleansed' southern Serbia, creating a landscape of burnt-out villages while 'by the roadside, in the Gudelica gorge and as far as Vranje and Kumanovo, you could see the abandoned corpses of children, and old men frozen to death.'[5] Those Albanians who arrived in Kosovo – together with Muslim Slavs who left Bosnia rather than live under Christian rule – brought with them increased hostility towards Christians, especially Serbs. So began another migration – of Serbs leaving Kosovo with its poverty, its Ottoman rulers and growing unrest, in order to become citizens of the newly independent Serbia.[6]

Serbia could not consider itself complete without Kosovo and was waiting for the right moment to expel the Ottomans. When it came, in 1912, King Peter called for a Holy War to bring 'freedom, brotherhood and equality' to all the inhabitants of 'Old Serbia' (Kosovo) – Christian and Muslim Slavs, Christian and Muslim Albanians. Such, however, was not the spirit of his forces. Rather they were the avengers of the 500 years of Ottoman occupation, bringing down an unprecedented terror on the population of Kosovo, Muslim and Catholic. The Serbian Social Democrat Dimitrije Tucović witnessed 'barbaric crematoria in which hundreds of women and children were burned alive' and reported that Serbian soldiers, urged on by their clergy, were obsessed with vengeance for the battle of Kosovo Polje. 'The historic task of Serbia', he wrote, was 'a big lie'.[7] Other observers noted that the Conference of Ambassadors in London intended to draw the borders of independent Albania according to ethnic and religious statistics:

> The Serbs have hastened to prepare the statistics for them with machine guns, rifles and bayonets ... Tens of thousands of defenceless people are being massacred, women are being raped,

old people and children strangled, hundreds of villages burnt to the ground, priests slaughtered. And Europe remains silent![8]

Serbian rule in Kosovo was soon interrupted by the First World War, a war claiming the lives of almost 1.3 million Serbs, a third of the population.[9] Recognising Serb heroism and suffering, the victorious Entente allies rewarded Serbia by granting its claim to Kosovo, now incorporated into the Kingdom of the Serbs, Croats and Slovenes. In 1929, this became known as 'Yugoslavia' – the land of the southern Slavs. At the time, two-thirds of the population of Kosovo were Albanian.[10]

Serbia ruthlessly put down the *kaçak* (Albanian guerrilla) revolts and set about reclaiming Kosovo both in terms of population and culture. It initiated an ambitious colonisation programme, offering incentives to Serbs and Montenegrins – especially former soldiers or members of *četnik*[11] bands – to settle. This 'Serbianisation' also involved naming new villages after heroes from epic poems – Obilić, Miloševo, Lazarevo – while Ferizaj (previously known to Slavs as Ferizović) was renamed Uroševac. The colonisation programme was widely deemed a failure. It seems that between 60,000–70,000 Slav colonists arrived in Kosovo[12] – a fraction of the number desired – and many failed to settle.

The other side of Serbianisation was that Albanians were treated as immigrants to be repatriated. They were expected to go 'back' to Turkey or south to Albania or to assimilate themselves. The new state had signed a Treaty for the Protection of Minorities, but – not recognising Albanians as a national minority – it denied them the right to education in their own language. In 1930 three Albanian Catholic priests submitted a Memorandum to the League of Nations examining article by article how Yugoslavia was violating the treaty – policies of 'forced emigration', the seizure of property, the replacement of Albanian municipal officials, dress restrictions, as well as a host of actions against Albanian education. They also complained about Serbian paramilitary groups.[13]

'Encouraged to emigrate' by such means, tens of thousands of Albanians left.[14] However, in 1938 in a desire to accelerate this, Yugoslavia made a deal with Turkey to 'repatriate' 40,000 Albanian families in the next six years. In 1937 a member of the Serbian Academy of Science and Arts (SANU), Vaso Čubrilović, had discussed this in a now-notorious memorandum frankly entitled 'The Expulsion of the Albanians'.[15] What he called 'Western methods', such as colonisation, were too gentle for 'the troubled and bloody Balkans' and had been defeated by 'the fecundity of Albanian women'. The answer was 'mass population transfers'. Čubrilović then went into detail about how to create 'a suitable psychosis ... [to] relocate a whole people'. The methods described by the three Albanian priests (including 'ill-treatment of clergy') should be extended and implemented more systematically. As well as harassment in the guise of health or educational measures or regulating business and property, he advocated arming settlers, secretly assisting *četniks*, and inciting local riots that could be 'bloodily suppressed'. He adds eerily: 'There remains one method Serbia employed with great practical effect after 1878, that is, secretly razing Albanian villages and urban settlements to the ground.'

When such schemes were being openly discussed in Belgrade, it is scarcely surprising that many Kosovo Albanians greeted the Second World War Axis occupation with some relief. In 1941, the bulk of Kosovo was re-united with Albania, under an Italian occupation later taken over by the Germans. The moment the invasion of Kosovo began, Albanians began to seek revenge, primarily against the colonists. Italian and German officials such as Carlos Umiltà and Herman Neubacher were shocked by what they witnessed. 'Slavs and Albanians had burnt down one another's houses, had killed as many as they could, and had stolen livestock goods and tools', reported Umiltà, who arrived in Kosovo at the end of May 1941.[16] Clearly, the Slavs were the main victims. 'From April until autumn the countryside was being burned and looted', wrote one Italian agronomist.[17] The German political officer, Hermann Neubacher, estimated that by April 1944, 40,000 Serbs and Montenegrins had been expelled.[18]

Communists later honoured the heroism of the multi-ethnic liberation struggle waged by the Partisans, drawing a veil over the ethnic bloodletting that took place in several regions of Yugoslavia during the Second World War – and in Kosovo during a bloody 'Pacification' campaign in 1944–45. (See Chapter 2.)

In most of Yugoslavia, the population declined during the Second World War. But not in Kosovo.[19] This revived fears of demographic de-stabilisation. The remedy was seen as a renewed programme of 'Turkification', pressuring families to register as Turkish rather than Albanian and in 1953 re-activating the 1938 Yugoslav-Turkish agreement to 'repatriate' 40,000 families to Turkey. Many Yugoslav Albanians were induced to register as 'Turks'. Probably 100,000

Kosovo Albanians left in this programme.[20] 'Turkification' was accompanied by a systematic programme of police intimidation, mainly on the pretext of searching for weapons. Creating a 'suitable psychosis', as Čubrilović might have said. Police would raid Albanian villages, cordon them off and beat the men.[21] This tactic was to be repeated in the 1990s.

At the federal level, several factors caused Communist distrust of Albanians: the low numbers who had joined the Party, their reluctance to be re-incorporated into Yugoslavia and, in view of the break between Tito and his former protégé, Albanian president Enver Hoxha, their potential as 'fifth-columnists'. However, in Kosovo the experience of Albanians was that this Communist repression was also Serbian – the secret police (Udba) in Kosovo were largely a Serbian force,[22] operating under the Serb Aleksandar Ranković, first Yugoslav Minister of Interior and then Vice-President, and carrying out policies of harassment and terrorisation advocated by Serb nationalists.

AFTER THE FALL OF RANKOVIĆ

The fall of Ranković in July 1966 and the purge of his allies in the provincial structures created fears that Serbs would now themselves be under pressure and without protection. Even in the Ranković era, the Orthodox Church reported 'disturbing levels of emigration' of Serbs from Kosovo. While acknowledging economic reasons, the diocesan reports mainly complained of 'pressure from *Shiptars*' (a derogatory term for Albanians) or Church harassment by the Udba and atheistic Communists.[23]

Many Yugoslavs, especially Kosovo Albanians, welcomed the fall of Ranković. In spring 1967, when Tito made his first visit to Kosovo for 16 years, things had changed so much that police took the precaution of detaining *Serb* extremists. Tito admitted mistakes: 'One cannot talk about equal rights when Serbs are given preference in factories ... and Albanians are rejected although they have the same and better qualifications.'[24] The provincial government now gained more autonomy, introduced secondary schooling in Albanian, accepted Albanian and Turkish alongside Serbo-Croatian as official languages, and began to administer the 'ethnic keys' that were a feature of Yugoslavia at this time.[25] For the first time, the majority of members of the LCY in Kosovo were Albanians.[26]

The period 1968–81 was seen as one of 'rapid Albanisation' of Kosovo, bringing Serbian resentment. In 1968 the LCY Central Committee expelled Dobrica Ćosić as a 'nationalist' for complaining that:

> Serbs and Montenegrins feel threatened, that there is pressure on them to emigrate, that specialists try to leave Kosovo and Metohija, that there is inequality in the courts and lack of respect for law and justice, that there is blackmail in the name of national identity.[27]

Instead of acknowledging the ethnic dimension, the Committee merely replied that many Albanians were also leaving Kosovo because of the weak economy. In 1976, the issue again threatened to surface when a Serbian LCY commission drew up a 'Blue Book' of arguments against autonomy, recommending that control of the judiciary, police and economic policies should revert to Belgrade.[28] This Blue Book itself was not publicly discussed during Tito's lifetime. Yet it was responding to a growing concern that was spread by hearsay.

The backlash was coming. The idea spread that Serbs were leaving Kosovo in large numbers, driven out by Albanian hostility. To Serbs, after the 1981 Kosovo demonstrations demanded the status of a full republic, everything seemed to fit the script that Kosovo Albanians wanted to purify Kosovo and secede. Demanding a republic was just a first step. The legalisation and increasing presence of the flag of Albania in Kosovo confirmed this suspicion.[29]

Serbian demographic analyses focused on the 'exodus' of Serbs. Propaganda figures of 200,000 'expelled' Serbs became common in the early 1980s, later doubling. The 1981 census indicated at least 85,012 Serbs and Montenegrins had left Kosovo since 1961.[30] Put in the context of similar scale migrations of Serbs from Bosnia and Croatia to Serbia, or from rural to urban areas, this might not have seemed too alarming.[31] Except that it was such a high proportion of the Serb population of Kosovo, shifting the ethnic balance dramatically. Kosovo Serbs became more outspoken in demanding the solidarity of their fellows outside Kosovo.

Economic factors contributed to the emigration. Although many in Serbia proper resented that Kosovo absorbed such a high proportion of federal development funds, Kosovo continued to fall further behind the rest of Yugoslavia. The percentage of unemployed in Kosovo rose to 36.3 per cent in 1987, against a Yugoslav average of 14.2 per cent. Statistically, Serbs in Kosovo were still far more likely to have a job than Albanians,[32] but the crucial factor was not statistics but perception. 'Affirmative action' to redress historic injustices was bound to bring allegations of Albanian discrimination against Serbs.[33] However, there was nowhere to discuss such problems openly. Eggert Hardten has observed that 'although "ethnic keys" have played a decisive role in Yugoslav politics, it is hard to find ... even the slightest reference to the system in the Yugoslav literature ... The organisation of ethnic relations on the local level was a taboo theme.'[34]

Towards the end of the 1980s, the Serbian Academy of Sciences and Arts (SANU) – as part of its campaign for the rights of Kosovo Serbs – commissioned a survey of 500 households to identify motives for emigration. Unsurprisingly, the migrants felt that 'a system of discrimination' existed.[35]

> The most crucial element for understanding the level and strength of discrimination was the numerical preponderance of the Albanians ... The critical point for deterioration of these relations was when the share of the non-Albanian population in a municipality or settlement was below 20 to 30 per cent.[36]

To counter the rising Albanophobia, the 'civic opposition' group the Association for a Yugoslav Democratic Initiative (UJDI) set up another commission in 1990. It offered this perspective:

> The core of the Serbian-Albanian relationship has been charac- terised by a pattern of domination – Serb over Albanian or Albanian over Serb – ever since Kosovo was part of the Ottoman empire. Under Tito ... whoever held power at any given time held absolute power, controlling the media, the police, the courts and the labour market. Although this dictatorship was theoretically a 'dictatorship of the proletariat' it was handily used as a thinly disguised dictatorship of the ruling ethnic group. This absolute domination, which Serbs exercised by controlling the Kosovo Communist Party from 1945 to 1966 and Albanians from 1966 to 1988, exacerbated inter-ethnic intolerance.[37]

Criticising talk of a Serbian exodus, the UJDI commission found that 'demographic shifts were not the result of an unusually large emigration of Serbs but of a surprisingly small emigration of Albanians.' Despite Kosovo's overpopulation, underdevelopment and high unemployment, there was 'extremely low Albanian mobility' and most Albanian men who went abroad to work returned to their families in Kosovo.

In managing the crisis of ethnic relations in Kosovo, the LCY faced a choice: work with the provincial leadership and seek to address the issues openly and without suppression; keep the lid on things bureaucratically; or move against the provincial leadership in support of Serb complaints. It opted for the bureaucratic solution, pushing the provincial leadership into a policy of self-administered repression and censorship, while at the federal level seeking to contain the Serbian reaction. This policy served to allow a head of steam to build up that would blow away not only Kosovo's autonomy but also the very federation.

THE RISING SWELL OF NATIONALISM

The founder of the country, Josip Broz-Tito, held the reins of power until his death, controlling the military, the state and ideology. Without him, the collective leadership did not carry conviction. Moreover, he died leaving a failing economy and with Serbs resenting 'Brotherhood and Unity' as a fraud. For them, the 1974 Constitution – in giving two provinces (Kosovo and Vojvodina) equal representation on the federal presidency to the republic itself – epitomised Tito's attitude: 'Weak Serbia, Strong Yugoslavia'.

Serbian nationalism in the years immediately after Tito's death was an opposition movement, dissident even. The Serbian reaction was mobilised around two main targets: the 'anti-Serbian' 1974 constitution and the lack of protection for Serbian minorities in areas dominated by other ethnic groups, especially Kosovo. Inside Kosovo, as the 1980s progressed, any form of bureaucratic insensitivity or corruption was interpreted by Serbs on ethnic lines. In a climate of mutual distrust, as long as the authorities seemed to be trying to hush up the problem of Serbian emigration, the complaints were bound to become more vocal. Increasingly lurid stories came out, especially complaints of crime and rape. By 1987 the idea that Albanians were rapists had taken such a hold that the Serbian criminal code (with effect in Kosovo) was amended in rape cases to take into the account the ethnic origin of the accused.[38] What the statistics show is that Kosovo had the lowest crime rate in Yugoslavia and little inter-ethnic murder or rape.[39] However, in the growing atmosphere of paranoia, rationality cut no ice.

The first mass public demonstration of Serbian reaction had been at the funeral of Aleksandar Ranković in August 1983. In the 17 years since his purge, Ranković had not ventured into public life. Yet his funeral in Belgrade attracted tens of thousands of Serbs, as if to say 'Who can protect us now?'[40] It was one of those moments when, no matter what official ideology maintains, people's feelings make themselves known – a 'hidden transcript' is revealed. At this time, the Party-aligned press still normally stood up for Titoite rectitude, reproaching overt expressions of nationalism. However, as the 1980s progressed, the Belgrade media turned towards nationalist sensationalism and Kosovo was their biggest running story. Rebukes from the media in Croatia and Slovenia mainly served to inflame matters further.

Perhaps the most explosive episode was the 'impalement' of Djordje Martinović. A Kosovo Serb farmer, in May 1985 he managed to crawl to the medical centre in Gjilan with a broken beer bottle in his anus. Horrified, the (predominantly Albanian) local authorities issued a statement calling this a 'pre-conceived barbaric attack'. Three days later, when the story was already news, they reported that he had admitted injuring himself in an act of self-gratification (sitting on a bottle on a stick). A medical examination in Prishtina bore this out. Serbs could not believe this change of story, and sure enough a subsequent medical examination in Belgrade concluded that the injuries could not have been self-inflicted. Indeed, his own version was now that he had been attacked by masked Albanians. Months later, the final investigation ruled that both explanations were possible, neither proven.

For Serbs, this incident became a symbol of how Albanians maltreated Serbs while the provincial authorities 'looked the other way'.[41] It was even debated in the federal parliament, not once but twice. While Albanians saw this as Serbs finding another excuse to incite anti-Albanian feeling, the Serbian press and population believed that Martinović had been 'impaled on a bottle' (recalling Ottoman impalings).

During the 1980s, successive layers of Serbian opinion were mobilised.

The Church

In April 1982, Serbian priests appealed to the Holy Synod that Kosovo Albanians were carrying out a systematically planned policy of 'genocide' against Serbs. In 1984 a book by theologian Atanasije Jevtić complained of the 'the rape of girls and old women in villages and nunneries' and of the emigration of 200,000 Serbs and Montenegrins in the previous 15 years.[42]

Local Serbs

The (Kosovo) Committee of Serbs and Montenegrins began with a petition with just 76 signatures: 'This is our land. If Kosovo and Metohija are not Serbian, then we don't have any land of our own.'[43] By autumn 1985, 2,016 Kosovo Serbs and Montenegrins had signed. In February 1986 there began a series of demonstrations by Kosovo Serbs and Montenegrins in Belgrade.[44]

Intellectuals

Ivan Stambolić, Serbia Party chief in the mid-1980s, claimed that the upsurge of nationalism was being directed by a group of high-level intellectuals in Belgrade. Apart from a growing number of books and articles from a nationalist point of view, there were two main manifestations of this. In January 1986, 216 prominent intellectuals signed a petition arguing that the Albanians' 'first goal is an ethnically pure Kosovo, to be followed by further conquest of Serbian, Macedonian and Montenegrin territories ... The case of Djordje Martinović has become that of the whole Serb nation in Kosovo'.[45] Later that year fragments began to appear of what was even more of an intellectual bombshell: the draft of a memorandum of the Serbian Academy of Sciences and Arts (SANU) in September 1986. SANU was the most prestigious non-party body in Serbia. While this was never officially published, it has widely been taken as the Serb nationalist manifesto.

> In the spring of 1981, open and total war was declared on the Serbian people, which had been carefully prepared for in advance in the various stages of administrative, political and constitutional

reforms ... It is not just that the last remnants of the Serbian nation are leaving their homes at an unabated rate, but according to all evidence, faced with a physical, moral and psychological reign of terror, they seem to be preparing for their final exodus.[46]

The conditions had ripened for a leading Communist politician to change his colours.

MILOŠEVIĆ MOBILISES

Slobodan Milošević did not create the rising tide of nationalism in Serbia, but he did decide to ride it, and to convert it into the force capable of sweeping aside the dams of ideology erected by Tito. The previously suppressed claims of 'blood and soil' thrashed against the very foundation myth of 'Brotherhood and Unity'. Kosovo had been the issue where the first cracks in the dyke were opened and from which the rising flood of Serbian nationalism gained much of its symbolic and emotive force. By 1990, a raging torrent of hatespeak beset the Kosovo Albanians. Writers describing the atmosphere in Serbia towards Kosovo at the time of the break-up of Yugoslavia tend to use words such as 'hysteria', 'fever', 'frenzy', 'delirium', and 'pandemonium'.

Milošević first emerged as the voice of Serbian nationalism in April 1987. Until then, he had been an LCY apparatchik, apparently with few friends and caring little for Kosovo. On 24 April, he was due to address a meeting in the House of Culture in Kosovo Polje when Serb protesters began hurling stones at the (predominantly Albanian) police. Seeing the police respond with batons, Milošević left the building and bellowed to the crowd – and on television, where the scene was repeatedly shown, to the whole Serbian nation – 'No one should dare to beat you!'

This apparently spontaneous event had in fact been stage-managed by Miroslav Šolević, an activist in the (Kosovo) Committee of Serbs and Montenegrins.[47] In June, when Milošević organised a session of the federal LCY on Kosovo, Šolević brought 3,000 Serbs from Kosovo to come and apply pressure. At a time when public demonstrations were still a major event in Yugoslavia, Milošević saw how to use 'the masses'.

In September, a 19-year-old Albanian conscript Aziz Kelmendi went berserk in Paraćin, killing four of his fellow soldiers before committing suicide. 'Kelmendi shot at Yugoslavia', blared the Belgrade dailies, *Politika* and *Borba*. The next night shops were damaged all over Serbia. A media orgy ensued, even the straightlaced *Politika* suggesting that today's Albanian graffiti-writers were tomorrow's mass murderers.[48] This created just the climate Milošević needed to remove his main rivals and gain complete control of the LCY in Serbia.

1988 saw the beginning of Milošević's 'anti-bureaucratic revolution'. His campaign machine organised mass rallies throughout Serbia and Montenegro, called 'Meetings of the Truth' and 'Solidarity with the Serbs and Montenegrins from Kosovo'. Milošević's aides set up a transport company to bus in demonstrators, especially Serbs from Kosovo; they paid unemployed people to protest; and they prevailed on state enterprises to send their workers. Most of the slogans were against Kosovo Albanians, with frequent threats of 'Let's go to Kosovo'. If the demonstrations had a 'rentamob' core, as well as intimidating non-Serbs, they were a powerful weapon in winning the internal fight inside the Serbian LCY. Their effect was contagious, spreading a promise among Serbs that change was coming. Among football fans in Serbia and Montenegro at this time, 'ethnic identity became the dominant theme' and fans increasingly found patriotic motives for their aggression.[49]

The climax was the 'Meeting of Meetings' in Belgrade in November 1988. Party press reported that a million people (add salt and divide by ten) turned up to demonstrate in favour of sacking the Kosovo provincial party leaders and changing the constitution. 'The people are happening' was how the Milošević organisation projected this, anticipating the 'people power' revolts elsewhere in Eastern Europe late in 1989.

The message was clear. The Kosovo Albanians were not the only enemies, but they were the No. 1 Enemy. Dirty, primitive and nasty, they were embarked on a campaign to make Kosovo ethnically pure, by driving out Serbs and Montenegrins by a variety of criminal means, and by maintaining their own birth rate, the highest in Europe.

Albanians were rapists. One Serbian psychologist claimed (not in the gutter press but in a philosophy journal) that 'Albanians rape every day and everywhere: in the streets, in the fields, in buses, hospitals, factories.' There were poems, paintings and even one sculpture about Albanian men raping Serbian women.[50] *They were baby-killers*. It is 'a psychosis that the whole Serbian nation seems to share', wrote Michel Roux, that Albanian medical staff were killing Serbian babies.[51] *And they were conspirators*. As one Albanian commentator has put it, 'all ongoing or planned activities of Albanians – be it in education, culture, science, economy or sports – are [seen as] concealed forms of hostility towards the interests of Yugoslavia and Serbia, which need to be uncovered.'[52]

In analysing the resurgence of Serbian nationalism, Renata Salecl notes how 'Serbian authoritarian populism has produced an entire mythology about the struggle against internal and external enemies.' She then goes on to point out (using a concept from Jacques Lacan) that, as well as defining itself against 'the Other', the nation needs 'the Real, that "something more" which designates the symbolic community.'[53] For this 'something more', the 1980s Serbian nationalists turned to the same source as the nation-builders a century earlier – the legend of Kosovo.

LAZAR'S CURSE: 'WHOEVER DOES NOT FIGHT AT KOSOVO'

Visiting journalists often write about the enduring power of the myth of Kosovo. In fact, its power waxes and wanes according to circumstances. It lies dormant – as it did throughout the Tito years – or it is re-activated when it suits somebody's political purposes. For Serbs, the battle of 1389 marks the beginning of five centuries of Ottoman occupation and oppression, with the willing collusion – they say – of Albanians. Some 300 years later, the story goes, Serbs again rose in alliance with invading Austro-Hungarian troops. When the Austro-Hungarians were repulsed by Ottoman forces in 1690, with them went thousands of Serbian families, moving north to Belgrade and beyond to Vojvodina. This was the Great Migration. Their cherished dream was to return and liberate Kosovo.

All this was captured and embellished in epic poems handed down in the oral tradition from generation to generation. Many of these were put into writing by one of the fathers of the nation – Vuk Karadžić. The day of the battle, Vidovdan (St Vitus' Day), was elevated into the Serbian national day. The Serb leader Tsar Lazar's choice – surrender and retain his 'earthly kingdom' as a Turkish vassal, or fight a battle he could only lose and inherit a 'heavenly kingdom ' – became known as 'the Kosovo covenant', a model for Serbs to follow. Stories of the past build today's nation: the historical record is less important than what the legend offers. What does it matter if there were battles more decisive than the battle of 1389? Or if the evidence indicates that Albanian Catholics were more active allies of the Austro-Hungarians in 1689 than were the Serbs? What matters is what is imprinted on the Serbian collective memory.

The nineteenth century Serbian nationalists were intent, like other Balkan nationalists, on creating an ethnic state based on one dominant nationality. Their ideas have disturbing overtones for the late twentieth century. The doctrine of *Načertanije* formulated by Ilija Garašanin (1812–74) shaped Serbian foreign policy: its basis 'is not to restrict [Serbia] to its present borders but to seek to embrace all the surrounding Serbian peoples' – in short, a Greater Serbia.[54]

According to Tim Judah, Bishop Njegoš's poem *The Mountain Wreath* (1847) demonstrates how in Serbian consciousness 'ideas of national liberation became inextricably intertwined with the act of killing your neighbour and burning his village.'[55] The soldier reports to the Metropolitian:

> Though broad enough Cetinje's Plain,
> No single seeing eye, no tongue of Turk,
> Escap'd to tell his tale another day
> We put them all unto the sword.
> All those who would not be baptiz'd …
> We put to fire the Turkish houses,
> That there might be nor stick nor trace
> Of these true servants of the Devil …
> Of all their mosques both great and small
> We left but one accursed heap,
> For passing folk to cast their glance of scorn.

The Metropolitan responds to this mass murder with joy.

The geographer Jovan Cvijić put forward the concept of 'Dinaric man', born in the shadow of the Dinaric Mountains. Consumed with a burning desire to avenge Kosovo …

> [he] knows not only the names of the heroes of Kosovo, but their qualities and faults; he is from regions where he can all but feel their wounds. To kill lots of Turks is for him not only a way of avenging his ancestors but of assuaging their pain which he shares.[56]

In 1889, the quincentenary of the battle of Kosovo had been a celebration of Serbia's recent emancipation. One hundred years later, the six hundredth anniversary provided the perfect opportunity to make the symbolic link with the heroes of the past. A year before that anniversary, what were said to be the bones of Tsar Lazar were put on public view for the first time. Taken from Belgrade, they were for the next year paraded around monasteries and graveyards throughout Yugoslavia – to many places claimed as Serb lands in the coming wars – in time to be restored to Kosovo for the big day.

In the course of the tour of Tsar Lazar's bones, the Yugoslav dinar fell to an eighth of its value.[57] Nevertheless, many Serbs felt that their nation was finally coming into its own. The Sunday before the anniversary, the Saint Sava Cathedral in Belgrade – honouring the founder of the 'autocephalous' Serbian Orthodox Church – was finally opened, some 55 years after the laying of its foundation stone. And then on Wednesday, 28 June, came Vidovdan. Not only the anniversary of the battle of Kosovo, this was the day in Sarajevo in 1914 when Serb nationalist Gavrilo Princip shot Archduke Ferdinand and the day of the first Yugoslav constitution in 1921. In 1989, the day belonged to Milošević. The new Serbian hero had already restored Kosovo to Serbia by annulling its autonomy, and in May had formally become Serbian President. A million Serbs gathered at the battle site, which 'was turned into an infinite expanse of Serbia's imagined glory, dominated by one image over all others – Slobodan Milošević.'[58]

Although the organising committee apparently 'went to some lengths to point out that the Battle ... involved an alliance of Serbs, Albanians, Bulgarians, Croats and Hungarians ... the overall tone of the celebrations was more narrowly nationalistic and these groups were virtually excluded,' reported Radio Free Europe. If Milošević's speech was mild by his standards, it 'will undoubtedly reinforce those feelings of both admiration and fear of the 47-year-old lawyer and banker turned politician.'[59]

'Serbs in their history have never conquered or exploited others', claimed Milošević with that propensity for speaking as if Serbs are always the victim, never the culprit.

> If we lost the Battle it was not only due to Turkish military supremacy but also to the tragic discord at the top of the Serbian leadership. This discord has followed the Serbian people throughout their history, including both World Wars and later in

Socialist Yugoslavia when the Serbian leadership remained divided and prone to compromises at the expense of the people. The moment has come when, standing on the fields of Kosovo, we can say openly and clearly: No longer … Today, six centuries later, we are again fighting a battle and facing battles. They are not armed battles, although such things cannot yet be excluded.[60]

There was no need to remind anyone present of the inscription on the monument at the battlefield, Tsar Lazar's curse:

Of Serbians by nation and by birth,
And by their blood and by their ancestry,
Whoever does not fight at Kosovo,
May he have no dear children born to him,
May neither boy nor girl be born to him!
May nothing bear fruit that his hand sows,
Neither the white wheat, nor the red wine!
His blight rot all his brood while it endures![61]

2
The Albanians in Kosovo

'What's the origin of these high walls surrounding the houses?' asked someone recently driving through rural Kosovo. 'They didn't want the Turks to see their women', replied the modern young Albanian woman. The walls around family compounds provide a symbol of impenetrability for the outsider, and reinforce the idea of patriarchal clannishness. Indeed, they are known as *havale*, the word also used for the seclusion of women and the veil.

This chapter follows the Kosovo Albanian experience of occupation since Ottoman times. It introduces their previous experience of resistance – armed, political and cultural – as well as some of their durable traditions, and the tension between conservative and modernising impulses. It concludes with the on-off process of 'national awakening' and modernisation since the Second World War and the widespread police repression in the period after 1981.

THE OTTOMAN EMPIRE

Throughout the Ottoman Empire, Albanians gained a reputation as travelling traders, as architects and builders, as soldiers and as administrators. Both because of the variety of relationships with the Empire and because of their strong clan loyalties, Albanians were later than their Slav neighbours in developing a national movement and it was not until 1912 that the Kosovo Albanians finally united to gain a short-lived autonomy.

In Kosovo, Albanians found Ottoman rule less oppressive than their previous incorporation into the medieval kingdom of Serbia. Serbs had sought to impose Orthodoxy on the predominantly Catholic population in much the same manner as other Christian rulers in the Middle Ages – with the death penalty or confiscation of property for those who refused to convert. In contrast, for the early Ottoman Empire the primary distinction was not religious –

Islam spread only gradually – but was between those who fought wars and those who paid for them. The Empire had two main categories of soldiers: those sent by local leaders in return for rank and favour; and sons 'collected' from families, taken to Turkey for training and then given a salary to serve the empire, either as soldiers or as administrators. If such conscription was oppressive, it could also be a source of privilege and promotion. From the fifteenth to the twentieth century, 42 Albanians (and some Serbs) rose to become Grand Viziers, including some from Kosovo.[1] From such heights down to local landowners, there were Albanians profiting from cooperation with the Ottomans.

There was also Albanian resistance to Ottoman rule, beginning with those who fought alongside Tsar Lazar at the battle of Kosovo, and continuing with the legendary Albanian hero Gjergj Kastrioti Skenderbeg. His 25-year revolt (from 1443 until his death in 1468) delayed the subjugation of Albania, and his red flag with a black double-headed eagle has remained the symbol of Albanian national liberation. Albanians continued to take part in conspiracies or military campaigns against the Empire – one estimate is 54 uprisings[2] – and there were frequent local revolts against new taxes, conscription, or attempts to disarm the local population (tradition-ally, Albanians prize highly the right to bear arms). Some would also interpret banditry as a form of defiance of all central power. However, there was no concerted movement of Albanians until the end of the nineteenth century.

Both the first Albanian national body, the League of Prizren (founded 1878), and its successor, the League of Peja (1899) tried to bring together metropolitan intellectuals with predominantly Muslim clan chiefs. While the educated elite wanted to integrate Albanian lands and introduce Albanian-language schooling, traditional landowners mainly wanted to protect their privileges and way of life from the expansionist designs of Bulgaria, Greece, Montenegro and Serbia. The Porte (Ottoman government) crushed the League of Prizren militarily in 1881; the League of Peja crisis was defused with concessions, including removing the governor of Kosovo.

The closing years of Ottoman rule (the first decade of the twentieth century) were a time of intrigue and treachery, when alliances shifted and when the hostility between Christians and Muslims in Kosovo reached a new intensity. The final Albanian revolt against the Ottoman Empire began in May 1912 spreading throughout Kosovo and much of Albania. By August the Porte was willing to concede the principal demands: autonomy for Albanian lands within the Empire, plus Albanian schools and the retention of Albanian 'religious and national laws' – a mixture of allowing the modern while protecting the traditional. This, however, was not to be.

Seeing the Empire's weakness, Serbia and Montenegro together with Bulgaria and Greece prepared finally to drive out the Ottomans. In October they declared war – the First Balkan War. In Kosovo, the Serbs quickly vanquished the Ottoman forces, but bands of Albanian rebels – *kaçaks* – continued to resist. As well as seeking control of Kosovo, Serbia aimed to gain access to the sea by taking the port of Durrës, ideally partitioning what became Albania between itself and Greece. Albanians responded by declaring their own state – at the Congress of Vlora, 28 November 1912, a date still celebrated by Albanians – and Austria-Hungary threatened military intervention if Serbian expansion proceeded. In order to prevent a wider war, the Conference of Ambassadors convened in London at the end of December 1912.

Albanians did not want 'a truncated state'. Their delegation in London included Albanians from Kosovo, Macedonia and Montenegro. However, when Albania was formally recognised, in the Treaty of London in May 1913, a decision on its frontiers was postponed. In the months that followed, Serbian forces continued to carry out atrocities in a systematic plan to reduce the Albanian presence in Kosovo (see Chapter 1). The frontiers finally agreed left more than half the Albanians outside their 'homeland', victims of a Great Power deal in the interests of European stability. This did not just fracture their 'imagined community', their inchoate sense of nationhood, but also had direct personal repercussions on many rural Albanians, cutting them off from traditional markets such as Peja, Prizren (both in Serbia) or Debar (Macedonia). They could be flogged or shot if they were caught trying to smuggle goods across the border.

THE FIRST WORLD WAR AND THE FIRST YUGOSLAVIA

During the First World War Kosovo Albanians fought at various times both alongside and against the Serbs, but ended once more under Serbia and again facing Serbian reprisals.

The leaders of the 1912 revolt and those Albanians displaced in the Serbian conquest saw the opportunity to free themselves from Serbian tyranny and therefore cooperated with the Austro-Hungarian war effort. At the same time, however, many Albanians enlisted in the Serbian army (they were not liable for conscription).[3] When Bulgarian forces entered Kosovo in autumn 1915, the entire Serbian army was forced into the Great Retreat (through Albania to the sea and Corfu). Not surprisingly hundreds of Albanian recruits in the Serbian army deserted and changed sides. Although Serbs still tend to blame Albanians for the atrocities committed during this period, it was above all the Bulgarians who followed the familiar and horrific pattern of Balkan wars, while the Austrians used the new technology of the epoch and bombed columns of Serbian civilian refugees.[4] If Albanians were reportedly reluctant to give Serbs food, Edith Durham commented that it was to their credit that 'they spared the lives of retreating Serbs who had previously [in 1912–13] shown them no mercy.'[5]

Austria occupied the north of Kosovo and Bulgaria the south. The harshness of Bulgarian rule soon prompted Albanian revolts, but there was also some resistance in the Austrian zone – sometimes even in cooperation with Serb *četniks*. As the tide of war changed and the Bulgarians and Austrians withdrew, Serbian forces re-entered, declared martial law and began meting out vengeance. In January and February 1919, Serbian troops were again burning down homes and massacring Albanians.

The Albanian resistance is known as 'the *Kaçak* movement'.[6] Its most famous military leaders were Azem and Shota Bejta,[7] while its political head was the Kosova Committee – the 'Committee for the National Defence of Kosova' – set up inside Albania by leaders of the 1912 revolt. The Committee existed to support rebellion inside Kosovo, and to lobby internationally for Kosovo's liberation and the re-unification of Albanian lands. It called for a general revolt to begin in May 1919, and at the same time drew up a general set of rules that counsel a self-restraint foreshadowing the 1990s:

1. No rebel will dare to harm the local Serbs, but only those who stand with weapons in their hands against the will of the Albanians.
2. No rebel will dare to burn down a house or destroy a church.

Belgrade, in response, brought in *četniks*, distributed arms to Serbs in Kosovo, imposed new collective punishments and took extended families hostage. In an abortive meeting with Serbs in autumn 1919, Azem Bejta made eight demands which again echo in the 1990s: recognise Kosovo's right to self-government, stop killing Albanians, stop taking their land, stop the colonisation programme, stop army actions on the pretext of 'disarmament', open Albanian schools, make Albanian an official language and stop interning the families of rebels.

In spring 1921, the authorities interned the women and children of suspected *kaçaks* in camps in central Serbia. It seemed a calculated provocation, as some of the women were wives of clan chiefs exiled in Albania who had sent messages urging *kaçaks* to restrain themselves. Predictably, resistance intensified – and, with it, repression. In July 1921 the Kosova Committee submitted a 72-page document to the League of Nations, describing Serbian atrocities and identifying victims. Since 1918, it claimed, Serbian forces had killed 12,371 people, imprisoned 22,110 and burnt down roughly 6,000 houses. Finally, the revolt was crushed with the aid of Albanian Minister of the Interior Ahmet Zogolli, later King Zog. Azem Bejta was killed in July 1924. Shota Bejta fought on until she was mortally wounded in July 1927, almost the last active *kaçak* leader. Malcolm's assessment is:

> In the final analysis, the *kaçaks* achieved just two things. First, they made a strong symbolic demonstration of the fact that many Kosovo Albanians did not accept the legitimacy of Serbian or Yugoslav rule. And secondly, they did in fact seriously obstruct the colonization programme, to the point where many would-be settlers were reluctant to go to Kosovo, and many who went returned home.

Parliamentary politics proved no more effective than other means in improving the situation of Kosovo Albanians. Although Yugoslav Albanians had the right to vote, only 20 per cent of them registered and just over half of those voted in the 1920 Assembly elections. Out of 18 Kosovo deputies, eight were Albanians, three from Xhemijet – the Islamic Association for the Defence of Justice. After first splitting on the question of allying with Muslims from other parts of Yugoslavia, Xhemijet then more or less dissolved in the face of the imprisonment or assassination of its leaders and intimidation during election campaigns.[8]

'Not a single Albanian organisation survived [the inter-war] period of Serbian repression to form the basis of a movement', Maliqi has commented. 'But the Albanian population remained strongly anti-Serb.'[9]

THE SECOND WORLD WAR

The Second World War again seemed to offer Kosovo Albanians a chance to end Serbian rule. In 1941, the Axis occupation unified Albanians in most of Kosovo, Western Macedonia and Albania. Resistance to occupation was much stronger in Albania than in Kosovo where, in the area under Italian jurisdiction, Albanians became citizens of Albania. For the first time Albanian became the language for local administration and education, and – a Communist intelligence report in 1942 estimated – there were between 4,000 and 5,000 Kosovo Albanians in 'quisling formations'.[10]

The major obstacle to the growth of a resistance movement in Kosovo was the prevalent anti-Serb feeling. Indeed, as we saw Chapter 1, both Italians and Germans were alarmed by the Kosovo Albanian campaign against Serbian settlers. By July 1941, all but two of the colony villages had been abandoned – the remaining two followed in October. Vickers comments that the Albanians were discriminate: 'Remarkably, it was only ... settlers who were attacked. Original Serbian communities ... were generally treated by most Albanians as traditional neighbours.'[11] However, a second, less discriminate wave of expulsions followed the founding of the Second League of Prizren.

The Second League was the creation of the Balli Kombëtar (BK – National Front). The BK began as a resistance movement against the Italian occupation of Albania, but in 1943 after talks broke down on cooperation with the Communist-led National Liberation Movement of Albania, their rivalry developed into open warfare, Communists increasingly interpreting 'anti-fascism' as fighting the BK. In response, the BK became openly collaborationist – its activity in Kosovo was directed against Serbs with the goal of the Second League being to maintain the unification of Kosovo with Albania.

At first, the Yugoslav Partisans, who had good relations with the Communists of Albania, found few Kosovo Albanians willing to join their Slav-dominated movement.[12] Activists such as Fadil Hoxha tried to build cells, but ultimately it was only by making 'self-determination' more central to their agenda that Partisans could enlist significant support. When a National Liberation Committee in Kosovo was set up at Bujan in January 1944, its closing declaration acknowledged the Albanian yearning for unification. It recommended Yugoslav Albanians to join in a common struggle against the Nazis so that 'all peoples, including the Albanian people, will find it possible to decide their own fate by exercising the right to self-determination, which includes the right to secession.'[13] Although the Bujan declaration was never adopted at a Yugoslav level, Kosovo Albanians took it as a promise of self-determination. More began to join the Partisans towards the end of the war.

German withdrawal from Kosovo began in September 1944 and was completed in November. In unison with the arrival of the Yugoslav People's Liberation Army, two brigades of their Albanian allies crossed into Kosovo 'in order to promote trust', in reality securing a Communist post-war victory. In December 1944 a general insurrection of Kosovo Albanians began, uniting the BK with some Albanian Partisan bands. What prompted Partisans to participate was their sense of betrayal at Tito's rejection of Bujan and the beginning of a Yugoslav military operation to 'pacify' Kosovo. The precise trigger, however, is unclear. Perhaps it was the Yugoslav military decision on 13 December to forbid the display of the Albanian flag, the Skenderbeg eagle.[14] Perhaps it was the refusal of Partisans from Drenica to go 350km north in the pursuit of retreating German forces, leaving their families defenceless. Perhaps it was that Yugoslav officers opened fire on a commission of (Kosovo Albanian) Partisans who returned to headquarters in Podujeva verifying the report that 250 Albanian men from Skenderaj had been killed, tied together in groups of six and dumped in the Klina river.[15]

The Yugoslav authorities declared martial law and with the 'fraternal assistance' of Albania's two divisions substantially quelled the insurrection. Official accounts spoke of 'a final attempt to raise a counter-revolutionary rebellion by remnants of the Ballists [BK] and other pro-fascist forces and a number of Albanians who had deserted from the brigades of the People's Liberation Army and become outlaws.' Vickers comments:

> What was really happening was a repetition of the hideous massacres that had occurred between Serbs and Albanians after

the First World War. Perhaps the worst atrocity occurred in Tivar in Montenegro, where 1,670 Albanians were herded into a tunnel, which was then sealed off so that all were asphyxiated.[16]

There seems to be no reliable figure for how many Kosovo Albanians lives were claimed in this 'pacification' programme.[17] Its history was not written in Tito's Yugoslavia. Instead the official narrative celebrated the contribution of Albanians to the Partisan struggle, naming schools after them and even at times inventing a personal history for certain 'heroes' who were not actually Partisans.[18] Yet in the close-knit society of Kosovo Albanians, this remained as a 'hidden transcript', each village and each family learning its own history.

A RESISTANT CULTURE

More significant for this study than Kosovo's armed revolts is the durability of their own traditions, something that in itself can be seen as a form of resistance. There are strong pressures to conform in Albanian society, each person feeling observed by their social circle (*rreth*), usually preferring to wait until it reaches consensus to change a norm rather than acting individually to breach it.[19]

Religion

Kosovo Albanians, including Muslim leaders, object to interpretations of the conflict emphasising religion. A traditional saying is 'Where the sword is, there lies religion', while a slogan of the nineteenth century League of Prizren was 'the faith of the Albanian is Albanianism'. Skenderbeg himself in the fifteenth century had been born an Orthodox, raised as a Muslim (at the Ottoman court) and returned to Kosovo as a Catholic.[20]

Under the Ottoman Empire, although conversion from Christianity was no shame, Islam spread relatively slowly. Mass conversions of Albanians occurred mainly in the seventeenth century, especially because of discriminatory tax legislation after 1690. Islam adapted to local traditions. For instance, in rural areas, Shariat law took account of the existing customary code. Although conversion to the official Sunni creed may have been a source of privilege, a more mystical unofficial Islam spread through Sufi dervish missionaries. Several Sufi orders existed in Kosovo, setting up lodges in towns and forming close connections with craft guilds. Norris suggests that 'since Islam in Kosovo was "sufi-conditioned" ... it displays certain characteristics and offers survival strategies more akin to those known in the Caucasus and Central Asia (i.e. "parallel Islam").'[21]

Catholicism did not die out, although the Catholic Church was usually in a worse position than the Orthodox (partly because of the Catholic allegiance to an earthly power, the Vatican). The Ottomans did not permit teaching in Albanian, but Catholics began to promote Albanian education, Jesuits setting up an 'Illyrian College' in Italy in 1574. There was also a phenomenon of crypto-Catholicism, families who publicly adopted Islam but received the Catholic sacraments in private. In some areas, women might remain Catholic while the men of their family formally adopted Islam.

The Kanun

The foundation of a social order for the clans in the rural areas of Northern Albania and Kosovo were codes of customary law, *kanuni*, transmitted orally. Even under the Ottomans, these held sway especially in relatively inaccessible villages. The most famous was the *Kanun of Lekë Dukagjini*, named after a comrade-in-arms of Skenderbeg.

> The highlanders who governed themselves by the *Kanun* for at least 500 years considered themselves in a perpetual state of war with the occupying power ... The *Kanun* of Lekë Dukagjini itself was an expression of the independence and *de facto* autonomy of the northern Albanian clans.[22]

The *Kanun* is an expression of four qualities that 'Albanians consider to be the pillars of their ethnic identity': honour (*nderi*), hospitality (*mikpritja*), right conduct (*sjellja*) and loyalty to one's clan (*fis*).[23] It laid down norms for most aspects of rural life – the family and marriage, work and trade, house, livestock and property – defining duties, procedures for the regulation of conflicts and penalties. Whatever others might try to impose, the oral customary law remained primary, and the population preferred to ignore the written law and avoid contact with the legislative authorities. Any doubts about the *Kanun*'s interpretation would go before the *Pleqëria*, the council of Elders (or sometimes of Neighbours). In the 1920s, when the *Kanun of Lekë Dukagjini* was first set down in writing, it included an annex illustrating contemporary judgements from the *Pleqëria*.

The potency of this code is expressed in Ishmail Kadare's novel *Doruntine*. A mysterious horse rider brings back Doruntine from her husband's faraway land to be with her dying mother. As rumours spread about the ghost rider, and the bards embellish the story, state and church press the investigator to explain it away rationally. Ultimately, he can offer no alternative but that the mysterious rider was Doruntine's dead brother, Constantine, who had returned from the grave to honour his *besa* – his solemn word of honour – to his mother that he would bring back Doruntine when she needed her. 'Each of us has a part in that journey, for it is here among us that Constantine's *besa* germinated and that is what brought Doruntine back.'[24] The *besa* transcends the mortal, its power is that of a value system rooted in community.

In the 1990s, the *besa* – the vow – remained the supreme expression of the Albanian moral code, while allegiance to a parallel code was the central feature of the movement of civil resistance.

Family

The basic social structure of the Ghegs of northern Albania and Kosovo was the *fis*, best translated as clan. In Kosovo, clans tended to disperse, hence increasingly the *fis* played a lesser role in daily life than the large extended family. In the villages both Serbs and Albanians used to live in multi-generational family communes – the *zadruga* (Slav) or the *shtëpia* (Albanian). Typically, an extended Albanian family would live in a group of houses, sharing a common courtyard and surrounded by a high wall. The headman – the *zoti i shtëpisë* (master of the house) – spoke in the name of all. His was not a hereditary position; rather he was normally chosen by his predecessor or elected by the men in the extended family. Every evening the men would meet in the *oda*, the reception area, and the *zoti* would assign work for the next day. His wife, or another senior woman, was mistress of the house, delegating chores among the women. Property was held in common, except for a wife's trousseau and a man's gun.

After 1945 the *zadruga* died out among Serbs in the face of urbanisation and socialist agrarian policies. In the villages of Kosovo, however, where most mothers tend to have more than six children, extended Albanian families of 15–20 members remain common, and there are many with 40–50.[25] As more men left the village looking for work in the city, elsewhere in Yugoslavia, or in the 1970s and 1980s abroad, they continued to contribute to the collective economy, and the family adapted. Many grew too big and divided into two, creating one source of pressure for property and land in Kosovo. A study concluded in 1990 found that the authority of the *zoti* is rarely questioned. 'His will extends into every aspect of communal life. In addition to making all financial decisions about marriage, education and relations with non-family, his personal ideology affects the lives of all members.'[26] Patriarchal familial relations remain the basis of Kosovo's social solidarity.

Schooling

Historically, there has been some ambivalence to schooling among Albanians. Rural patriarchs were wary of its 'modernising' influence believing that the creation of an intelligentsia would erode their own authority. This is the basis for the insinuation that Albanians traditionally have an aversion to education (one of the excuses Yugoslav officials gave in the 1920s for failing to provide Albanian-language education was that this was not a right denied but a right not claimed). On the other hand, an increasing number of Albanians saw Albanian-language schooling as central to their advancement as a people.

The first Albanian language school inside Kosovo did not open until 1889 and operated illegally. During their occupation in 1916–18, the Austrian authorities encouraged the opening of more than 300 Albanian-language schools. However, contrary to the 1919 Treaty of Saint Germain on the Protection of Minorities, Yugoslavia did not allow Albanian-language education, closing the Albanian schools or converting them into Serbian-language schools. The Muslim political party Xhemijet demanded Albanian schools, and for this reason its parliamentarians opposed the 1924 Yugoslav budget. Xhemijet and Catholic churches also set parallel schools in the 1920s. The 1930 memorandum to the League of Nations by three priests lists 28 towns in which Albanian private schools had been closed down.[27]

Until 1940, the only elementary schools allowed in Kosovo taught in Serbo-Croatian; few Albanians attended. At the same time, Albanian-language publishing was also illegal. Consequently, illiteracy was widespread. When, during the Axis occupation, the first four-year elementary schools opened in the villages, attendance was compulsory but there was strong resistance as boys in rural areas needed to work. The expansion of Albanian education continued in socialist Yugoslavia, recruiting some teachers from Albania to make up the shortfall in Kosovo, and in the 1950s and 1960s opening eight-year elementary schools. Nevertheless, there remained strong suspicions in rural areas – be they of modernisation, atheism or Serbianisation.

Schooling for girls was a particular struggle. Shahe Berisha, later to become one of the Kosovo's first Albanian women schoolteachers, was one of the first girl pupils in the Deçan area. She was sent to school in Prishtina.

> People from the neighbourhood did not talk to my father for years as he had let his daughter attend school ... They did not understand my school as an educational issue, but they interpreted it as 'getting the school to become a cafe singer,' which at that time was considered something shameful.[28]

The attitude changed dramatically and almost at one blow in the 1960s, when the belief 'Only in education is there a future' caught the popular mood – a sudden shift in social consensus coinciding with greater self-government. Secondary schools were set up and illiteracy rates dropped from 94 per cent before 1950 to 30 per cent in the 1970s.[29] The economic crisis of the 1980s brought disillusion as the newly educated Albanians still had problems finding employment, and there was a particularly high drop-out among girls.[30]

Population

The value attached to education by many Albanians and the hostility to schooling for girls both relate to the high proportion of young people and the high birth rate. While a people's future may depend upon developing the potential of youth, the traditional rural way of life and patriarchal dominance depends on women staying at home, having babies.

Both Serbs and Albanians in Kosovo had a high birth rate in the early 1950s (41 births per year per 1,000 population for Serbs and 46 for Albanians). Subsequently, the Serbian birth rate fell rapidly, although not to the level of their neighbours in inner Serbia. However, the Albanian rate fell more gradually and remained the highest in Europe, higher than in Albania. Within Kosovo, the central factors were clearly the slower rate of Albanian urbanisation and the restrictions on education. Illiterate women are likely to have more than three times as many children as more educated women.[31]

Kosovo Albanians resent the priority Serbs give to this topic. True, Kosovo's poverty made its burgeoning population a burden on the rest of Yugoslavia, but it is hard to deny that some arguments carried more than a tinge of racism. Thus, another topic not discussed openly in the years of autonomy was the reluctance of the Albanian-dominated authorities to try to curb population growth or support family planning.

Migrant Labour

From the Ottoman Empire onwards, male migration has been an economic survival strategy for Albanian families. In socialist Yugoslavia, this initially took the form of migration to other parts of Yugoslavia or the Balkans, but from the 1960s onward, increasing numbers of Yugoslavs sought work in Western Europe. The pattern for Albanians was normally that a man would leave his family behind,[32] but send back money, and in particular invest in a house or extravagant weddings. The Opoja/Dragash area studied by Reineck is particularly noted for the opulence of some homes financed by migrant workers.

While Rugova and Maliqi have both suggested that migration has had a modernising impact, exposing the 'guest-workers' to European ideas, Reineck's study suggests that this was not the case for rural areas. Migrants frequently displayed a tendency to insist more strictly on adherence to family traditions, while few contributed to economic innovation on their return.[33]

TITO'S YUGOSLAVIA

If Kosovo Albanians were ushered into Tito's Yugoslavia through a bloody 'pacification campaign', at least they got Albanian language schools. Any hopes for self-determination, however, were dashed in 1948 when Stalin expelled Tito's Yugoslavia from the Cominform. At one blow, former allies ostracised Yugoslavia – and the most virulent denunciation came from Tito's erstwhile protégé, Enver Hoxha. Albanians were already not trusted to play a full role in Yugoslavia, but now their situation worsened. The claims that Albania was infiltrating agents into Kosovo[34] gave free rein to the Udba (Ranković's secret police) in Kosovo as protectors of Yugoslav 'security'. It also affected economic policy. Until 1957, the federal government did not invest in industrialising Kosovo. Then, instead of promoting forms of development appropriate for the territory with the fastest-growing potential labour force, it concentrated on industries supplying raw materials or energy for use elsewhere in Yugoslavia.

There was no high-ranking Albanian member of the Politburo until 1978 and no Albanian member of the Yugoslav Communist Central Committee until 1953, and in the 1950s the local Party and leading positions were dominated by Serbs and Montenegrins.[36] The option of full integration into Socialist Yugoslavia was not open to Kosovo Albanians. Even if it had been, traditional distrust of both Serbs and Communism would have created a strong reluctance to integrate. Rural Kosovo was suspicious of 'modernisation'. State campaigns against 'backwardness' did not only address the problem of illiteracy, but tried to 'secularise' Kosovo, forbade women wearing the veil, suppressed Shariat courts (1946) and closed mosque schools (1950). If there were now Albanian language publications such as *Rilindja* (Renaissance), and cultural societies and reading rooms opened throughout Kosovo, the limits of this social space could shift arbitrarily and suddenly. For instance, the Albanological Institute, founded only in 1953, was closed in 1955 along with a number of other recently established cultural bodies whose existence was held to impede Albanian 'assimilation' into Yugoslavia.

The worst period for Kosovo Albanians in Socialist Yugoslavia was 1953–56, the height of the campaign for 'repatriation' to Turkey and its accompanying police terror (see Chapter 1). These stimulated nationalist sentiment more effectively than any amount of propaganda. The protest they provoked took the form of small, symbolic actions – mainly unfurling the flag. The first recorded unfurling was by four youths in Gjakova on 1 May 1956. In the following months, others followed: 'Unable to assemble and speak freely, high school and college students took the lead by secretly unfurling Albanian national flags over government buildings, schools, and at nights on trains travelling all over Yugoslavia.'[36]

Suspected unfurlers were arrested and interrogated about 'irredentist' plots. The Udba – as well as keeping files on some 120,000 Albanians, half the male adult population – tried to extort 'confessions' incriminating leading Kosovo Albanian Communists. They assassinated 19 Albanians in Gjakova, eight in Prizren and an unknown number elsewhere. They tortured people to the point of suicide or insanity. They set fire 'to houses and committed acts of sabotage in factories, and then assigned responsibility to innocent Albanians.'[37]

Meanwhile Albanian-language education was creating potential for new leadership in Kosovo. The first arrest of Adem Demaçi (born 1936) followed his criticism of the policy of 'repatriation' to Turkey. Later to be Kosovo's most famous political prisoner, in November 1958 he was sentenced to three years in prison. On his release, he founded the clandestine Revolutionary Movement for the Unification of the Albanians – the first known group of its kind. He and other leaders of the group were arrested in 1964, Demaçi himself receiving a ten-year sentence.

The fall of Ranković in 1966 triggered a wider movement of Albanian self-assertion. The programme of Turkification was ended, prisoners released – including nine 'spies' whose famous trial in 1956 was now denounced by the Kosovo Assembly as 'staged and mendacious'.[38] As the authorities began to purge the secret police, the state-controlled press – in Belgrade as well as in Prishtina – published detailed accounts of their activities. *The Times* of London commented that 'the almost daily disclosures of brutal acts of repression, murder and torture by members of Mr Ranković's police against the Albanian minority ... are astonishingly frank.'[39] Repishti speaks of 'a political catharsis, bringing to the surface the emotions of the local population silenced since 1945.'[40]

Tito's 1967 visit gave a cue to Kosovo Albanians to voice their own demands. A senior Communist, Mehmet Hoxha, spoke for all in April 1968 when he asked: 'Why do 370,000 Montenegrins have their own republic, while 1.2 million Albanians do not even have total autonomy?' By the end of 1968, students – some marking

Skenderbeg's quincentenary by sporting badges with a double-headed eagle – were on the streets demanding 'We want a republic' and even chanting pro-Tirana slogans. There were violent clashes at demonstrations in October and November in 1968 in six Kosovo towns, police killing one student demonstrator in Prishtina. In December, Albanians in Tetova (Macedonia) demolished a hotel and several shops after a Macedonian removed an Albanian flag from a shop. In the demonstrations that followed, 22 people – mostly students from Prishtina – received prison terms of up to six years.[41]

EVERYTHING BUT A REPUBLIC

The Kosovo Albanians were refused a republic, and also any expansion of provincial borders to include Albanian communities in Macedonia and Montenegro. However, they did gain concessions. 'Metohija' was dropped from Kosovo's official name, while the province gained greater governmental autonomy, their own police and even a Supreme Court. Equality of status was now granted to three languages: Albanian, Serbo-Croat and Turkish. While secondary schooling (for pupils aged 15–18) became available in Albanian, the four Faculties established in the 1960s were expanded and upgraded into the University of Prishtina. Inaugurated in February 1970, this offered teaching in both Albanian and Serbo-Croat. In Prishtina, the Rilindja printing house began to publish a stream of books on Albanian history and culture. Kosovo was also now to have priority in the distribution of central funds for economic development. Most provocatively, Kosovo Albanians were now allowed to fly the flag of Albania.

The 1974 constitution defined Kosovo as a 'constituent element' of the federation with rights and responsibilities equal to those of a republic including a veto within the presidency – except, crucially, the right to secession. In 1978, a Kosovo Albanian – the former Partisan leader Fadil Hoxha – had his turn in the rotating vice-presidency of Yugoslavia, while under the rotating presidency system following Tito's death, Kosovo too had its turn, Sinan Hasani being president in 1986. In place of the 'assimilationist' policies of the Ranković era, the new decentralisation favoured 'national affirmation'.

The theoretical justification for denying Kosovo the right to secession was that each republic was considered a homeland for one of Yugoslavia's six *narodi* (nations). Albanians, on the other hand, were a *narodnost* (nationality) – their homeland was outside Yugoslavia. Despite their numbers – and by 1974 they outnumbered two nations who had their own republics (Macedonians and Montenegrins) – they were denied a republic.[42]

In view of the rights Kosovo had under autonomy, it was not surprising that the Slavic nations of Yugoslavia should see the demand for a republic as a demand for secession. The other side of that coin, however, was that denying Albanians their own republic signified refusing their full integration into Yugoslavia. The Kosovo Party leadership backed off the demand, taking the attitude 'What's in a word?' However, while Kosovo's autonomy and accompanying 'affirmative action' was to provoke a Serbian backlash, among Kosovo Albanians learning about the history of their people it fuelled their aspiration to recognition. Anton Logoreci comments:

Having been denied for many generations everything that helped to nourish a people's national consciousness and identity, the Albanians living in Yugoslavia, especially the post-war generation, were by the 1960s like a very parched sponge, immensely avid to absorb anything that helped to illuminate their past history and made some sense of their current situation.[43]

The University of Prishtina, the Prishtina Radio and TV centre, and the Rilindja publishing house were the institutional symbols of the cultural revival. In addition, there were many cultural activities outside the framework of the provincial administration. Ibrahim Rugova sees the beginning of the 1970s as a time when Kosovo Albanians discovered themselves. He fondly recalls 'Shtefën Gjecov evenings' (honouring the priest who wrote down the *Kanun* and who was later assassinated) and literary festivals, especially in Prizren, attended by thousands of villagers.[44] 1970 also brought a campaign to end the blood feud. (See Chapter 3.) The 'normalisation' of relations between Belgrade and Tirana in 1971 allowed Kosovo Albanians to reconnect with their supposed 'homeland', whose teachers and textbooks were essential in the expansion of Kosovo education. At the same time, Kosovo – and especially the university – were attracting Albanians from other parts of Yugoslavia.

This cultural and national renaissance was accompanied by a 'political emancipation of the Albanian nationality in the period 1968–81 [that] was almost vertiginous, creating whole new strata of state and party officials, industrial managers and university lecturers, teachers and policemen, radio and television personalities.'[45] The growing Albanian membership of the LCY in Kosovo – as much a source of advancement as Islam ever was – reflects the progress.[46] Yet, economically, this was a time when Kosovo was falling even further behind the rest of Yugoslavia (see Appendix I, Table 2). If the University of Prishtina was the pride of autonomous Kosovo, its expansion was also being used to postpone young people's entry into the labour market, a policy that merely deferred the problem. Kosovo was gaining a large group of discontented but articulate unemployed young people with a growing awareness of Albanian culture and history.

Throughout the 1970s there were repeated symptoms of unrest. 'Between 1974 and 1981, 618 persons were accused of various nationalist and irredentist activities in Kosovo.'[47] There were few known nationalist groups, but a number of small cells, usually nameless and mainly passing propaganda to each other.[48] Police brutality to those arrested or sentenced served as a reminder that, despite autonomy, this was nothing like freedom, and prisoners periodically protested with hunger strikes and riots. In 1978, centennial celebrations for the League of Prizren brought a spate of illegal leaflets and graffiti and the death of an Albanian student at the University of Zagreb, killed by police in a skirmish after an evening of Albanian literature and songs.[49]

In October 1979, Tito paid his fifth and final official visit to Kosovo and was perturbed at what he found. The local Party warned him of the slow pace of the socioeconomic development, and he duly promised increased economic aid. However, he also denounced the 'various nationalists, irredentists, hostile clergy and other ideological enemies ... [trying] to provoke dissatisfaction among the Albanians in Kosovo and to stir up disunity among its multinational population.'[50] A wave of 52 arrests followed, 19 receiving prison terms.

1981 AND AFTERWARDS

With such a background, the eruption of student protest in March 1981 – less than a year after Tito's death – seems predictable. That is hindsight. In reality, it shocked Yugoslavia to the core. On 11 March 1981 a student in the University canteen found a cockroach in his soup. This sparked a protest that converged with a crowd leaving a football match. As the day progressed it grew in militancy, ultimately being dispersed with arrests and tear gas. Hardly a word appeared in the Yugoslav press. On 26 March, the annual Youth Relay was due to arrive in Prishtina. The day before students in Prizren had demonstrated. Now Prishtina students gathered in front of the university to argue with professors and politicians. This time, they had placards, with a range of slogans that went far beyond university conditions. Special units of Serbian police drove the students from the streets and into the student residences which police then stormed. Belgrade TV news pretended nothing had happened, broadcasting footage from the arrival of the previous year's Youth Relay in Prishtina.

Demonstrations spread throughout Kosovo and were joined by workers. On 2 April, the army sealed off Prishtina, federal troops were also deployed in Podujeva and Ferizaj, a curfew was imposed and schools closed down. While the protesters were unarmed, they were far from nonviolent – for instance, throwing stones at the police. The state response, however, was on a different scale. Hundreds were wounded. The official death toll was 11 (including two policemen); however Amnesty International cited an internal report for the LCY suggesting over 300 Albanians were killed.[51] Now the protests were big news.

The last large student protest was on 19 May – an occupation of student residences dispersed by tear gas. After this, students were sent home and the University Council suspended. General Herljević, reporting to the federal Parliament in June, spoke of armed clashes the week before in villages in Drenica, and announced an expansion of the Kosovo police force by 1,000 and a doubling of its plainclothes branch.[52]

Between March and June 1,700 people were arrested. Between July and 9 September, 226 – mostly under 25 years old – received sentences of up to 15 years' imprisonment, nearly all found guilty either of 'verbal offences' or 'hostile propaganda'.[53] Throughout the year, sporadic protests would flare up – such as school pupils stoning cars – against a continued backdrop of graffiti calling for a republic and various acts of agricultural or industrial sabotage.[54] Subsequent public demonstrations were rare – just a thousand-strong rally in Prishtina in 1982 on the first anniversary of 11 March. By then, police claimed to have uncovered 33 'illegal groups', two of them 'massive'.[55] Occasionally police alleged that groups were planning arson, but above all it seemed that they were writing slogans: has there ever been such a detailed public police report on graffiti writing as this? From 1981 to 1983 in Kosovo, '8,567 hostile slogans were written'.[56]

At the level of inter-ethnic relations within Kosovo, 1981 marked a watershed. Despite social engineering to encourage an ethnic mix – arranging for different ethnic groups to live side by side in socially-owned flats or grouping conscripts from different ethnicities in the same army units – the ethnic boundaries in Kosovo were always stronger than in other parts of Yugoslavia. Inter-marriage was never common, not even among the urban elite. After 1981, inter-ethnic suspicion became an even stronger barrier to friendship and both Serb and Albanians communities in Kosovo each had its own homogenous recollection of divisive events.[57]

For many Kosovo Albanians, the events of 1981 mark the beginning of what they consider an 18-year terror – their experience is well captured in Ishmail Kadare's *The Wedding Cortege Turned to Ice*.[58] Many Albanians, especially political activists, left the country. In Switzerland, the Movement for an Albanian Republic in Yugoslavia began publishing its magazine. While one of its founders was killed in Prishtina in January 1984, apparently in a shoot-out with police, in Belgium and Germany Yugoslav agents are suspected of killing other exiled nationalists.[59]

Inside Kosovo, the repression was primarily administered by Albanians. The Kosovo LCY began an inquest, aiming to stamp out separatism. There were some expulsions from the Party, and some people lost their job through 'differentiation' (being declared politically unfit). That 'nest of nationalism', the university, was reined in. Student numbers were cut back by 25 per cent and the curriculum was re-oriented away from the humanities towards the sciences, a move seen as more in line with Kosovo's economic needs as well as reducing the dangerous zone where nationalistic ideas thrived.

Compared with the 1971–72 purge in Croatia, the Kosovo purge did not seem as far-reaching to some observers.[60] However, the scale of police harassment had a powerful impact on the population as a whole. From March 1981 to November 1988, '584,373 Kosovars – half the adult population – were arrested, interrogated, interned or reprimanded.'[61] The whole of Kosovo was under suspicion. Symptomatic of this was the federal abolition of the province's territorial defence – supposedly an integral part of Yugoslavia's then system of general people's defence – and removal of the weapons caches.[62]

The Communist leadership in Kosovo maintained that socioeconomic grievances had been exploited by 'enemy activity'. Some suggested that bodies in Albania had conspired to organise the protests – be they opposition circles or the secret service.[63] Reaction from the government of Albania was schizoid: domestically, unlike in 1968, most of the press supported the demonstrations, if some suggested an element of Serbian-Soviet provocation.[64] Nevertheless, those Kosovo 'troublemakers' who sought shelter in Albania (249 cases in 1981–83) were promptly handed back to the Yugoslav authorities.[65]

Many people were bewildered by the 1981 events: Slavs fearing that Albanians were demanding unification with Albania; Kosovo Albanians at the ferocity of repression unleashed against them. On all sides, it seemed to have got out of control. Some points, however, are clear.

First, the demonstrations were not orchestrated by dissident cells inside Kosovo. Of the 'counter-revolutionary groups' in Kosovo detected by Yugoslav police in 1985, more than two thirds were formed *after* the demonstrations.[66] Rather, the process has been likened to a 'national awakening'.

Second, while the demonstrations were sparked by socioeconomic grievances, the aspirations they expressed were national – for a republic and in some quarters for unification with Albania. While the LCY in Serbia denounced 'irredentism', the provincial Communists did not want to acknowledge the presence of nationalism among the population at large, yet the central call for a republic became the symbol for Yugoslav Albanian discontent.

Third, no matter how many small groups adopted names echoing Enverist ideology, the fierce atheism and general authoritarianism of the Hoxha regime and the country's poverty made immediate unification unattractive. A placard such as the reported 'We are Enver Hoxha's soldiers' was not proposing a political programme, but striking a pose. Tirana itself was more interested in improving relationships with Belgrade than in backing the aspirations of Yugoslav Albanians. Nevertheless, there is also no denying that many, if not most, Kosovo Albanians retained the historic aspiration for Albanians to be ultimately united in one country.

AN AFTERWORD ON COMMUNISM IN KOSOVO

For a number of reasons, it is common to treat Kosovo Albanians as victims – their comparative poverty, high unemployment, long-term denial of the right to education, appalling treatment by the Yugoslav police and prison system, and the visceral propaganda against them by Serb ultra-nationalists. This all goes to confirm a view that Kosovo should never have been made part of a state of 'south Slavs'.

Historian Marco Dogo has accused Kosovo Albanians of having 'constructed a historical pedagogy based on self-pity', avoiding sensitive topics and exacerbating 'backward-looking bitterness',[67] while the anthropologist Reineck observes that Kosovo Albanians:

> ... cope with marginality by cultivating their identity as oppressed and suffering 'outsiders'. *Vuajtje*, suffering, is considered a fact of life ... They identify themselves as a backward, forgotten, plundered people, characteristics which they feel make them special.[68]

Unfortunately, this victim attitude persisted with Albanians even when they controlled the provincial government in Kosovo. It made them over-protective about problems in their own community – the treatment of women, the rates for birth and illiteracy, the existence of nepotism in the provincial Communist Party, and the popular hostility towards Serbs. It made the Albanian leadership of the Kosovo Communists unwilling to try to allay Serbian fears – for instance, by not discussing the Blue Book compiled by Serbian Communists in 1976, or by their lack of transparent guidelines for the 'ethnic key system' (albeit a lack shared by every other administration in Yugoslavia).

Ultimately, the Kosovo Communists found themselves repressing their own young people while becoming hate figures for the rising Serb nationalism. They were not a base from which to defend Kosovo against the imminent attack. On the other hand, the traditional Kosovo villages, extended families and migrant workers and the rising generation of educated youth were to show stiffer resistance.

3
The Turn to Nonviolence

Nobody knows how or exactly when the Kosovo Albanians decided to adopt a policy of nonviolence. A rebellion that seemed increasingly violent in January 1990 transformed itself in spring, to a point where by the end of 1990 Kosovo Albanian identity was somehow linked to their nonviolence, and villages were giving their football teams names such as *Durim* (Endurance) or *Qendresa* (Standing firm).[1] Old traditions were being re-cast as the aspiration to be 'modern' and 'European' took hold of a younger generation who hoped they could emulate people power movements elsewhere in Eastern Europe. A vacuum of political organisation left by the rapid disintegration of the Communist Party created space for new initiatives, particularly from a new generation of activists linked with those elsewhere in Yugoslavia struggling for pluralism and a non-nationalist democracy.

The impulse towards nonviolence came at the height of the hate campaign against Kosovo Albanians and when the extreme nationalism of Serbia's plans for Kosovo was unfolding. If there was no one turning point, no key strategic decision, there were a series of formative experiences – the miners' actions of November 1988 and February 1989, low-risk but morale-building forms of 'semi-resistance', the foundation of a variety of new organisations, the inspiration of change in other parts of Eastern Europe and the Campaign to Reconcile Blood Feuds of 1990–92. These are the subject of this chapter. The attack on Kosovo Albanians that then ensued and their response at the political level are described in Chapter 4, while Chapter 5 surveys how they survived at the level of every day life by maintaining or constructing their own institutions.

MINERS DEFEND AUTONOMY

While Milošević was consolidating his hold on the leadership of Serbia, his public project was 're-unification' – revoking the

autonomy of Vojvodina and Kosovo, and creating a centre of power
that would dominate Yugoslavia in the name of protecting Serbs.
On 5 October 1988, the 'Yoghurt Revolution' – so called because
Milošević's mob pelted the Assembly building in Novi Sad with
yoghurt pots – brought down the provincial government in
Vojvodina. Milošević replaced them with appointees ready to accept
the annulment of Vojvodina's autonomy. Two days later in
Montenegro, steel workers clashed with police at the beginning of a
process which three months later would install Milošević's allies in
power there.

The leaders of the LCY in Kosovo – Azem Vllasi and Kaqusha
Jashari – could see the writing on the wall. Throughout Serbia, the
Titoite Vllasi was personally demonised for the oppression of Serbs
in Kosovo: from 'Meetings of Truth' to football matches, nationalist
crowds were demanding his arrest or even execution. The federal
level offered no defence. There, Kosovo always had a weak position
because of its poverty, its dependence on federal subsidies for
economic investment, administration and the welfare state.
Slovenia, Kosovo's main ally in the federation, was expanding its
own democracy and protecting itself from federal interference, but
at the price of limiting the scope for federal interference in Serbia's
treatment of the autonomous provinces inside Serbia. Vllasi and
Jashari knew that they and Kosovo's autonomy were doomed if the
terrain of struggle was limited to an intra-Party dispute, and so they
insisted that all the organs of the 'Socialist Alliance'[2] inside Kosovo
– the municipalities, the organs of self-management, professional
associations, as well as Party branches – should publicly debate the
proposed constitutional changes. And they opened up the
provincial media.

It was rather late in the day for Kosovo's Communist leaders to
turn to the people. Nevertheless, a substantial consensus emerged
rejecting Serbia's proposals. People – above all, miners – insisted on
making their opinion felt. Preparing for the annulment of Kosovo's
autonomy and under pressure from Belgrade, the provincial Party
board was ready to dismiss Vllasi and Jashari. The meeting was
scheduled for the evening of 17 November 1988. At dawn that day,
3,000 miners from Trepça left their pits and set off to march 45
kilometres (28 miles) to Prishtina. They were marching not for an
extension of Albanian rights, but in defence of Yugoslavia and the
constitution of 1974. The front row of the march signalled this by

holding a picture of Tito, two miners' flags, the Party flag and the Yugoslav, Albanian and Turkish flags. Throughout Kosovo, other marches formed to join in – perhaps 300,000 people.

The genuine spontaneity of the demonstrations contrasted with Milošević's 'Meetings of Truth', with their core of workers brought in by factory buses. Their nonviolent character was also a revelation. Shkëlzen Maliqi later wrote:

> Trepça miners – who inspired hundreds of thousands to repeat their brave deed in cold and snowy weather for five full days, so that the roads of Kosovo were day and night full of protest columns – in all aspects of their conduct, attempted to prove that the Albanians were not as the Serbs presented them and, still more importantly, that the Albanians were different and better than the Serbs. This entire manifestation, which involved the participation of some 400,000 people, went without a single incident, a single act of vandalism or destruction, and even without a single broken window. It took enormous self-control and high motivation to hold back the powerful internal destructive instincts and check the eruption of hatred, anger and rage. We are not as you choose to present us, we do not rape and do not kill but only 'with dignity' express our political will which is different from yours. This was a reflection of the Albanians' fanatic self-control. Moreover, the miners tried to avoid any gesture or slogan which could insult the Serbian people. At the demonstrators' main meeting place in Prishtina one could even hear the slogan 'Long live the brave Serbian people' which attempted at making a distinction between the regime and the Serbian people.[3]

One demonstration could not halt the dismissals of Vllasi and Jashari. Overshadowed by Milošević's 'Meeting of Meetings' in Belgrade, it was hardly reported in other parts of Yugoslavia. Yet inside Kosovo and at the federal level of the LCY it gave notice of the struggle to come if Milošević persisted in his plans. Warned to desist by the provincial LCY leadership, the miners were resolute. Asked by a journalist about the Special Police in wait, one 'grim-faced' miner retorted with a traditional saying: 'Journalist, have you ever seen a wedding without meat?'[4] Perhaps they trusted in their self-discipline and their dignity to inhibit violence against them. In so doing, they set a tone that in the coming years would become widespread among Kosovo Albanians. Or perhaps they trusted in their organised strength, that the provincial leadership would simply not dare to order an attack.

In place of Vllasi and Jashari, Milošević now appointed three 'placemen' – a category referred to in the Serbian press as 'honest' or 'loyal' Albanians: Rrahman Morina (who as Kosovo Minister of the Interior had called in federal troops to crush the 1981 protests), Husamedin Azemi and Ali Shukria. Their job was to see through the constitutional amendments brought before the Serbian Assembly on 25 November, annulling Kosovo's autonomy.

On 20 February, with the constitutional amendments due for final approval of the Serbian Assembly, the miners again acted. Their strike – the focal point of a general strike – became the stuff of legends. As Polish shipworkers were aware when they founded Solidarnosc in Gdansk in 1981, it is harder for police to break up a strike when workers have shut themselves inside their workplace. As the days progress, this site itself becomes a focus for external solidarity while inside the workers are together, feeling their common strength. So it was that a total of more than 7,000 workers are said to have shut themselves in Kosovo mines – 1,300 in Stari Tërg in the Trepça complex. Some were even on hunger strike.

For three days, the authorities ignored them – 'until the miners issued their warning that they would remain underground as long as was necessary, even to the point of death' and presented ten demands.[5] Oxygen was scarce, the air dusty, and in Trepça at the depth of the ninth level the heat was sweltering, already 50° C (120° F). A makeshift hospital was set up on the surface, for people suffering from respiratory, stomach or eye problems. After treatment, most returned down the pit, although by the end of the strike 180 miners had been taken to hospital in Prishtina, some in intensive care.

Local Party branches were instructed to oppose the workers' action, but few obeyed, and within days the Party youth organisation and then local secretaries began to demand the resignation of the 'placemen'.[6] A general strike spread throughout Kosovo, shutting down schools and factories – everything except the power stations. 'All life has been paralysed,' reported Maliqi:

> ... a kind of Albanian *Intifada* has begun. Thousands of solidarity meetings are taking place, supporting and expanding the miners'

demands. Schools throughout the province are not working, while in Prishtina students have entered their sixth day of peaceful demonstration in the 25 May sports centre. Writers are holding daily protest meetings. All socio-political organisations are in permanent session.[7]

Intellectuals, too, took action: on 22 February a petition by 215 intellectuals appealed to the Serbian Assembly not to revoke Kosovo's autonomy.

The miners urged 'no retreat from the fundamental principles of the 1974 constitution' and the resignation of the 'placemen'. They showed distrust of the provincial Party leadership, demanding that in future it should 'be elected by the Kosovo base and not by the bureaucracy of other republics.' Since 1981 it had been primarily Albanians who had been repressing other Albanians, and now it was common to hear miners remark 'We'll be screwed by the Albanians, it's the Albanians who'll do us in, we know it.'[8]

The strike continued. Down underground there was talk of self-immolation; furnace stokers spoke of committing collective suicide if Trepça was stormed.[9] More than a strike, reported Maliqi, this was an act of national rebellion:

> Milošević's extreme Serbian nationalism made them react not only as workers, but as Albanians, since they were being threatened and denounced as Albanians. They consequently resorted to the ancient ethos of resistance against an enemy that was attacking their national, workers' and human integrity. And the thing that gave them power, that integrated their internal strength, was their solemn vow to defend the truth. There awoke among them that supreme expression of the traditional Albanian moral code – the oath, the *besa*. For no one could take from them that which for Albanians is holy above all: the word of promise, the *besa*.[10]

On 26 February – the sixth day of the strike – the provincial LCY announced that the 'placemen' had submitted their resignations. The following day the miners emerged into daylight. Their victory, however, was short-lived. On 1 March, Belgrade rejected the resignations and imposed a State of Emergency, and on 2 March the arrests began – first with Azem Vllasi and 15 managers and miners from Trepça.

Throughout the Yugoslav federation, the strike had been headline news. In both Slovenia and Croatia there were demonstrations of public support. The head of Belgrade TV decided to broadcast the 27 February rally in Slovenia, sensing how it would inflame Serbs to hear remarks such as 'Albanians are in a position similar to that of the Jews in World War Two'.[11] Milošević and his allies quickly mobilised hundreds of thousands of people for an enormous rally in Belgrade that proclaimed 'We will give our lives but not Kosovo'. The federal Presidency said it possessed 'the plan of the Albanian separatist headquarters' for an armed uprising (a plan never published and probably non-existent). The crowd would not disperse until their hero, Milošević, addressed them, and so he kept them waiting. When he arrived, he promised to fight ('for peace and unity') and agreed to arrest Azem Vllasi.

Strikes resumed in Kosovo, in the mine at Golesh on 10 March, and in three others on 12 March, while in Trepça itself workers occupied the canteen. What broke the general strike at this stage was the authorities sending a letter to every striker warning that unless they returned to work, they would be sacked or arrested.

In response to the State of Emergency in Kosovo, a reported million Slovenes – half the population – signed a declaration warning that Yugoslavia faced a choice between recognising the Albanians' legitimate aspirations or permanent military occupation and the extinction of democracy.[12] This is sure evidence of how at this time Slovenes saw their fate inside Yugoslavia linked to that of the Albanians. However, alarm about Kosovo in Slovenia and Croatia served to accelerate their own trajectory towards secession and hence severance from Kosovo. When the Slovenian government banned a 'Meeting of Truth' in Ljubljana planned for 29 November by the Kosovo Serb group *Božur*, the Serbian government retaliated by encouraging businesses to cut links with Slovenia. Yet ultimately, no matter how sincere the popular sympathy in other republics, the republican leaderships knew that, in Magaš' words, 'to endorse Albanian mass resistance would have involved taking responsibility for Kosovo's economic problems. Slovenia and Croatia were not willing to do that, Bosnia could not.'[13]

THE PARTY CRUMBLES

The next major confrontation came on 23 March 1989, the day the Kosovo Assembly was to ratify the constitutional changes. With armoured cars and tanks outside, helicopters overhead, and members of the security police and Serbian LCY officials inside, this has entered Kosovar lore as 'the Constitution of the Tanks'. Albanian accounts tend to concentrate on the Assembly's irregular procedures – the lack of a voting register, the presence of outsiders (including armed police), the ineligibility to vote of those who did raise their hands, the majority abstention. Indeed in June the Constitutional Court of Kosovo initiated a review of proceedings with the power to invalidate them – except that the Court itself was promptly abolished. Delegates with a firmer will to resist could no doubt have found more scope for action on 23 March. However, the present delegates had been elected in December 1989 under Serbian scrutiny and Albanians already 'considered them to be the most pro-Serbian parliament elected in the last 30 years'.[14] At this symbolic moment, their want of courage and leadership made a shameful contrast with the epic resistance of the miners. One of the LDK founders later called it 'treason' that they were so easily intimidated.[15]

Outside the Assembly, the protests had little of the miners' nonviolent discipline. Riots erupted in Prishtina, Ferizaj and some other towns. Stone-throwing was common and some demonstrators made molotov cocktails, while in Podujeva both sides used firearms. For the next six days, spontaneous mass demonstrations met with brutal suppression, tear gas, water cannon and bullets. Official figures reported 24 people killed, including two police officers. Amnesty International noted estimates of 140 killed based on a coffin count, several hundreds wounded and 'over 900 demonstrators, among them school pupils, were jailed or fined, sacked or disciplined for taking industrial action.'[16]

There were stories of units from Slovenia and Croatia refusing to shoot. In Ferizaj, women and children were at the head of the march. When security forces from Macedonia began to club them (there is as much hostility towards Albanians among Macedonians as among Serbs), apparently Kosovo Albanian police stepped in and themselves fought the Macedonians.[17] In general, however, the protests had little organisation, involving mainly the poor and young with little middle class participation.

As well as deploying federal security forces, the authorities tried to 'decapitate' the emerging Albanian movement by a practice known as 'isolation' – a form of arbitrary detention without contact with the outside world, usually including torture. From March to June 1989, at least 237 people were 'isolated', including at least 65 who had signed the petition of 215 intellectuals, and some who were 'accused' of taking food to the Trepça miners during their strike.

One of those 'isolated' was the philologist, Rexhep Ishmajli. Until the miners' action, he suggests, most people felt it was impossible to find a means of struggle that would not lead to war or else they were deterred by possible condemnation within the LCY or investigation by the police. 'After this strike, that was over, people said "OK, me too". Everybody came to declare openly their support for an independent republic of Kosovo and against Serbian domination.'[18]

The miners' strike was also the catalyst for the disintegration of the provincial LCY. Sickened by the Party's deception of the miners when the 'loyal' Albanians tendered false resignations, journalists in the *Rilindja* branch immediately drafted a statement of collective resignation from the LCY. Within half an hour 40 people had signed it. They took this to TV Prishtina whose more liberal editorial remit allowed it to be broadcast on the main news that evening. 'This was enough', recalled one of its authors, 'to make the majority of the basic organisations [branches] of the LCY in Kosova fall apart in the following days, with an incredible speed.'[19]

Even with an apparent vacuum of organisation, there were fresh waves of protests. The next came when Azem Vllasi was due to face trial in October for 'counter-revolutionary' and nationalist activity in purportedly organising the miners. A further and more violent wave came in January 1990 following an incident in Macedonia, where an Albanian died trying to stop local authorities bulldozing the traditional high wall surrounding his house. Veton Surroi commented that 'the situation in which Kosovo lives – a state of isolation maintained by police terror – simply generates demonstrations'. That January, however, he also saw a pattern of provocation. In Rahovec, police had opened fire without warning on mourners returning from a non-political funeral, killing three and wounding about 20. In Malisheva a convoy of armoured personnel carriers opened fire randomly – even spraying the local police station with bullets, killing three and wounding about a dozen. Such incidents suggested 'a conscious policy of trying to provoke a national rising … The Kosovo Party committee had sent a warning to the hospitals, even before the demonstrations began, that they should prepare themselves for a lot of casualties.'[20]

In 1989, it was common to compare events in Kosovo with the Palestinian *intifada*, although Albanian rioters did not have the sense of strategy shown by Palestinians.[21] After events elsewhere in Eastern Europe at the end of 1989, Surroi was one of those who feared that Albanians might draw their inspiration from Romania 'and the fact that Ceausescu's regime was overthrown precisely by a popular uprising':

> We are, therefore, engaged in a desperate race not only against Milošević's policy of constantly raising the stakes, but also against sheer time in our efforts to create an organisational base for the genuine pluralization of Albanian political life. We do not wish to see a party-based monism replaced by one based on nationalism.[22]

ORGANISATION AND PLURALISM

Yugoslav democrats stayed well informed about progress towards pluralism in other Communist countries, learning from the opposition to totalitarianism there about the consolidation and expansion of 'safe spaces' and the delicate balance between testing what could be risked and provoking repression. The alternative to Communism that came to dominate Yugoslavia, expressed most virulently in Serbia and Croatia, was nationalism, accentuating ethnic differences, reviving past grievances and bringing war. There were, however, attempts to develop a non-nationalistic, democratic and pluralist alternative process.

Regionally, the counter-culture in Slovenia was the most successful endeavour and played an important role in supporting Kosovo Albanians, for instance through publishing articles or books by Albanians. At an all-Yugoslavia level, the Association for a Yugoslav Democratic Initiative (UJDI) aspired to be an equivalent to the East German New Forum. Widely seen as a belated effort to prevent the disintegration of Yugoslavia, it was an important forum for non-nationalist ideas and a space for dialogue between ethnic groups. Nevertheless, UJDI in Prishtina failed to gain a multi-national membership, attracting only two Serbs alongside hundreds of Albanians. Chaired by Veton Surroi, it was closely linked with the Association of Philosophers and Sociologists, an oppositional body with left-democratic leanings. Shkëlzen Maliqi, one of UJDI's founders, has claimed 'in Kosova, as nearly everywhere else in the former Yugoslavia, it was the UJDI that shattered the political monopoly of the LCY.'[23]

The other influential centre of Albanian opposition in Kosovo was the Writers Association. In the 1980s, the Writers Associations throughout Yugoslavia aligned themselves with intellectual freedom. The most celebrated freedom of expression case – the Trial of the Belgrade Six in August 1984 – encompassed defendants ranging from the ultra-nationalist Vojislav Šešelj (later a notorious paramilitary leader and vice-president of the Serbian republic) to the social democrat and consistent anti-nationalist Milan Nikolić. In Kosovo, however, the people who the Writers Association defended were invariably alleged 'separatists' now facing 'differentiation' (expulsion from positions of responsibility). The Kosovo Writers Association's representatives at the 1985 federal meeting were themselves accused of 'separatism'.[24] In 1988, the Serbian members (27 out of a total of 150) resigned from the Kosovo Writers Association, intending to destroy it. Instead, they opened the way for the Association to express Albanian aspirations and in April 1988 it presented a draft Albanian programme. Its president, Ibrahim Rugova, now became one of the main voices of Kosovo to the international and domestic press. Attacked both by his Serbian counterparts and by voices in Tirana critical of 'decadent modernism',[25] he was one of the first to call for the independence of Kosovo.

The period December 1989 to February 1990 saw the foundation of a variety of organisations in Kosovo. Springing from the environment of UJDI were several groups with the attitude 'First democracy, then the status of Kosovo' – the Social Democratic Party (initially led by Muhammed Kullashi, then Shkëlzen Maliqi); the Youth Parliament (initially led by Blerim Shala and Veton Surroi, later to become the Parliamentary Party – PPK); a Green Party and a feminist group. These can all be identified with the 'Kosova Alternative'.

On 17 December 1989, the Council for the Defence of Human Rights and Freedoms (CDHRF) was founded. This became the main monitoring and collection centre for details of human rights violations and police maltreatment. Theoretically open to Serbs, it was always an Albanian body. While its board was strictly above party politics for the first several years of its existence, its network in the municipalities depended on former political prisoners. After so many years of police harassment, Kosovo Albanians finally had a body to make an issue of that.

The dominant force in the Kosovo political scene for the next eight years was founded on 23 December 1989 – the Democratic League of Kosova (LDK). Its founders looked outside their own circle for a president and asked Ibrahim Rugova, who was becoming increasingly prominent and whose premises at the International PEN club were already well known to the press. Recruitment to the LDK was spectacular. Even if its claim of 700,000 members in the first five weeks is far-fetched, there were queues of people signing up. 'This was not a classical membership in parties', recalls one of its founders; rather 'it was a referendum, a political declaration'.[26] Surroi, who estimated the LDK membership at 200,000 in February 1990, described it 'as not so much a party as a product of the popular response to so many years of repression'.[27]

Maliqi and Surroi from the outset were clear that the role of smaller groups was to try to set an agenda. While recognising that the question of national oppression was bound to take precedence at this time, people in their Kosova Alternative circle launched a number of groups in a deliberate effort to raise issues that went beyond 'the national question', and – like the Belgrade UJDI Commission on Kosovo (see Chapter 2) – they were concerned to end the cycle of domination in Kosovo. Asked by Magaš in February 1990 who would win if free elections were held in Kosovo today, the urbane 'left democrat' Surroi was frank:

> Those individuals who have actively resisted repression. And in this regard, we are all different. There are democrats, but also old village chiefs. The provincial assembly is very large and it is possible that we will see elected to it quite a few village characters who have made their name by being more Albanian than the next man. These people would not concern themselves too much with the content of new laws, but would shout about Albanianism just like those who today swear by Serbianism. This is a real danger.[28]

In January 1990, various small groups and the CDHRF called for Albanians to refrain from street demonstrations. Without success. There were at least 32 deaths from police violence in January and February.[29] Maliqi, Surroi and others therefore had a series of meetings with the LDK leadership.

Rugova didn't say much at the time, he waited to see what would happen, but the then-ideologists of the LDK were saying: that's the people's will, if they want to, they can die, we can have an uprising, 50,000 people will die, but we will be free.[30]

In fact, following this, the LDK did join the call for restraint. However, the continuation of the demonstrations showed its lack of influence at this time.[31] The LDK initially was designed more to express public sentiment than to direct it, although soon it would establish a strong network of branches and sub-branches throughout Kosovo and among the Albanian diaspora in Europe and the USA.

'The main instigators of demonstrations', according to Maliqi, were militant 'Marxist-Leninists',[32] some even calling for armed insurrection. Although they had borne the brunt of repression in Kosovo throughout the 1980s, now – in the westward-looking climate after the fall of the Berlin Wall and when Kosovo Albanians were also beginning to understand more of the reality of Albania itself – such groups were a dying breed. Two additional factors ended this influence. Perhaps most important was a statement issued by Adem Demaçi – then serving his 28th year as a political prisoner – supporting nonviolent resistance and the democratic opposition. He reiterated the dedication in his book *The Serpents of Blood* (1958): 'Not to those who raise their hand in crime, but to those who extend their hand in reconciliation.' The other factor was the activity of other groups, especially the Youth Parliament, in offering an alternative.

An important organising tool in the first half of 1990 was the declaration *For Democracy, Against Violence*, coordinated by UJDI, the Association of Philosophers and Sociologists, the CDHRF and, in practice, also supported by local LDK organisers. This gathered 400,000 signatures. As Veton Surroi, the main organiser, commented: 'the very act of signing, with full name and address, concretizes the individual political demands and provides a solid basis for collective negotiation.'[33] Along with this came a commitment from the organisers 'to make each death a public act'. Rather than riot on the streets, this would take a form that could be termed 'semi-resistance': activities that strengthen the morale and unity of people and which they can take up with little risk in the course of their everyday life. These 'homages' initially took the form of the sounding of factory hooters and car horns at a specific time on a 'day of sorrow'. In the second half of 1990 these became five-minute protests in the streets. Other forms of symbolic semi-resistance were developed: in February and March thousands of people put candles in their windows or balconies, and they would mark the beginning of curfew by rattling keys in a tin, a symbolic expression that despite the state of emergency, Kosovo Albanians still held the key to the situation.

International Women's Day, 8 March, is generally celebrated in Kosovo more as a Mothers' Day than as a day when women make their demands. However, in March 1990, Prishtina women used the space provided by this occasion to protest.[34] In response to police firing on student residences and expelling students, they pledged to house students in their own homes, and they also protested against the violence of conscription: in the 1980s 54 Albanian conscripts returned home from the army in coffins, purportedly from suicide, but in any case the victims of systematic bullying.[35] If these concerns were acceptably maternal for a patriarchal culture, the women's insistence of having their message heard was a sign of change.

Towards the end of March two events confirmed the Albanians' worst fears of Serbian policy. In Belgrade, on 22 March, Milošević unveiled and the Serbian Parliament adopted his blueprint for Kosovo: *The Programme for Achieving Peace, Freedom, Equality and Prosperity*. This was largely a programme for changing the ethnic balance in Kosovo (see Chapter 4).

At the same time, a mysterious episode, apparently of poisoning, provoked fury among the Albanian population. Between 18–23 March, some 7,000 children in 13 communities reported symptoms of neuro-intoxication. The authorities did not permit a proper investigation by Albanians but offered a diagnosis of mass hysteria. However, the then federal president (the Croatian Stipe Mesić)[36] and a number of international observers believe that this might have been caused by an agent such as Sarin, used in chemical weapons and known to have been manufactured by the Yugoslav People's Army.[37] According to the Zagreb daily *Vjesnik*, at least 50 personal attacks on Kosovo Serbs took place within days of the alleged poisoning.[38]

Dušan Janjić describes this incident as 'the "trigger" case which generated massive emotional-political mobilization of the Albanians and got them ready for abandonment of institutions and norms of Serbia and Yugoslavia.'[39] It fitted the growing Albanian analysis that Serbia wanted to provoke an armed uprising for only a war could shift the demographic balance decisively in favour of Serbs. On 16

April, Serbia abolished Kosovo's own Ministry of the Interior and began the process of Serbianising the Kosovo police force by purging Albanians – initially suspending 200 Albanians and drafting in 2,500 Serbian police.[40] However, the Albanian self-restraint was now becoming an organised phenomenon. 'In some towns', reported Shkëlzen Maliqi, 'furious mobs tried to lynch "suspicious" Serbs, but were prevented through the interventions of activists from political organisations, especially the Youth Parliament.'[41]

It became the pattern that, whenever there was an incident of violence, activists from the CHDRF or the new parties would go to the scene, partly to document what had happened and so to highlight the violence of the regime, but also to urge restraint or to explain the idea behind nonviolence. A detailed series of reports of Serbian police activity in Kosovo began to flow out of Kosovo once the CDHRF was established and LDK branches began to keep 'a chronicle of repression' (a sub-title in the daily KIC bulletin). Sometimes fear of reprisals deterred people from reporting violence against them. However, the act of naming this violence could have a transformative impact, at best converting an attitude of resentful submission into a durable resistance.

Visits to villages by educated urban activists, oriented towards the future and Europe rather than to tradition, were a sign of social solidarity. If Ibrahim Rugova himself decided not to visit rural areas personally for risk of providing the occasion for an incident, the LDK had an increasing presence:

> When the police make incursions into the villages and terrorise them, we – the people of the LDK – try to be the first ones to speak with the police so they can see we are there. For example, we went to Gllogovc when we had been warned. Not to calm the people – that was impossible, the police had already done their work – but to make an act of solidarity, to witness. That's very important. Otherwise, the police or army can take advantage of some piece of stupidity.[42]

What was emerging was a set of methods and organisational structures to identify violence with the Serbian oppressor while restraining counter-violence from the population, to strengthen social solidarity while emboldening the population to use the limited space available to communicate their defiance. The new Kosovo

Albanian movement also directed its attention to the violence inside their own community, notably the blood feud.

THE CAMPAIGN TO RECONCILE BLOOD FEUDS[43]

Kosovo remained blighted by the blood feud. In the late 1980s, this practice threatened the lives of as many as 17,000 men,[44] more or less confining them to their homes. Blood feuds in Kosovo were regulated by the code of customary law in a particular area. This included some provision for resolving feuds, by offer of payment or arbitration, and for periods of truce – for 30 days after a killing, the killer had a period of truce before he became liable to be shot. Some feuds went back generations. Along with the classic motives for vendettas, there were feuds that began accidentally, for instance with the killing of an animal, especially a sheep dog, or that grew out of everyday conflicts, for instance over water or boundaries. A visitor could trigger a blood feud, as the Albanian code of hospitality would make the host responsible for any offence to the guest or caused by the guest. Once caught in the traditional logic, young men were trapped. They would stay behind their family walls (it is forbidden to kill someone in his home), venturing out at risk of death. The campaign sometimes found men who had not stepped outside the family compound for decades. If there was not a man in the family, daughters might have to assume the duty to kill. In this case, they cut their hair, dressed like a man and could not marry. The last case where Çetta was present was of a woman with the duty to avenge her brother's death.

Adem Demaçi's 1958 novel *The Serpents of Blood* is said to be a 'powerful condemnation of vendetta ... as well as an accusation against a society that does little if anything to stop it'. Its hero is a young man 'who broke the rules of patriarchal life by a decision "see the world" outside the eggshell in which he lived.'[45] The classic blood feud novel is Ishmail Kadare's *Broken April*. This begins with Gjorg – having once failed in his duty by only wounding the man he has to kill – lying in wait to redeem himself. It ends later, in the month of April, with all the rules having been observed and the cycle complete. Gjorg now lies dead, it is his corpse being turned onto its back and his dignity being respected as his rifle is laid by his side – the very rites he had observed for the man he killed.

He lost consciousness for a moment, then he heard the footsteps again, and again it seemed to him that they were his own, that it was himself and no one else who was running now, leaving behind, sprawled on the road, his own body that he had just struck down.[46]

When Albanians try to reconcile blood feuds, some people say they are preparing for war. More accurate for modern times would be to say that they are preparing to take charge of their own destiny. Thus the first modern movement against the blood feud arrived with self-government, in the years immediately after the fall of Ranković. In 1970 two historic *kuvends* (tribal meetings of elders) had gathered thousands of people to end feuds at Tuz in Montenegro and in the Rugovo mountains. The elders gave their *besa*:

> ... to unite in their fight to end the feud, to denounce and to boycott those men who would not listen to reason and compassion. This stance was to reverse the historic idea of shame and dishonor in Albanian society: it would be shame now to kill, to seek revenge.[47]

The Montenegro *kuvend* was the subject of the first big production of Kosova Filmi, a documentary 'Pacifying Blood'. Although the blood feud survived this campaign, the spread of secondary education increased the questioning of the practice.[48] In the 1980s, there were occasions when political prisoners involved in feuds persuaded their families to 'pardon the blood', while in 1989 the family of a hunger striking miner released him from the obligation to kill a fellow Albanian. However, there was no concerted effort at eradication. In 1989, there were 15 deaths by blood feuds, including the death of students. This prompted a group of students from Peja to approach the CDHRF in Prishtina. The CDHRF in turn called on Anton Çetta (1920–1995) at the Albanological Institute, someone renowned for his knowledge of the villages and folklore as well as being a CDHRF board member. A living legend inside Kosovo and immersed in its traditions, Çetta was not a parochial figure, rather he had a passion for social reform and spoke French and Italian fluently.

Declaring 1990 the Year of Reconciliation, every weekend from 2 February onwards, campaigners would visit villages, seeking out families in a blood feud. Students gave up the first term of 1990 to do the legwork for the campaign. The need was to convince the victim's family, for only a 'magnaminous pardon' can absolve the blood. It often took several visits to persuade a family to offer this and at least one visit by an 'elder' in the Campaign – often Çetta himself. Some 500 youths and intellectuals devoted themselves to this campaign, using television and radio as long as that was allowed.

Çetta would try many lines of arguments: 'Don't you see that this is a kind of suicide?', 'Don't you have other problems?', 'Aren't you aware of the situation?', 'Isn't it important for us to have our population living and united?', and 'If we want to become part of Europe, do you think Europe will accept such barbaric and medieval traditions?' Anything to start the discussion. He would urge people to free themselves from the stone in their hearts, to free the younger generation. Many teachers in higher education had the experience of a promising student 'disappearing'. The newly-educated generation was a powerful resource in the campaign. As well as the student volunteer workers, within each family there was likely to be a young ally – most families had some high school students and virtually all had someone who had finished elementary school (eight grades).

Not simply the 'master of the house', but at least the male side of the family, had to accept reconciliation. Frequently, visitors from the campaign found they would embolden a woman in the family to seize this chance to put her arguments against the hated custom. Çetta spoke of sisters, aunts and mothers who, out of his earshot, made the decisive intervention.

The campaign also involved enlisting local support and trying to set up structures to arbitrate on future disputes: any quarrel, not just those that might lead to blood feuds. This sometimes meant reviving a Council of Elders/Neighbours or forming a new reconciliation council. One of these, the Gjilan Community Council to Avoid Negative Phenomena reported in 1998 that it had settled 541 of the 778 disputes brought before it in the past six years.[49]

Once a family had agreed to give their *besa*, they would attend a public ceremony organised by the campaign. Here they would meet the other family and 'pardon the blood'. While the *Kanuni* stipulated a feud could be ended with money or with a guarantor who might become responsible to carry on the feud if the pardon was violated, on these occasions families were invited to 'put your hand forward and forgive in the name of the people, youth and the flag'. All present stood as witness. At each ceremony, several feuds would be publicly reconciled. Because maintaining a feud was a sign that a family had not forgotten the death of a son, the ceremonies of reconciliation were emotional occasions. Sometimes they inspired others to come forward spontaneously and offer their *besa*.

Families from Macedonia, Montenegro, Albania itself and throughout the diaspora attended the largest public gathering – at Verrat e Llukës on the plain of Deçani on 1 May 1990. Even the official Tanjug agency reported a crowd if 100,000 people (Çetta himself guessed at 500,000). Participants were not immune from police attention – Amnesty International reported beatings of some young people who attended, and later that month when police found a young man with a photo of Çetta, they reportedly beat him and forced him to swallow his engagement ring.[50] At the end of August, the authorities banned large gatherings and police broke up a ceremony in Peja.[51] The campaign proceeded, but now by holding smaller ceremonies, for instance behind the walls of family compounds. These were all arranged by word of mouth and secretly, often with participants pretending that they were going to a wedding.

Some 1,000 feuds involving death, 500 of wounding and 700 other disputes, for instance about water or women, were reconciled in the course of this campaign (1990–92). A few blood feuds remained unreconciled – 'We cannot force reconciliation', said Çetta – but for the time being, the tradition was all but eliminated. Subsequently, only a few isolated incidents have been reported in Kosovo. This was a campaign for self-reform and modernity but, like the miners' *besa*, it evoked positive aspects of traditional Albanian values. Çetta offered this interpretation of the quality of *Burrnia* (literally 'manhood', more denoting 'strength of character'):

> *Burrnia* has three levels. The first is the person who resists evil, suffers and endures heroically without suicide. The second is the person who removes themself from evil without provoking violence and war. The third is the Strong who pardons the Weak.[52]

Çetta felt that the blood feud campaign set the tone for Albanian civil resistance. 'The enthusiasm and sense of fraternity that spread', he said, 'gave courage to our politicians and also encouraged the self-organisation of our population.' His own concerns made him the first president of the humanitarian Mother Theresa Association, founded on 10 May 1990, and later to become the backbone of Albanian healthcare in Kosovo. But he also saw a pressing need to address illiteracy, polygamy, the education and rights of women in the villages and in general to oppose repressive aspects of culture and tradition.

Mirie Rushani explains the significance of the movement for reconciliation:

> First of all, as an act of self-defence, not a call to unite in arms, as nearly always in the historic campaigns of General Reconciliation [for instance 1444, 1703 and 1878], but to unite in a general resistance without arms, with the awareness that nonviolent resistance could carry enormous suffering and a high price.[53]

MILITARY REALISM

At the beginning of 1990, some Kosovo Albanians did favour the option of an armed uprising. Most of these accommodated themselves to the new policy but did not necessarily abandon the belief that ultimately war would be necessary. Especially in the diaspora Kosovo Albanians could be heard expressing scepticism about nonviolence, and inside Kosovo in 1993 preparations began for the formation of the Kosova Liberation Army (UÇK). There were also occasional armed clashes with police. The analyst Zoran Kusovac considers the incidence of these 'surprisingly low', citing Serbian police figures which can be assumed to be exaggerated – 136 attacks in the first 18 months after the Declaration of Independence,[54] mainly consisting of potshots. The serious incident – when two police were killed and five wounded near Gllogovc on 22 May 1993 – was later said by a Serbian police inspector to have been staged by the police themselves.[55]

It is also believed that Croatia's Franjo Tudjmann offered help if Kosovo would open up a second front during Croatia's war with Serbia.[56] While this may have been in Croatia's interest, it was certainly not in Kosovo's. Both had had their territorial defence suppressed for fear of nationalism,[57] but Kosovo would have been much more vulnerable than Croatia, militarily weaker, with a smaller population and higher proportion unable to take part in armed defence. Therefore the dominant feeling at this time was that any armed uprising would have been suicidal.

If the people embraced nonviolence with optimism, among the LDK leadership there were nevertheless secret discussions about improving Kosovo's military defences. Ferocious police campaigns in 1993 and 1994 were targeted against people suspected of trying to organise a parallel Minister of Defence and Minister of the Interior in Kosovo, including some LDK branch officials, former soldiers and former police officers. A series of mass trials attracted attention outside Kosovo mainly for the blatant use of torture to extract confessions. But five years later, in October 1999, Hajzer Hajzeraj – the person accused of having been 'Minister of Defence' but who denied this at his trial – confirmed the broad case made by the prosecution: namely that there was an attempt, authorised by the LDK leadership, to reconstruct the territorial defence system.[58] According to reports in winter 1992–93 – strenuously denied by the government of Albania – there were even military training camps in Albania for Kosovo Albanians.[59] Rather than being part of a plan for an uprising, these seem to have been part of a contingency plan, in case of a Serbian military attack on Kosovo, to withdraw to the borders and fight to defend the population until the promised international military intervention arrived.

'Impenetrable' as Kosovo Albanian society may appear to outsiders, there was no way that such a large operation could be organised secretly. Indeed, it provoked the heaviest police repression before the arrival of UÇK. Judging from the lack of effective military defence against the Serbian offensives of 1998 and 1999, it can be assumed that the plan was abandoned. As an armed uprising would bring catastrophe and as even the insurance policy of reviving territorial defence structures was impossible, Rugova began to speak not only of a policy of nonviolence in pursuit of independence, but also that independence itself should be combined with demilitarisation.

If this seemed to be dictated by realism, nonviolence occupied a more important place in popular consciousness: it was, said Rugova, 'a necessity and a choice'.[60]

> The practice of nonviolence in this situation corresponds to an aspect of our character, to a tradition of patience and prudence in the face of all domination … By means of this active resistance based on nonviolence and solidarity, we 'found' ourselves. Today, we have succeeded in touching this point of the spirit of the Albanian people.[61]

NONVIOLENCE IN KOSOVO ALBANIAN IDENTITY

In a phrase that Shkëlzen Maliqi has often used, nonviolence 'imposed itself' on the Kosovo Albanians. Faced with an opponent whom they perceived to be genocidal, who seemed to want to provoke war, nonviolence was an option for survival. They decided to trust in their own social solidarity and to look for allies outside, rather than to confront directly the armed power of Yugoslavia's largest nation. 'The strategy of nonviolence was somehow self-imposed as the best, most pragmatic and most efficient response to Serbian aggressive plans.'[62]

If certain Albanian traditions were conducive to adopting nonviolence, the importance of weapons in Albanian culture and the celebration of *kaçak* resistance were quite the reverse. But Kosovo Albanian society was ripe for innovation. The spread of schooling and literacy had given intellectuals an increasing influence. Rugova saw himself as belonging 'to a generation that has evolved in relation to the traditional way of life: the intellectuals have experienced modernity, society follows.'[63] Nonviolence was more than a counsel of realism because it became part of the construction of a 'modern' Albanian identity. Somehow it drew together both the village patriarchs and the urban intelligentsia in a common effort to avoid a tragedy. It suited a patriarch that a key point in the struggle would be to maintain Albanian society in Kosovo. It suited the outward-looking urban intelligentsia that Kosovo was moving closer in attitude to the rest of Europe.

In 1990, some Kosovo Albanian Muslims even discussed the idea of a collective conversion to Catholicism as a demonstration of their Western orientation.[64] They rejected the suggestion as opportunistic, but repeatedly the movement rallied around Catholic symbols, above all Mother Theresa (herself an Albanian), observing Catholic holy days and attending Catholic ceremonies, forming a Christian Democratic Party (with a majority membership of Muslims) – a demonstration that they were not the Muslim fundamentalists portrayed in Serbian 'hatespeak'.

The Kosovo intelligentsia had attentively followed the disintegration of Communist regimes in other parts of Eastern Europe and the activities of people's movements there. One journalist was taken off the foreign desk at *Rilindja* for being too interested in Lithuania's struggle for independence and the possible disintegration of the Soviet Union.[65] However 'the 1989 factor' – from the outcry at the slaughter of nonviolent demonstrators in Beijing to the celebrations at the end of the year as one European Communist regime after another collapsed in the face of 'people power' – fired the popular imagination. The drama of the collapse of a series of regimes fostered the illusion that people power could win quickly in Kosovo, ignoring – as did the most of the media – the years of erosion of the edifice of Communist rule and the long struggle of civil society groups. It also encouraged the idea that movements against Communist dictatorship could count on Western support.

'We have learnt', said Rugova, 'that nonviolence is the modern European preference.'[66] Indeed, nonviolence became linked to 'modernity' for many, especially youths with their aspirations towards being contemporary Europeans. The slogan of the women's illiteracy programme, Motrat Qiriazi, on its foundation in 1990 was 'To Europe with a pencil!'[67] The most dynamic section of the movement in this initial phase were those who used the language of pluralism, democracy and a greater say for women – the Kosova Alternative circle, city-dwelling modernisers. Certain factors that helped the long-term adherence to nonviolence – internally, the patriarchal discipline of the extended family system and externally, the exhortations of Western political leaders – do not seem to have played such a significant role in the popular adoption of the policy.

In 1990, nonviolence became a fashion in Kosovo. The modern-day bards made up songs about Rugova, Çetta and Demaçi. Suddenly, Rugova was talked of as an Albanian Gandhi, rather to his embarrassment: 'I'm not too keen about talking about passive or Gandhian resistance. I say it's about a political resistance, not passive and so not Gandhian.'[68] If certain methods and themes emerged in 1990, there was still no overall strategy. The only idea for how the regime might yield was through international pressure. If the danger of the war option was obvious, the level of repression that unarmed resistance would entail was not. Yet, for all the underdevelopment of the concept, the population had swung behind 'nonviolence' as their hope.

Shkëlzen Maliqi has written:

The key to the sudden shift [towards nonviolence] might be sought in the process of structuring of an identity in contrast to 'the Other', in this case a rival and enemy nation … The Albanians have, therefore, asserted themselves by emphasizing their difference from Serbs, by proving themselves before and against

them ... All that the Serbian propaganda had assigned to the
Albanians for years appeared as a projection of their own desires
and evil hegemonic intentions. The victim and the villain from
the perspective of a Serbian chauvinist exchanged roles in reality.
Prejudices against the Albanians served as justification for the
most horrible of crimes against them, including unprecedented
ill-treatment and torture. Thus Kosova became a fantastic crossing
of two confronted national self-perceptions: if an Albanian raised
two fingers, a Serb had to raise the third; if the former opted for
democracy, the latter considered the establishment of democracy
in Kosovo equal to the loss of it; if one was freed of traditional-
ism, folklore and inherited prejudices, the other sank into myths,
restoration of the Serbian military glory and revenge of Kosova.[69]

The practice of nonviolence served to validate the self-worth of
Kosovo Albanians at a time when they were being vilified. However,
the dangers of deriving one's identity from a matrix of antagonism
are evident – a lack of flexibility, an inability to appreciate what is
held in common, ultimately a manichean worldview where one is
always the victim or martyr, the Other always the villain. Self-
awareness also requires some notion of reciprocity and some element
of respect for the rights and person of the Other. These are values
often associated with nonviolence, yet underdeveloped in the
Kosovo Albanian self-understanding. The Campaign to Reconcile
Blood Feuds itself has sometimes been represented as primarily a
'closing of ranks'.

From Gandhi onwards, many opponents of colonialism (including
advocates of violence such as Franz Fanon) have avowed that
nationalism – in the sense of reconstructing a national identity and
establishing a basis for self-determination as a nation – is not an
exclusivist impulse but a step towards a wider identity. The new
identity can emphasise inclusive values and independence/liberation
is not a form of introversion but the beginning of a fuller participation in the world. For Kosovo Albanians, their own self-determination
was inextricably linked with becoming European – with all the
illusions about 'Europe' that were common in the East European pro-
democracy movements of the 1980s. However, on the questions of
how their imagined Kosovo related to its Yugoslav past, its neighbours
in Serbia and its potential Serbian citizens, the new identity was being
constructed in conditions that militated against openness.

Maliqi in his essay on Self-Understanding was primarily celebrating the changing identity. One of the LDK founders later praised Maliqi and Veton Surroi as 'the main carriers of the initial and transitional process of positive changes in Kosova.'[70] Yet, because of their 'Yugoslav' background,[71] they themselves were in a prime position to realise the limitations of Kosovo Albanian identity. Among the most dialogue-minded of all Kosovo Albanians (I first met them in Belgrade in December 1991 when they were calling for a dialogue with Serbian opposition groups), both were thrown into the political wilderness in the early 1990s for being too open towards Serbs.

The intuitive nonviolence taken up by Kosovo Albanians and absorbed into their identity and culture at this time was a durable basis for protracted civil resistance. However, this was a narrow nonviolence, especially compared with the Gandhian concept where non-cooperation with evil is combined with a willingness to seek truth with the Other, where self-development and constructive action are part of a process of empowering a population, making it capable and worthy of self-rule. Moreover, much work remained to be done to develop an adequate strategy.

Certain central strategic themes were clear: the need to avoid offering a pretext for Serbian military action; the value of 'naming the violence'; the importance of involving international support. Also, there was an analysis of the limited social space available and of some of the strengths of the people. Events, however, were to plunge the emerging movement into a struggle where ending Serbian rule became seen as a matter of survival, under which the objectives of the Kosova Alternative were submerged.

4
Two Sovereignties

For Kosovo Albanians, the Serbian nationalist project was akin to an occupation, aiming to recolonise Kosovo, arming the Serb civilians while denying basic rights to Albanians and threatening population transfer. There were differences of degree between Serbian nationalist politicians and a range of motives from heartfelt nationalism through power-political manipulation to crime.[1] Its explicit goals were to reclaim Kosovo as part of Serbia, to increase the numbers of Serbs and Montenegrins living there and to reduce the numbers of Albanians, but the regime's main interest was quite cynical – to have Kosovo as a card in its hand, a situation of tension to be exploited when domestic needs required. Its strategy towards Albanians only had the dimension of threat. After the collapse of the LCY in Kosovo, it did not cultivate 'loyal' Albanians leaders with any significant support. Rather, the script of 'getting tough' with an ethnically homogenous and separatist bloc suited the regime.

Inside Kosovo, however, the 'occupation' schema presented by Albanians was too simple. The shrinking Serbian minority indigenous to Kosovo and other ethnic groups – Slav Muslims, Roma/Gypsies, Turks and Croats – had rights too. Safeguards were needed for the Serbian cultural heritage. Moreover Kosovo – for all the problems of its annexation in 1912 and its incomplete integration into Yugoslavia – had still been part of a state that was now breaking up. This permitted certain claims upon other members of that polity, offered alliances and even demanded some responsibility towards the future of the whole. However, the politicisation of inter-ethnic relations – and ethnicisation of politics – inside Kosovo seemed to allow little scope for inter-communal initiatives, as shown by UJDI's failure to attract Serbian support in Kosovo. The vehemence of the regime's project for Kosovo forced the Albanian movement to concentrate on issues of their community's survival. Four primarily defensive objectives for civil resistance became explicit:

– To contest the legitimacy of institutions imposed by Serbia and counterpose the legitimacy of institutions supported by the Albanian population of Kosovo.

– To refuse to be provoked to acts of violence by the vandalism and brutality of the Serbian police or paramilitary, but rather to name that violence.

– To mobilise international support.

– To maintain the life of the Albanian community in Kosovo, including its social solidarity, sustain its intellectual life and so defeat the perceived Serbian objective of 'quiet ethnic cleansing'.

This chapter treats the first three of these objectives, Chapter 5 the fourth. It looks at Serb and Albanian attempts to establish their own sovereignty in Kosovo, describing the two major forms of repression used by Serbs – mass dismissals from work and police and paramilitary intimidation – and the political strategy pursued by Albanians to challenge Serbian domination.

A SERBIAN RECIPE FOR ALBANIAN 'SEPARATISM'

'Unification' with Serbia involved a range of measures revoking gains made by Kosovo Albanians since 1966: one official language (Serbo-Croatian); street names changed; Albanian statues and monuments taken down, and figures from Serbian history (or mythology) erected in their place; shops ordered to have signs in Cyrillic; the reinstatement of 'Kosovo and Metohija' as the territory's official name; reversion to the derogatory *Šiptar* to refer to Albanians – such changes at the symbolic level were a way of saying to Kosovo Albanians: 'This is not your home, this is part of Serbia.' However, they were just the surface. The Kosovo lawyer Nekibe Kelmendi has written a detailed analysis of the welter of decrees and laws passed by the Serbian parliament in the period 1990–92.[2] She describes 32 laws and more than 470 decrees or special measures listed, plus two programmes – the Orwellian *Programme for Peace, Liberty, Equality, Democracy and Prosperity* (PPLEDP) of March 1990 and the *Development Programme to Stop Emigration and for the Return of Serbs and Montenegrins* of July 1992. These:

– transferred responsibility for policing to the Serbian Ministry of the Interior and revived the militia, a force of special police disbanded after Ranković's fall;

– dissolved Kosovo's constitutional and judicial systems and integrated Kosovo into the system of the Republic of Serbia;

– put Kosovo information media under the control of Belgrade;

– repealed various laws on education and imposed a uniform educational curriculum for schools;

– established Serbian controlled municipalities;

– instituted new forms of 'emergency management' to supersede 'self-management' in Kosovo and facilitate mass dismissals;

– permitted the transfer of assets from provincial institutions to the Republic of Serbia while restricting even further the sale of Serbian property to Albanians and the participation of Albanians in the privatisation of socially-owned businesses;

– offered incentives for Serbs and Montenegrins to settle in Kosovo; and

– promised investment programmes building new factories and homes for Serbs and Montenegrins.

The ostensible goal was nothing less than to change the ethnic structure of Kosovo permanently, bringing in Serbs and Montenegrins while 'inducing' Albanians to leave. Albanians were offered advice on relocation to other parts of Yugoslavia, while Article 91 of the PPLEDP promised 'the necessary activities' to bring down the birth rate in Kosovo.[3] The promises to Serbs and Montenegrins, as events were to prove, were completely unrealistic, more a public relations exercise than a serious intention. The threats against the Kosovo Albanians, however, were serious. Article 6 warned: 'If Albanian nationalists and separatists continue to oppose the approved policy ... they will be stopped by all means ... Society is obliged to protect members of the Albanian nationality from this kind of primitivism and the violence of Albanian nationalism.'[4]

This anti-Kosovo Albanian onslaught was guaranteed to unite them behind a banner of 'nationalism and separatism'. Their very future was at stake. It is a measure of the change of atmosphere that in June 1990 nearly all the Albanian delegates to the Kosovo Assembly – the selfsame people who 15 months before had been intimidated into accepting the 'Constitution of the Tanks' – occupied the Assembly building for three days and nights, prepared to adopt a Declaration of Independence. At this stage, they demanded 'an equal unit in Yugoslavia' with 'Albanians as a nation and not a national minority'. The delegates – the direct link back to the constitution under which they were elected – now performed their duty to withdraw legitimacy from Serbia and bestow it on the emerging Albanian leadership.

The following week, on 2 July 1990 – locked out of the Assembly building – 114 out of the 123 Albanian Assembly members met in the street symbolically to vote in a new status. This unilateral declaration, parallel to that enacted by Slovenia on the same day, was a sign of the resolve of the whole Albanian population of Kosovo to reclaim their self-determination. Even if their signatures to the Declaration on Independence had not been 'at all easy to collect',[5] members of the province's 'most pro-Serbian' parliament now stood for independence.

Also on 2 July, while Kosovo and Slovenia were declaring sovereignty, a referendum in Serbia resoundingly endorsed imposing direct rule on Kosovo and Vojvodina. Three days later, the Serbian parliament voted to dissolve the Kosovo parliament and government and on 26 July the *Law on Labour Relations under Special Circumstances* expanded powers to dismiss workers arbitrarily. At the constitutional level of the conflict, the next round came three months later. On 7 September 1990, the Albanian delegates of the Kosovo Assembly gathered in Kaçanik, near the border with Macedonia, to proclaim the new Constitution – Article 2 declared Kosovo 'a sovereign and independent state' – and to nominate their own government. The meeting was clandestine in one sense, but Tirana TV cameras were there to broadcast the proceedings. Three weeks later, the Assembly of Serbia passed its own new constitution, annulling the autonomy of Kosovo and Vojvodina yet claiming their votes on the federal presidency so that, combined with Montenegro, Serbia now had a bloc of half the votes on the federal presidency.

Earlier in the year, there had been a moment of relaxation of the repression. In April 1990, pressure from other republics – especially Slovenia and Croatia – ended the State of Emergency and withdrew federal forces. Also, some political prisoners were released – the charges against Azem Vllasi and the mine officials fell (for lack of evidence), while Adem Demaçi was released several months ahead of the completion of his sentence. This easing was temporary – a pause before the full weight of 'unification' with Serbia was to be felt.

Every public act asserting the right to self-determination, every challenge to the legitimacy of Serbian rule, brought repression. Three days after the 2 July 1990 Declaration of Independence, police stormed Radio and TV Prishtina, shutting out journalists. In September, Serbia immediately condemned the declaration of the

Kaçanik Constitution as a 'criminal act' and brought charges against participants, many of whom had left Kosovo for their own safety. Zenun Çelaj, secretary of the CDHRF, was detained for a month just for reporting on the meeting.[6] In the meantime, on 9 September, police went on the rampage in Klina and Pollata, killing four Kosovo Albanians.[7] In November 1990 six town councillors in Deçan were arrested for 'preparing to change borders ... in an unconstitutional way' – revising the town constitution to reflect the Kaçanik constitution.[8]

WHOLESALE DISMISSALS

Sometimes the strongest weapon of nonviolent struggle is the mass withdrawal of labour. For the Milošević regime, however, calculations about the public economy were secondary. In the years to come, it ran the economy for its own benefit, which was better served by printing money and black marketeering than by taking care of industrial production. However, in 1990, the nature of Milošević economics had not yet fully revealed itself.

Early in 1990, the Union of Independent Trade Unions of Kosova (BSPK) formed. It had seemed a natural development, in keeping with transitions from Communism elsewhere. Their members were proud that, unlike in Slovenia, these independent unions were initiated from below. A steering committee began work in April 1990 and, by its founding Congress in Gjakova, 30 June–1 July, they had recruited 14,900 members. They proposed a weeklong series of half-hour strikes, taking place the following week – almost an announcement of BSPK's arrival on the scene. From 10 to 10.30 a.m., workers would leave their factories and process in the streets used for the evening *korzo* (promenade).

Although BSPK had permission for this Congress, on the second day police broke it up. A foretaste of what was to come. Within a year, more than 45 per cent of Albanians in employment would lose their jobs and ultimately nearly 90 per cent (a total of 146,025 out of the 164,210 Albanians in employment in 1990).[9] Already, the first Albanian police had been suspended: eventually 3,709 were dismissed, and replaced by many more Serbs and Montenegrins, many brought in from outside. Henceforth Albanians were systematically removed from positions of influence. In the media, Albanian workers for Radio and TV Prishtina and the now-banned daily *Rilindja* were dismissed.

Medical personnel were a particular target. Their response to the alleged poisoning episode was just the latest irritation from a body seen as colluding with demonstrators and refusing to control the growth of the Albanian population. First, teams of medics from Serbia arrived to 'offer their professional help' – that is, to supervise. Then, in August, 'emergency management' was installed, Albanian directors were replaced by Serbs and the sackings began. By June 1991, over 1,211 medical workers had been fired because they refused to accept these measures.[10]

In August, the dismissal of municipal officials began with Podujeva where, Kelmendi points out, only two of the eight new Serb chiefs actually lived in Kosovo. Serbian control of the municipalities further facilitated dismantling other 'Albanianised' structures, including the withdrawal of Albanian teaching.

The theme of mass dismissals is one subject where Serb authorities accused Kosovo Albanians of bringing suffering on themselves in order to make Serbia look bad. They say – and most Serbs believe it – that this was all a 'boycott', Albanians obeying 'their leaders' orders' to stay away from work. Certainly some workers left their jobs rather than work under the new conditions or as a protest against the sackings of colleagues – BSPK advocated that kind of solidarity. However, the mass dismissals were real enough. This is indicated by the copies of redundancy notices on file, for instance with BSPK branches, the tens of thousands of complaints submitted to industrial tribunals yet never heard, and the personal testimony of people dragged from their workplace or physically barred from entering either by police or by a lock-out.

People were sacked on a variety of pretexts. Some were overtly political – participating in demonstrations or strikes, collecting humanitarian aid for dismissed workers. Some were petty offences such as bad timekeeping and many workers were declared 'technologically surplus' or sent on 'indefinite (unpaid) leave'. For some people, losing a job could also mean losing their home.[11] A common pretext for dismissal was if a worker refused to sign an oath of loyalty to Serbia. Refusal was widespread. Yet Brian Hall recounts a friend in 1991 taunting some university professors for arriving at their jobs at 7 a.m. every morning to sign the loyalty oath.

When the Serbs introduced the loyalty oaths last year, our leaders and our intelligentsia told people not to sign, so many workers were fired. Then it was the turn of the intelligentsia to sign, and suddenly there was talk of "pointless gestures", and a lot of them signed.[12]

However, their time would come. Signing loyalty oaths neither saved their jobs nor protected the education of their students.

What came as a particular shock was the wholesale sacking of industrial workers. Kosovo Albanians, if asked what Serbia wanted from Kosovo, sometimes answer its mineral wealth. Yet all but 300 Albanian miners (94 per cent) were dismissed, 90 per cent of chemical workers and nearly 60 per cent of metal workers. Newly imposed 'emergency managers' locked workers out and then put up a list of those who could return. Even when their name appeared on that list, it was rare for an Albanian to go back to work. In the coming weeks, or in some cases months, the 'emergency managers' would issue dismissal notices.[13] Workers fired in this way lost their rights to social security payments.[14]

Either individually or collectively, half of those sacked lodged an appeal to the Kosovo labour court. This court was then abolished and its cases transferred to Serbia proper. Many workers were never summoned to a hearing and – of those who were – few went. There were about 70,000 complaints lodged in court, according to the BSPK, few of which were heard.[15] Even on those occasions when courts heard a complaint and overruled dismissals, there are reports of managers not accepting workers back in factories and hospitals.[16] Any strategy based on the 'organised strength of the working class', as Maliqi and Magaš had discussed[17] or as BSPK might have envisaged, was in disarray. Far from being able to threaten withdrawing the fruit of their labour, soon the main task of the new unions was keeping count of those dismissed and raising solidarity funds.

On 3 September 1990, BSPK called a one-day general strike demanding the reinstatement of the 15,000 workers already dismissed and the respect of trade union rights. Those doing work considered 'vital' showed their support by wearing green armbands (a non-provocative choice, rather than the Albanian national colours). This strike itself served as a pretext for the dismissal of a further 5,000 BSPK members. Whilst the temporary measures of 'emergency management' hit ethnic groups other than Albanians, suspended Serb and Montenegrin managers tended to be reinstated, whereas Albanians hardly ever were. In their place 'loyal' Roma or Turks (usually trying to stay out of the conflict) were likely to be promoted.

It was rare that Kosovo Serbs would protest at the removal of Albanian colleagues, even where there had been friendships across the ethnic divide. There were a few cases of Serb managers or school principals refusing to implement the new policies, usually leading to their resignation. At the university in 1991 at least two Serbs stood up for Albanians: a music teacher (who later taught at the parallel university) and the Dean of Philosophy who insisted on respecting his sacked Albanian colleagues by publishing their articles.[18] Under authoritarian Communism, most people had learnt 'prudence' when 'provocateurs' were repressed, but this was also an ethnicised situation where any gesture of solidarity to a friend would be interpreted as treason to one's own community. Ethnic polarisation was imposing its own discipline on members of both communities and the mass sackings intensified the bitterness.

POLICE AND PARAMILITARY

Any resistance movement has to weigh up its ability to withstand the types and scale of repression it could face and develop strategies either to inhibit repression or to make sure that the oppressor pays a political price for it. If Albanians could not anticipate that the Milošević regime would be willing virtually to write off industrial production in Kosovo, history made them only too well aware of the police and paramilitary operations they could expect. The Serbian authorities had no use for Albanians in Kosovo, hence the security organs worked in the spirit of Čubrilović's advice to create 'a suitable psychosis' to encourage them to leave.

As a counter to a resistance movement, this was less effective than a more selective strategy trying to exploit divisions among Albanians. It actually served to strengthen Albanian unity. But for the Belgrade regime this was not a time for half-measures. From 1989 onwards, it seemed as if the Serbian population were being prepared for war. Arms were distributed increasingly openly and Serbian 'village guards' formed.[19] The group *Božur* had the frank aim of restoring a Slav majority in Kosovo and was rumoured to include former Ranković special police. As well as its role in the Meetings of

Truth around Yugoslavia, it was notorious inside Kosovo for terrorising peasants.[20] Its leader Bogdan Kecman, soon to be head of the Serbian Red Cross, displayed a clear orientation towards war: 'I want to see the day when Kosovo is populated with Serbs who were forced to leave their land, and fewer Albanians. Who knows it could come to a big battle here.'[21]

Later, the famous paramilitaries – the Tigers (Serbian Volunteer Guards) of Željko Ražnjatović (Arkan) and the White Eagles of Vojislav Šešelj – arrived. In April 1992 Kosovo's senior Serbian official announced a recruitment centre for these in Prishtina's Grand Hotel.[22] While Arkan was to become Prishtina's representative to the Serbian Assembly, Šešelj was made a lecturer in, of all things, law at the Serbian University of Prishtina.

The main fear for Kosovo Albanians, however, was of the police. In January 1992, I heard that the sacked Albanian police had been replaced by double the number of Serbian and Montenegrin police, some 7,000. Later there were to be much higher estimates as Milošević built up the police force, trusting the police more than the army. Albanians believed that the police in Kosovo numbered around 40,000 in the early 1990s.[23] The US State Department's 1994 report described police violence as 'routine and capricious'. A former Serbian police officer recollected in 1996:

> If there was anyone who did not want to beat the old people, spill their hay onto the road or their wheat across the courtyard, while searching for arms, or who did not want to break into houses at three o' clock in the morning and smash everything in the way with rifle butts, people's heads, televisions, even remote controls, or if there was anyone who happened to take pity on these people, he was immediately branded as an inadequate Serb and a poor patriot, and the other policemen would turn on him with contempt.[24]

The main form of terror was the traditional 'search for arms', punitive expeditions mainly into villages and usually in the early hours of the morning. Police, sometimes accompanied by irregulars, would pick a village – often arbitrarily – and surround it with cars. A group would then go to one house, order the men to one side of the courtyard and the women to the other, while they conducted the search. Not finding weapons, they would begin to beat the men, demanding to know where the weapons were 'hidden'. Sometimes they would take a woman or child to the police station, telling the family s/he would be released if they reported to the police station with the 'hidden' weapon. The family then had to find or buy a weapon, perhaps from a Serb neighbour at an extortionate price. The whole search was designed to demean the people and offend against their culture. Women would be told to sing Serbian songs while serving the police with coffee; there are few reports of sexual molestation – a matter of social stigma.[25] Having some idea of the importance of honour to Albanians, the police would often try to humiliate the 'master of the house' in front of his family. The death of an 80-year-old woman illustrates the impact of this random terror. Police raided the village of Çabër on 30–31 August 1993, searching 150 families for weapons. They beat people, smashing up homes and furniture. It was on seeing her sons beaten that Grisha Kamberi fainted and died four days later.[26]

The CDHRF recorded incidents of arms searches in more than 20 villages and in some of the main towns in 1992; some were visited more than once. The next year, CDHRF began to keep a tally of the number of homes thus raided: 1,994 in 1993, 3,553 in 1994, 2,324 in 1995 and 809 in 1996. Few arrests resulted, yet each raid gave rise to brutality.

The police had a licence to vandalise, terrorise and plunder – especially hard currency brought back from working abroad. Any Albanian gathering – be it a wedding or a football game – ran a risk of police interference. Men of conscription age were especially vulnerable to being picked up on a bus. Many of that generation simply fled Kosovo to avoid conscription papers. It was not that they were wanted in the army, but this was another way to harass them.[27]

As each phase of Albanian resistance developed, people suspected of involvement were taken in for questioning and were often beaten. The CDHRF office in Prishtina had a grim photo album the size of a large telephone directory, packed with pictures of bruised torsos, faces or feet. The CDHRF and, after 1992, the Humanitarian Law Centre in Belgrade, collected horrifying testimonies about police sadism. Some people died under torture in police custody – two a year in 1991, 1992 and 1993, eight in 1994, five in 1995. In June 1992, Amnesty International issued a report with 15 illustrative cases of how police were ill-treating Kosovo Albanians. Helsinki Watch (later Human Rights Watch) published reports in 1992 and 1994.[28]

Following the 'isolation' campaign of 1989, there was no new effort to 'decapitate' the movement. Nevertheless, between 1989 and

1992, an estimated 20,000 Kosovo Albanians served 30–60 day prison sentences.[29] This number dropped, but such summary sentences continued to be handed out arbitrarily to 'wrongdoers' such as teachers in the parallel system, volunteer tax collectors and soccer club secretaries. However, before arrival of the UÇK the only major trials were those connected with the investigations into the parallel Ministries of Defence and the Interior from 1993–94.

The most prominent leaders of the struggle – Rugova, Agani, Demaçi – enjoyed an immunity within limits. If offices of the CDHRF and BSPK occasionally suffered raids (or the LDK's and their branch offices), Rugova himself and the LDK headquarters remained unmolested. Every Friday in the PEN club, Rugova or another LDK leader held a press conference. With voluntary labour and donated materials, people built magnificent houses for Rugova and Demaçi, standing next to each other, landmarks in their neighbourhood. Rugova, of course, would always be escorted. While he himself avoided going to villages so as not to cause a stir, vice-presidents and other members of the LDK board went to the scene of police raids and other events, and rarely suffered repercussions.

Over time, the Albanian resistance through their resolution and self-control gained more space and made their treatment a point of international pressure against the regime. In Kosovo's cities, it became second nature for Albanians to walk home by back routes to avoid the police, especially after dark. Every car driver seemed to have a personal strategy when stopped by the police. People learnt to live with tension. Doubtless, too, the wars in Croatia and Bosnia made Serbia's ultra-nationalists less interested in provoking a war in Kosovo. The harassment did not stop throughout the period of Serbian rule – brutal, random and racist – but, thanks to their human rights monitoring work, Albanians were able use the widespread violence against them to increase international goodwill towards their nonviolent policy.

THE CONTEST FOR LEGITIMACY

In the face of the unfolding threat, it was clear that a new level of coordination was necessary. So, towards the end of 1990, a Coordinating Council of Political Parties was formed. Although the LDK was by far the biggest party, the Council's practice of making decisions by consensus gave a voice to smaller bodies, such as those represented by the left democrats Maliqi and Surroi, as well as non-party figures such as Demaçi as head of the CDHRF and trade unionist Hajrullah Gorani of the BSPK. Henceforth, even the pluralistic Kosova Alternative groups went along with a 'united front' strategy, sinking differences in the interests of unity against military administration.

According to Gene Sharp, in the first phase of what might be called a 'close encounter defence', such as an occupation, the basic objective is to deny legitimacy. Nonviolent strategy suggests two main options. One is a 'nonviolent blitzkrieg' – the suspension of daily life during an intense period of all-out general strike, demonstrations and total non-cooperation. The other is 'communication and warning' – using low risk and sustainable actions to warn of the will to resist and to build support and morale among the home population.[30] A 'nonviolent blitzkrieg' is hard to sustain, especially without preparation. In 1989, the attempted general strike at the time of the miners' strike and the violence in the demonstrations after the 'Constitution of the Tanks' showed weaknesses both in the Kosovo Albanian organisation and the nonviolent discipline at that time. Nevertheless the miners' strike had the effect of signalling that an aggression was taking place. What followed can then be considered a phase of 'communication and warning'. The various forms of semi-resistance practised after the State of Emergency in 1989 served to mobilise the community while warning the occupiers. In 1990, when the January demonstrations threatened much wider bloodshed, collecting signatures for the declaration *For Democracy, Against Violence* strengthened organisation and communicated a new tone, internationally and within the Albanian community.

What demonstrations there were in 1991 were carefully designed to contrast the nonviolence of the Albanians with the violence of the Serbs.

– At the beginning of 1991, a sacked radio journalist – Afërdita Saraçini-Kelmendi – called an hour-long silent demonstration in which more than 1,000 women took part in Prishtina, their posters demanding 'Stop the Violence'. This represented a new step in women organising themselves in Kosovo.[31]

– On 13 June, 40,000 people (some reports estimate 100,000) took part in the 'Quiet Burial of Violence' – an event organised by the

Youth Parliament. Carrying an empty coffin, a procession resembling a funeral made its way from the Catholic Church in Prishtina via the mosque to the cemetery. Using the funeral theme helped establish a different tone among the demonstrators and to inhibit police violence.

– On 1 July, actually during the war with Slovenia, the BSPK organised a one-day general strike accompanied by massive demonstrations with the slogan 'We are for dialogue. And you?'

The next step in contesting the legitimacy of Serbian rule was to demonstrate democratically the aspirations of the overwhelming majority of the people of Kosovo. In this, the central idea was to prepare a referendum on the future of Kosovo.

The Coordinating Council of Political Parties did not include any member of the old provincial representatives, but stayed in touch with Jusuf Zejnullahu, former president of the Executive council, nominated prime-minister-in-exile at Kaçanik in September 1990. A year later, on 22 September 1991, Albanian delegates to the 'dissolved' Assembly met again, this time to call a referendum. The proposal was to proclaim Kosovo a sovereign and independent state with the right to take part in any eventual association of sovereign states within Yugoslavia. The referendum, organised by the Coordinating Council, took place a few days later, between 26 and 30 September at a cost of more than 40 organisers imprisoned for up to 60 days.[32] Its predictable result was that, of the 914,802 votes counted (87 per cent of the electorate), 99.87 per cent favoured independence. Without Slovenia and Croatia, Kosovo Albanians did not want to be part of Yugoslavia.

On 19 October, the members of the former provincial Assembly duly amended the Kaçanik constitution and declared Kosovo's independence. Now the Coordinating Council of Political Parties appointed one of the LDK's founders, its General Secretary Bujar Bukoshi, as prime minister, tasked with establishing a government-in-exile. Rugova as LDK president would stay in Prishtina to carry out his responsibilities openly. Therefore it was essential to have a legitimate voice operating from the safety of the diaspora.

Kosovo Albanians were also aware that their fate was relevant to Albanians elsewhere in Yugoslavia. LDK leaders began to meet with leaders of Albanian parties in Macedonia, Montenegro and southern Serbia. In Macedonia, Albanians boycotted the republic's referendum on independence in September 1991 and in January held their own referendum on the right to autonomy (political, not territorial). The Yugoslav Albanians agreed a set of common options: first, based on existing frontiers, independence for Kosovo with Albanians being recognised as a constituent part of Macedonia, and some self-administration in Montenegro and Serbia; second, if frontiers inside Yugoslavia changed, to have an Albanian republic, including parts of Macedonia; third, if external borders eventually changed, the unification of Kosovo and parts of Macedonia with Albania. This final part, emphasised Rugova, was a long-term option, not for tomorrow.[33]

Inside Kosovo, on 24 May 1992, the Coordinating Council organised elections for a parliament and president of Kosovo. Again, the turn-out of registered votes was overwhelming – 766,069 voters inside Kosovo, 105,300 in the diaspora. Some 24 parties and associations took part. The results underlined the LDK's dominance, it was more of a national movement than one party among several. The LDK with 76 per cent of the vote gained 96 out of the 100 single constituency seats, Slav Muslims one, and the Parliamentary Party (PPK – successor of the Youth Parliament) one. Some eyebrows were raised at the defeat of two constituency candidates, the leader of the Social Democratic Party Shkëlzen Maliqi and mine manager Bruhan Kavaya, recently on trial as an alleged organiser of the Trepça strike.[34] The remaining 42 seats were allocated on the basis of proportional representation, the PPK thus gaining another 12 seats, the Democratic Action Party (Slav Muslim) a further four and the Turkish Popular Party one seat.[35] Ibrahim Rugova as the only candidate for president registered 99.5 per cent of the vote.

There was little police interference with these elections, although there were contingency plans: for instance organisers prepared 'decoy' ballot boxes already filled with papers so that police would seize them in mistake for boxes with valid ballots.[36] Also, occasionally the election centre would have to be moved in view of police interest. Journalists from Tirana were not allowed in and a team from Croatia was ejected, but it was a sign of the Kosovo Albanians' attempt to 'internationalise' the issue that the parallel elections were observed by eight monitoring teams from the West and covered by 82 international news agencies.[37] The elections, as Veton Surroi observed were 'neither free', because Kosovo is not free, 'nor democratic … because there were no possibilities for them to be properly organised'.[38] However within the limits that existed, they were a successful demonstration.

While the regime had not prevented the elections, it did not intend to allow the parliament to meet. Police entered the Muslim seminary where the parliament was due to meet on 24 June 1992, smashing furniture. Then they sealed off the area and took in LDK vice-president Fehmi Agani for 'informative talks', warning him of the consequences of proceeding with this endeavour, and arrested several of those responsible for the building and some parliamentarians.

No attempt was made to hold local elections, but municipal structures with mayors were revived. If 'most are multi-party', Rugova explained, 'the LDK also functions as the local authority because with the party it is easier to organise life', thanks to its moral standing.[39]

While the elections gave legitimacy to the LDK, and in particular to Rugova as the recognised voice of his people, they also marked a shift away from the previous all-party cooperation. One outcome was that the Coordinating Council of Political Parties was now treated as meaningless, but unfortunately it was not replaced by the parliament. Unable to meet in plenary, 13 parliamentary commissions were appointed on a range of subjects, but only four seemed to have functioned in any way and they were all far from controlling policy.

The LDK exercised a dominance over Albanian political life that the LCY in Kosovo never had. It had far more members. Moreover it had assumed the position not only of rightful heir to the former authorities, but also to those outside the Party who had expressed the aspiration for a republic. Unfortunately, its style of operation was increasingly akin to that of other one-party states. As well as questions about the organising style of the LDK, and indeed the personal style of Ibrahim Rugova, this raises strategic issues about the role and structure of leadership in the conduct of a nonviolent struggle – especially in a context where self-restraint is so central.

THE ELECTORAL BOYCOTT

The alleged poisoning episode of March 1990 and the mass dismissals intensified inter-ethnic hostility in Kosovo. Nevertheless, in formal terms, there was an endeavour to somehow include Serbs in the emerging structures. The parallel parliament left seats vacant for the Serbs/Montenegrins who did not vote, while the CDHRF claimed to be monitoring the rights of the whole population of

Kosovo and invited Serbs to nominate members for its Board. Adem Demaçi, CDHRF chair from 1991–96, was only the most prominent of those who said that, while Serbs had imprisoned him, it was also other Serbs who had helped him to survive that imprisonment.[40] However, it was not to be expected that Serbs would participate in 'separatist institutions' – and nor would Kosovo Albanians participate in the institutions imposed by the 'occupier'.

Initially, where they could, Kosovo Albanians continued to participate in *federal* structures. Although in March 1990 their representative on the federal presidency was replaced by a Serbian-appointed 'loyal Albanian', in the federal Assembly even as late as 13 December 1991 16 Kosovo Albanian deputies appealed to the Secretary-General of the United Nations, accusing the Serbian authorities of an 'armed massacre against the Albanians' and calling for a UN peace-keeping force.[41]

However, the Coordinating Council of Political Parties – refusing to accord legitimacy to the Serbian structures that had taken over Kosovo – called a boycott of the December 1990 Serbian elections and later the census of 1991. The electoral boycott was maintained in subsequent federal, Serbian and local elections, a policy greatly criticised by members of the democratic opposition in Serbia and by international politicians. It was taken as a sign of nationalist intransigence and that Kosovo Albanians were not willing to do what was constitutionally open to them to moderate Serbia's policies.

For Serb oppositionists, such as those in UJDI, the Albanian abstention seemed to aid and abet Milošević's design. They argued that Albanians should demonstrate a willingness to resolve the issue through democratic processes and that only the full participation of ethnic minorities in Serbian politics could roll back the prevailing ultra-nationalism and create a democratic, multi-ethnic polity. The multi-ethnic Vojvodinans, who had also lost their autonomy, accepted these arguments but Kosovo Albanians were bound to find them unpersuasive. They were allergic to the term 'minority'. Far from seeing themselves as a 'minority' in the Yugoslav sense, they were – along with Slovenia – the most ethnically homogenous population in Yugoslavia, entitled by their numbers and their 'ethnic compactness' to be regarded as a 'nation'. Their previous experience of working through Yugoslav institutions – going back to Xhemijet in the 1920s – made them sceptical of participation in parliament, even more so now that they were the main hate objects of Serbian nationalism. The 1990 Serbian elections in Serbia were for an

Assembly that unconstitutionally usurped the functions of Kosovo's own Assembly and had imposed discriminatory legislation against Albanians. The clearest signal they could therefore give was a complete boycott of illegitimate institutions.

Their view would be shared by many who have studied civil resistance to occupation. Jacques Semelin – in his study of movements of resistance to Nazi occupation in the Second World War – suggests two related questions: 'What particular political behaviour of a militarily conquered nation would lead to its political submission?' and 'What would best activate civil society's potential to resist?' His analysis suggests 'a general axiom':

> Denouncing the illegitimacy of the occupier's power, which was acquired through force of arms, was the first way in which a conquered society could resist the conqueror's determination to control ... The founding act of a resistance process against an occupation is basically an affirmation of the superiority of the *de jure* authority over the *de facto* one ... The creative dynamic of resistance derives, above all, from this initiating and declaratory act of noncooperation politics ... The more the question of legitimacy is muddled ... the less chance a civilian resistance has to develop quickly.[42]

The strategic argument might shift later, but at this early stage the point was to announce – and indeed denounce – the 'crime' for a primarily international audience and to develop strategies based on mobilising their own population. This is not to deny the value of any connection with opposition groups in the opponent's society – in this case in Serbia – but to offer a perspective on strategic priorities. At a time when Milošević's Socialist Party of Serbia (SPS) could win 192 out of the 250 seats in the Serbian Assembly, Kosovo Albanians saw that Serbia was in thrall to a nationalism against which they needed to protect themselves.

The boycott, however, also raises an issue about considering this situation as an 'occupation'. Straightforward resistance to occupation seeks to defeat the occupier. Any question of subsequent relationships with the occupiers or with any collaborating minority or settler population is subordinate to that. Kosovo Albanians, however, were bidding for a status they had never had before, and therefore needed to build confidence in how inter-ethnic relations would be conducted in Kosovo – especially in view of the previous grounds for complaint. The Kaçanik constitution guaranteed rights for other ethnic groups, including reserving seats in the parallel parliament. That showed good intent at a formal level, but it was not enough. This issue affected the outlook of different camps of opinion. Those who saw themselves in the camp of 'coexistence' naturally sought dialogue with Serbs and cooperation with non-nationalist Serbs who were committed to democracy and pluralism. The dominant opinion, however, concentrated on defeating the occupier and claiming long overdue Albanian rights; it shunned contact with Serbs. The LDK leadership contained both views.

Although the boycott issue arose repeatedly in Serb oppositionist-Kosovo Albanian relationships in the years to come, few Kosovo Albanians could see anything to gain by voting. People in the camp of 'coexistence' – Maliqi and Surroi, for instance – were willing to consider the issue of voting in the context of maintaining some dialogue, but there was little basis for any electoral cooperation.

The greatest effort to secure Albanian votes came in December 1992 when Milan Panić challenged Milošević for the presidency of Serbia. Installed by Milošević as federal prime minister earlier in the year, Panić had asserted himself against Milošević in the London Conference on the Former Yugoslavia in August 1992. The West saw him as genuinely committed to making peace with Croatia and ending the war in Bosnia-Herzegovina, while on Kosovo he had crossed Milošević by agreeing for the CSCE to send a long-term mission of human rights observers and accepting internationally-mediated negotiations on education. Was this the occasion for a strategic alliance to defeat Milošević? Most Serbian democratic oppositionists genuinely concerned for the human rights of Albanians (not a large number) tended to feel that it was.

An LDK Board member who attended the negotiations with Panić explained the boycott of the 1992 elections in terms of practical politics.[43] The problem in taking part was not so much of conceding legitimacy to the process – 'We could have got around that.' It was more an assessment of what Panić could offer and what he could deliver. They felt he was not offering much, but worse 'he was so weak'. Milošević, with the media and police apparatus under his control, would not sit meekly by and allow himself to be voted out of office. While Albanians would run the risk of reprisals, they would still not advance significantly towards achieving their aspirations.

Some Serb democrats suggested that if Albanians boycotted the first round of the presidential elections, they could still vote for Panić in the second round.[44] It is unlikely that their pleas would have been persuasive, but – as it turned out – Panić's challenge fell in the first round, gaining 34 per cent of the votes against Milošević's 56 per cent.[45] At the same time, the federal and the Serbian parliamentary elections – also boycotted by Kosovo Albanians – showed overwhelming support for ultra-nationalists. The main anti-war party, Depos, gained fewer than half the seats of Milošević's SPS, fewer even than more extreme bodies frankly advocating expulsion of Albanians from Kosovo.[46]

As well as Milošević's own capacity for electoral fraud, the LDK negotiators were also mindful of the presence in Kosovo of more extreme nationalists. The likes of Šešelj and Arkan (who was elected as a deputy for Prishtina) have played an invaluable role for Milošević. On the one hand, their extremism allowed him to pose as a moderating influence. On the other, they had the arms and paramilitary organisation to do his bidding as the occasion demanded – including if that had meant intimidating Albanian voters in Kosovo, or even expelling them. Against all this, Panić's hastily scrambled together organisation lacked credibility.

LDK leaders may have been deceiving themselves in thinking at this stage that they were flexible enough to assess tactics such as the electoral boycott according to their merits. Attitudes in the movement were hardening, even rigidifying. For this reason, in 1993 both Veton Surroi and Shkëlzen Maliqi left party politics. Surroi quit the leadership of the Parliamentary Party (PPK), dismayed by the 'radicalisation' of its rank and file.[47] Maliqi stepped down from the Social Democratic Party leadership following 'fierce' reactions to his proposal that 'a list of independent citizen candidates ... go to the Serbian parliament with the programme for Kosovo independence.'[48] Maliqi's proposal was a far cry from deploying the Albanian vote to support any Serbian politician, indeed his judgement remained 'there are no conditions whatsoever for Albanians to take part in Serbia's political life, either directly or in large numbers'.[49] Nevertheless, simply proposing this tactic had put him beyond the pale. Not in the eyes of Ibrahim Rugova who calmed the furore, nor of some of his long-term friends in the LDK leadership. Rather it was the mood of most of the population. Looking back in 1996, one local analyst commented that, 'burdened by vital problems of survival and fierce Serbian repression, the Albanian public was not in a mood for such ideas nor thoughts about more complex forms of struggle.'[50] When Slovenia, Croatia

and Bosnia apparently had to go to war for independence, participation in the charade of an Assembly that existed in Belgrade was
not likely to appeal to many Kosovo Albanians. However, the
boycott – a tactic appropriate for the early mobilisation of opinion
– began to assume the status of an immutable strategic principle.

INTERNATIONAL SUPPORT

From the outset, the Kosovo Albanian strategy relied heavily on
international support. Here they had two great assets: a diaspora
ready to campaign for them, and the clear-cut character of the
human rights abuses. On the other hand, they were greatly
handicapped by the situation in the region – not only that Kosovo
was overshadowed by larger populations actually at war, but also
that international policy towards the disintegration of Yugoslavia
was incoherent. The Kosovo Albanians were more successful in
securing statements of concern from bodies with moral authority
than in influencing states whose main interests in the region were
to restore stability and to return refugees.

Perhaps the greatest success of Kosovo Albanian lobbying was also
the most damaging delusion. On 27 December 1992 outgoing US
president George Bush promised that the USA would not let Kosovo
become a second Bosnia. Receiving intelligence reports on a planned
crackdown, he threatened unilateral air strikes against strategic
targets in Serbia. Clinton re-affirmed this in February.[51] This
promise that Kosovo would not become another Bosnia could not
be kept and was irresponsible, while the threat of air strikes
suggested that Kosovo had a much higher level of priority than
events were to bear out. Among the population of Kosovo, this
reinforced their faith that some kind of international intervention
would resolve their situation.

The US lobby for Kosovo was ahead of its European counterparts
as there are more than 350,000 Albanian-Americans who in October
1986 had formed the Albanian-American Civic League.[52] Thanks to
its influence Ibrahim Rugova and Veton Surroi attended Congressional hearings on human rights violations in Washington in April
1990. In turn, Congressional representatives – including House
leader Robert Dole – visited Kosovo at various times, sent monitors
for the parallel elections and in 1993 decided to provide Kosovo with
humanitarian aid. The declaration *For Democracy, Against Violence*,

taken to the UN in June 1990, helped Albanians to claim the moral high ground.

The Kosovo Albanians' international outreach operated at every level from grass-roots circles through links with trade unions and humanitarian organisations up to the diplomatic level. Not receiving recognition as an independent republic (Albania aside), Kosovo joined the Unrepresented Nations and Peoples Organisation in 1991. Activists from Kosovo were also busy making links with trade unions, with peace groups, with whatever counterparts they could find – but with one exception: they were determined to be seen as Western-oriented and therefore avoided cultivating links with the Islamic world. Where previously Kosovo Albanians had taken part in Yugoslav delegations, now they formed separate groups. Trade unions from other countries began contributing to the teachers' solidarity fund, and from 1994 onwards a few international humanitarian organisations – such as Catholic Relief Services, Médecins sans Frontières, Médecins du Monde, Mercy Corps and Oxfam – began making funds available for projects in Kosovo.

Bujar Bukoshi, as prime-minister-in-exile, set up office in Bonn, while information minister Xhafer Shatri was based in Geneva. There were soon other active offices in Brussels, London and Stockholm, charged with spreading information about what was happening inside Kosovo and in organising the diaspora and 'guestworkers' to support the movement, especially financially.

In terms of opinion-forming, international press coverage was sporadic. With no demonstrations to report after October 1992, it was rare for any newspaper to have more than an occasional feature article on the remarkable nonviolent struggle that was avoiding war. However, a stream of resolutions condemned Serbian human rights violations, some praising Albanian self-restraint and some making a vague reference to the right to self-determination.

The European Parliament took up the issue of Kosovo early on: its first resolution protesting at repressive measures in Kosovo was on 13 April 1989. In December 1991, it awarded Adem Demaçi its Sakharov Human Rights Prize. He became the first Albanian to make a speech in the Palais de l'Europe – a symbolic moment.[53] Various UN bodies passed resolutions. In 1992, both the Commission on Human Rights and the General Assembly passed the first of several resolutions.

In August 1992, Kosovo Albanians were invited to be observers at the London Conference on Former Yugoslavia. Sidelined, they nevertheless claimed two modest gains: agreements for a mission of the Conference (Organisation after 1995) for Security and Cooperation (CSCE/OSCE) and for internationally mediated negotiations on education.

The primary international security body to deal with the Kosovo issue until the NATO intervention of 1998 was the CSCE/OSCE. In July 1991, during and after the war in Slovenia, its Meeting of Experts on National Minorities heavily criticised Serbia for its Kosovo policy. In July of 1992, as well as sending exploratory missions to Kosovo in May, August and September, the CSCE called for 'immediate preventive action' in Kosovo, urging 'the authorities in Belgrade to refrain from further repression and to engage in serious dialogue with representatives from Kosovo, in the presence of a third party.' This meeting also temporarily suspended FRY's membership in the CSCE (FRY had claimed the seat previously held by the Socialist federation). In 1993 it installed a 'long-term mission' to Kosovo, Vojvodina and the Sandžak. This mission lasted six months, after which FRY – in protest at being excluded from the CSCE – refused permission for its extension.

The UN Security Council's first resolution on Kosovo called upon FRY to reconsider the refusal to permit the extension of the CSCE mission. In future, UN Human Rights rapporteurs Tadeusz Mazowiecki and later Elisabeth Rehn would recount in detail the information they received from local human rights activists, including the CDHRF.

Kosovo Serbs would have welcomed the continuation of the CSCE mission, regarding its reports as more objective than others coming out of Kosovo.[54] The Kosovo Albanians, too, would have welcomed its continuation, for all its failings. Belgrade decided on this stance, however, in response to a CSCE decision motivated by events in Bosnia, not Kosovo.

If Kosovo was subsidiary to Bosnia, the problem was exacerbated by the CSCE's own weakness in the post-Cold War battle for institutional responsibilities in European security. The USA and Britain were determined that the military alliance NATO would play the prime role, rather than building up the CSCE into a body adequate for the challenges of the times. Caught between the lack of interest from states, the predominance of the war in Bosnia and the debilities of Europe's 'security architecture', Kosovo was left waiting.

Rugova began to receive diplomats in Kosovo and to tour foreign capitals, visiting leaders or foreign ministers. However, the reports of his meetings in the bulletins put out by Prishtina Kosova

Information Centre (KIC) were tediously repetitive and misleading. They reported what Rugova told the diplomats and how they in turn praised the Kosovo Albanians' nonviolent policy and condemned Serbian human rights violations. However, they did not convey the unpalatable truth that every foreign government said they would not recognise the independence of Kosovo. While Kosovo Albanians received little more than expressions of sympathy, gestures of concern about human rights and promises of 'preventive action', Rugova and the LDK-controlled media in Kosovo tried to disguise this fundamental problem and so avoid discussion of negotiating strategy.

INDEPENDENCE: A 'MAXIMALIST' GOAL?

The turn-out for the referendum in September 1991 and for the parallel elections in May 1992 indicated that Kosovo Albanians had achieved the greatest degree of unity in their history behind the demand for independence. For some, independence was a step towards the unification of Albanians. For others, it was the natural consequence of the break-up of Yugoslavia. Kosovo had been a federal unit and, ran the argument, now that the federation had ceased to exist, then Kosovo too had good reason to opt for independence. However, internationally, this was seen as a maximalist demand, while in terms of strategic objectives it shifted the ground from reclaiming what the regime had taken away towards demanding a degree of self-determination to which Kosovo Albanians had aspired but which they had never had.

Because of the break-up of Yugoslavia, there was no possibility of a return to the *status quo ante*. The Serbian regime's violence in Kosovo and wholesale denial of rights on an ethnic basis made it quite unacceptable to Kosovo Albanians that they should live 'under Serbia'. Their logic therefore led them to call for an independent, neutral and demilitarised Kosovo with open borders to FRY, Macedonia and Albania, and with constitutional guarantees for the rights of Serbs and other ethnic communities.

The problem was that *de jure* Kosovo had not been a republic and that the only state to recognise its claimed 'independence' was Albania. Its former allies inside Yugoslavia, Slovenia and Croatia were now prepared to let Kosovo be treated as an internal affair of FRY. The Badinter commission of the European Community (since

1994 European Union, EC/EU), hurriedly reviewing the question of sovereignties in former Yugoslavia at the end of 1991, decided to treat only republics as 'federal units', ignoring the practice of the 1974 constitution. Hence it accepted 'the right of Kosovo to autonomy' but 'as a non-sovereign territorial unit with national characteristics'.[55] Nobody was prepared to go back to the 1974 Constitution, let alone address the argument that the Albanian borders of 1913 were themselves unjust, or that Socialist Yugoslavia should have granted Kosovo the republican status that almost its entire Albanian population wanted.

Badinter recommended withholding recognition of Croatia (which failed to meet human rights criteria) yet – in an example of the inconsistency that has dogged international policy-making on the succession to Yugoslavia – the EC overrode this. Although the Serbian-occupied areas of Croatia had declared their own Serbian Republic of the Krajina, Croatia gained independence by presenting a *fait accompli* – and going to war. The Kosovo Albanians – although determined to avoid war – were also trying to make their own independence a *fait accompli*. However, without the numbers or the wealth of Croatia, there was no member of the EC promoting their case.

Without foreign support for independence, the Kosovo Albanians nevertheless decided to internationalise the issue. On two occasions – 22 May and 10 June 1992 – when the government of Serbia summoned representatives of the newly elected 'parallel' parliament to Belgrade for talks, the Kosovo Albanians ignored the invitation. Instead – based on their distrust of the regime and their desire to involve international bodies as guarantors of any agreement – they set a precondition that any formal negotiations with Serbia should have international mediators.[56] During the 'Panić Interlude' (July 1992–February 1993), the FRY government accepted this demand.

There was deadlock over the question of a final status. Serbia had unilaterally and unconstitutionally repealed an autonomy that it claimed the Albanians were abusing. For the Kosovo Albanians, accepting an autonomy on sufferance from Serbia, in a rump-state dominated by Serbia, would have been seen simply as accepting defeat, while for FRY to offer any more would be seen by Serbs as once more abandoning the Kosovo Serbs to the hateful Albanians. Therefore the Special Group on Kosovo (of the International Conference on the former Yugoslavia, ICFY)[57] adopted a step by step approach. Instead of dealing directly with the question of Kosovo's status, the group offered to mediate negotiations on education. (See

Chapter 5 for an account of the closure of Albanian schools and the establishment of a parallel system.)

Negotiations on education began in Prishtina from 13–15 October and continued in Belgrade on 22 October, scheduling the re-opening of the elementary and secondary schools for 2–3 November.[58] This did not happen. Regardless of how sincere Panić's desire to resolve this conflict may have been, it was not actually in his power. He was an official of FRY, not of Serbia, and in any case his position was precarious. When the Special Group on Kosovo was due to meet in Geneva in November, on three separate occasions the Serbian delegation failed to arrive. Serbia also obstructed negotiations by denying one Albanian delegate a passport – teachers' union leader Rexhep Osmani – and in March 1993 arresting another – university rector Ejup Statovci. Eventually a dozen or so internationally mediated meetings took place in Geneva until June 1993 when FRY pulled out.

Yugoslav negotiators had offered two substantial concessions – to permit teaching according to the 1990 Kosovo curriculum and to recognise the credits earned by pupils in the 'illegal' schools. However, they insisted, any qualification had to be issued by Serbian officials using the seal of their republic. In other words, Kosovo Albanians could only pursue their own educational curriculum in state schools if they recognised that Kosovo was under the authority of Serbia.[59] Such an insistence defeated the object of trying to negotiate step by step on single issues without prejudicing any solution to the overall problem of the disputed status of Kosovo. This negotiating process ended in June when, at the same time as it refused to renew the mandate of the CSCE mission, FRY took a strong stand against any international interference in 'internal affairs'.

By the end of 1992, the Kosovo Albanians had succeeded in persuading foreign governments that Serbia's violation of their rights was more than an 'internal issue' and that the annulment of Kosovo's autonomy had been an illegitimate act. What they still had to achieve was either to convince foreign powers of their case, or to press them for a concerted effort to agree on a process for resolution. In Washington in May 1993, the foreign ministers of the USA, Russia, Britain, France and Spain stated their determination that Kosovo should have a high level of autonomy within Serbia. Foreign powers refused to accept that – if FRY continued to refuse international mediation and continued to abuse the Kosovo Albanians – they should reconsider the insistence that Kosovo 'remain' inside FRY.

5
Parallel Structures

'Each day that passes without an explosion is a victory for the Kosovo Albanians', commented the Serbian oppositionist Ivan Djurić in 1992.[1] Certainly, in the early years of the nonviolent struggle, the Kosovo Albanian leadership projected the idea that time was on their side. As long as they refused to be provoked to violence, they could organise their own lives and build up international support. They needed a strategy that would avoid either war or submission to the regime while progressing towards their aspiration for independence. The key to this was the parallel institutions – either the transfer of the former autonomous organs to the self-declared Republic of Kosova or the construction of new systems.

Some Kosovo Albanians were sceptical that such a strategy could succeed. However, the enthusiasm for a type of struggle new in Albanian history swept along even the sceptics. Many share Igballe Rogova's recollection: 'At that time there was great solidarity. All of Kosovo was doing some work in the parallel society, volunteering. The Serbs tried to kill our society, but we woke up instead.'[2] There was not only a sense of emergency but also a desire to show social solidarity and to participate. While there were no major demonstrations in Kosovo, the everyday maintenance of Albanian community structures – above all education – took on the character of civil resistance.

This chapter concentrates on the first half of the 1990s, a period when Kosovo's 'parallel structures' took shape. While the regime had established its monopoly over state structures, Kosovo Albanians counterposed their own self-organisation and self-activity. In 1993, Ibrahim Rugova was able to claim that 'in Kosovo only our system functions'.[3] The Kosovo Albanian community was surviving the Serbian assault, yet was showing few signs of being able to stop it. In the words of a CSCE report in June 1993, 'the situation in Kosovo is stable *and* explosive.'[4] The parallel structures were probably the most stabilising element in the situation.

95

SCHOOLS IN STRUGGLE

The struggle for education became a central symbol for the Albanians of Kosovo. The proudest achievement of the parallel system, it was a defence of the gains made in the years of autonomy and a guarantee of the maintenance of Albanian society in Kosovo.

Serbian measures against education began in September 1989 with the introduction of ethnic segregation in schools. Sometimes the segregation was physical – Serbs using one floor, Albanians another, or partitions were erected. Sometimes there was a shift system, Albanians holding classes at times when Serbs were not using the school. The first school closures began a year later. On 8 August 1990, the Assembly of Serbia repealed the entire body of educational legislation passed by the Assembly of Kosovo in order to impose a uniform curriculum on the whole of Serbia, with only the most token concessions to the presence of Albanians in the republic. Going on strike would actually have served Serbian purposes. Therefore, teachers decided to work on without compliance. Instead of teaching the uniform curriculum, they carried on in Albanian with the curriculum approved by the now-disolved provincial administration.

The first of the parallel schools was in the Peja municipality, named 7 September in honour of the Kaçanik Constitution. When a school with a Serb majority announced in September 1990 that it would no longer provide teaching in Albanian, every day for two months teachers and children gathered in the school yard to protest. Then they began to have classes in private homes. In January, the principal of the parallel school was sentenced to 31 days in prison for inciting civil disobedience.[5] This was a foretaste.

The Serbian authorities ceased to pay Kosovo Albanian secondary schoolteachers in January 1991 and elementary schoolteachers in April.[6] In May, they announced a plan to abolish half the secondary schools (15–18 years old), in future providing places for only 28 per cent of Albanians finishing elementary school, while offering more places for Serbs than the number finishing elementary school.[7] Three Belgrade groups – UJDI, the European Movement and the Forum for Ethnic Relations – joined the Kosova Helsinki Committee and the CDHRF in sending a letter to the Serbian Assembly on 26 July pointing out that these breached the international standards agreed by Yugoslavia.[8]

By August 1991, the authorities had dismissed 6,000 secondary schoolteachers as well as the principals and deputies of 115 elementary schools. Finally, at the start of the 1991–92 school year, the authorities moved to exclude Albanians from all schools in Kosovo. All over Kosovo, there were similar scenes: children, teachers and parents arriving at schools on 2 September to find armed police blocking their entry. Often there would be beatings and detentions. In many places, the protests were repeated day after day. The principal of the Luigi Gurakuqi high school in Klina recalled:

> Armed police were waiting at the school entrance on 2 September 1991. They cursed us in the yard and said we couldn't go into the school unless we accepted the education of the Republic of Serbia. We continued our peaceful protest. Then the police started beating us. Some of the teachers were detained. Non-teaching staff who were still working at the school told us the Serbian management burned all the Albanian-language books on 19 September. On 1 October, together with parents and students, we staged a protest. The police blocked the streets and tension ran high. We continued our protest against being barred from the school for the next three days. There were about a thousand of us and we protested peacefully. But the police beat us anyway. On 16 October, we tried again to get into the school but couldn't even get near the building. It was guarded by police and Serbs from Klina.[9]

Similar scenes were repeated that term outside elementary and secondary schools throughout Kosovo.

The Yugoslav Constitution both guaranteed elementary schooling and made it compulsory, and therefore in the second term, most (about 90 per cent) of the elementary schools were re-opened. However, they remained segregated – Serb pupils having better facilities and more space. Also, the authorities had no intention of spending any money on Albanian education – not even for heating, let alone for teaching. Even when pupils used the same building, there was little contact between Serb and Albanian youngsters. The language of the other ethnic group was no longer on the school curriculum.

At the secondary level, there were three choices: to succumb to the Serbian curriculum; to keep protesting and being beaten; or to find some alternative. The teachers' union began compiling an inventory of private places where classes could meet – empty houses, warehouses, garages, basements and mosques. In January–February 1992, secondary teaching resumed in these. In Ferizaj – after just a week in private homes – parents, teachers and students again organised nonviolent protests at their schools. As a concession, the municipality designated three of its school buildings – rather inadequate for the total of 10,180 Albanian pupils from grades one to eight, and they were emptied of all but the oldest equipment and furniture.[10]

At the start of the 1992–93 school year pupils and parents again tried to re-enter the schools. In August 1992 FRY prime minister Panić had expressed his hope that they would be open, but again police blocked the entry to secondary schools and even some elementary schools. Demonstrations at schools continued in the next few weeks, despite police beatings. These culminated on 12 and 13 October with massive demonstrations throughout Kosovo just before their negotiators were due to meet with their federal counterparts. Perhaps a quarter of the population participated. The first day, police dispersed the demonstrations with beatings and tear gas, arresting members of the local Protest Organising Committees. The second day with less media attention, police were reportedly still more brutal, while in Mitrovica Army units helped clear the streets.

Without Albanian pupils, some schools were simply not viable and had to close. In others, the overcapacity was ridiculous – eight Serb pupils used one village school with nine classrooms, a gym, a science laboratory and two offices.[11] The situation also created a choice for members of other minority groups. Turks often joined the parallel system to continue with their own 1990 curriculum,[12] while Slav Muslims were more likely to opt for the Serbian curriculum. Despite having more in common with the Albanians culturally, Roma/Gypsies tended to align themselves with whichever nationality was dominant.[13]

From 1992–98, some elementary schools (41 out of 441) and nearly all secondary schools (60 out of 66) functioned in makeshift classrooms.[14] In the early years, some 900 sites were used – a number that dropped as more buildings were found with several classrooms and the situation stabilised somewhat. Many classrooms lacked writing surfaces for the pupils; in some the only equipment was a black rectangle painted on the wall to serve as a chalkboard; nearly all were desperately over-crowded. Initially, some did not have chairs or benches, although as the years progressed, parents tended to make some improvements in the equipment. Nobody would say that education in these conditions could be adequate. The initial perspective was that the most they could achieve was to stop the children forgetting what they had already learnt, and most teachers did not expect to have to endure these conditions for more than a year or two.

After the Kosovo textbook publishing house was closed, textbooks were smuggled in – some on mules from Albania – but gradually Kosovo Albanians were able to produce more of their own. In the period 1990–97, they produced 156 new text books for schools and the university, often printed outside, smuggled in and distributed illegally.[15]

Also, as time progressed, more secondary schools began to use the empty elementary school classrooms. According to local conditions, there would be quiet attempts to regain the use of school buildings.[16] Some succeeded; others were baulked by police, even after parents and teachers had repaired the buildings and re-equipped classrooms. However, there were no coordinated demonstrations for the right to education from the massive protests of October 1992 until the student protests of October 1997.

The numbers of pupils dropping out from elementary schools rose – by 1997 about 25 per cent of pupils did not finish – and there was another dip between those who completed elementary and those who registered for secondary school. This especially affected girls: it was not unusual for economic hardship to reinforce or revive patriarchal patterns. A special concern was for girl pupils who had to travel from villages to their schools, distances sometimes of 20 km. Over the years, the numbers of both teachers and pupils fell somewhat. Nevertheless it was a remarkable achievement that by 1997 some 18,000 teachers and 330,000 pupils (compared to 376,000 before) were still able to carry on with school.

OPEN BUT ILLEGAL

In the early days, police often harassed children to find out where their 'private' schools were, and classes would shift from place to place to avoid disruption. Later their whereabouts became something of a public secret, yet still with the persistent threat of police intervention. Police visits to schools tended to come in spates – and then they would confiscate teaching and other materials and any money found on the premises, sums as large as DM 53,000 were reported.[17] There may have been a pattern for more raids towards the end of the school year, seizing diplomas, class registers and official stamps. The harassment of teachers, pupils and sometimes owners of the premises also tended to be spasmodic, although most likely at the beginning of a school year. To greet the 1993–94 school year, the Republic of Kosova issued an appeal to international associations and institutions, stating:

> The educational process for Albanians in the period 1991–93 was followed by appalling repression. As a result of Serbian state terror, 18 pupils were killed, two teachers, one principal and three parents, while a further two parents were wounded. Serbian police beat up and maltreated 2,000 teachers and principals and more than 400 pupils of primary and secondary schools. 140 teachers and six pupils were sentenced to 20–60 days imprisonment.[18]

CDHRF began to keep a separate tally for the number of people maltreated by the police in the course of educational activities.[19] In cities, it was risky to organise any outdoor activity. A music teacher I met in Podujeva had had the temerity to hold a celebration of the school anniversary in the schoolyard: it was interrupted by police and the teacher was taken for interrogation. She was lucky – many teachers were badly beaten for doing less. An increasing proportion of teachers went into exile, seeking paid work in order to support families, and by 1997 over 20 per cent of teachers were not qualified.[20]

In general, Albanian persistence had gained them the space to maintain something as vulnerable to attack as an educational system. The Yugoslav authorities tried other tacks. From November 1993 the offer stood that individual Albanian pupils who wished to abandon the parallel system for the Serbian one could do so and their credits would be recognised. There would also be some Albanian-language instruction in official schools in music, arts, history and geography. The few pupils who attended those classes were mainly of mixed Serbian and Albanian marriages.[21]

THE UNIVERSITY OF PRISHTINA

The University of Prishtina, wrote Ibrahim Rugova on its 25th anniversary, has 'contributed immensely to the cultivation ... and consolidation of national consciousness, as well as to the intellectual and civilised development of Albanian people'.[22] Not surprisingly, Serbs saw it as 'the nest of Albanian nationalism', especially because of the 1981 revolt. Following that, there had been a purge of staff and a reduction in the annual intake of students.

The Medical Faculty was the first part of the university to feel the impact of the new repression. While it was purged in August 1990, the dismissal of other lecturers mainly took place the next year. When the 1991–92 academic year was due to begin, as with schools, police blocked entrances to the faculties. By the end of 1991, 984 teachers and other Albanian employees had been sacked.[23] The Serbian rector from 1991–98, Radivoje Papović, referring to the university as 'this factory of evil', explained 'our first task was to remove the hatred for all that is Serbian and which has been accumulated here for decades'.[24]

Barred from any state buildings, the university's 13 departments and the seven associated training colleges had to rely on facilities in 250 private buildings. The day the university re-opened in private premises, 17 February 1992, it was choreographed 'like a ballet, in minute detail' – the places people had to wait, at what times – all organised by word of mouth, with a more or less coded message the evening before in Radio Zagreb's Albanian broadcast.[25] This was organised not by the LDK, but by the recently elected university bodies, despite the rector's imprisonment in January.[26] Inevitably student numbers fell: enrolment in the 13 faculties dropped from 19,620 in 1991–92 to 13,805 (full-time and part-time) in 1996–97.[27] While in secondary schools the most obvious fall in numbers was among female pupils, at the university level there was more pressure on young men to drop out. Many went abroad to earn money for their families or to avoid conscription. In April 1994, the first issue of the revived student newspaper, *Bota e re*, appealed to students 'to continue their studies because their presence keeps alive the University and the difficult life in Kosova.'[28] Because of the closure of university residences, the university had to find student accommodation in private homes and adapt the timetable to reduce travel.

Some medical students managed to find internships inside Kosovo, for instance in Mother Theresa clinics.[29] Often, however, it was necessary for science students to go abroad to complete their studies, especially to Albania. As well as the two week visits made by up to 200 students per year to use medicine, physics and chemistry facilities in Albania, there were a number of full-time students in

Albania (47 in 1995–96).[30] Albania was willing to grant more scholarships and some West European universities offered scholarships. These were especially welcome for graduate students, whereas for undergraduates the rector explained that 'our University is interested to send to Albania only [undergraduate] students of deficient faculties'.[31] What was important was to maintain life inside Kosovo.

Despite the adverse conditions, the parallel university succeeded in opening new departments, such as pharmacy in the Faculty of Medicine, veterinary medicine in the Faculty of Agriculture and drama in the Faculty of Fine Arts.[32]

As in elementary and secondary schools, there has been some questioning of the quality of teaching. In the rest of Yugoslavia, the University of Prishtina did not enjoy a very high reputation in the days of autonomy. This was not just Slavs looking down on Albanians, but also because of the problems faced in the rapid expansion of a new university. Following 1990, the poor conditions obviously hampered academic work and science students were particularly handicapped by the lack of equipment. Yet Rector Zenel Kelmendi, formerly Dean of the Medical Faculty, insisted that standards remained rigorous. In fact, he joked, students complained they suffered a double repression – from the Serbs and from their own teachers.[33] The Zagreb philosopher Lino Veljak was one of a few foreign academics who went to Kosovo to give some lectures in 1997. He was surprised and impressed by the quality of discussion he encountered with students: 'none of the reputable European universities would be ashamed of such a level'.[34]

FUNDING EDUCATION

Financing this educational system required a major effort. At first teachers worked on unpaid, or with a few 'hardship cases' receiving support from their union. In 1993 the Republic of Kosova began to pay wages – initially token wages of DM 20 per month but by 1997 rising to DM 150–160 for schools and DM 180 for higher education.[35] This was not enough to support a family and there were complaints of teachers being paid late. Nevertheless, both the wage level and the regularity of pay compared well with what Serbia could manage to pay teachers, such was Serbia's economic crisis. Although parents were expected to pay a small amount each term, the financing of the schools was primarily a mark of the success of the system of voluntary taxation.[36]

Foreign reports normally referred to the 3 per cent suggested contribution requested of Kosovo Albanians working abroad, but the bulk of the Republic's income was actually raised *inside* Kosovo. By September 1994, the government-in-exile had raised less than a third of the amount raised inside Kosovo;[37] subsequently the proportion raised outside increased but it never equalled the amount raised inside. Each municipality had a multi-party Council of Finance whose volunteer tax collectors – sometimes people involved in similar work in the days of autonomy – assessed how much each family should contribute, agreed this with the family and then collected it, usually monthly. They tried not to accumulate too much at one time for fear of confiscation by the police. The local finance councils were also in charge of the distribution of tax money, about 90 per cent of which went to support the parallel educational system. Naturally, according to the resources and needs of a municipality, there were local variations in the balance between income and expenditure, and a need for greater or lesser support from central funds.

Although volunteer tax collectors took precautions such as sewing hidden pockets into their coats, inevitably there were incidents of police catching them, beating them up and, of course, taking the money. This seems to have been especially severe at the start of the system, but remained a risk. One was beaten to death in 1995.[38] Most of the taxes collected came from small businesses – Prishtina businesses in 1998 were placed in five categories, their taxes ranging from DM 100 per month to DM 1500[39] – but most families paid something.[40]

Podujeva was able to give small grants to 30 university students, while the LDK Youth Forum would organise free bus vouchers with private companies. Organising vouchers or discounts was also an important activity for the students' union (UPSUP).

Primarily, then, the educational system depended on social solidarity. Nevertheless, it could not be completely self-reliant. The teachers' unions were active in approaching Western counterparts for funds or materials. Foreign governments were reluctant to aid schooling; it was too much a symbol of the state Kosovo Albanians wanted to create. However, towards the second half of the 1990s international donors such as Mercy Corps, Norwegian Church Aid and Oxfam began to contribute, while the Open Society Foundation (Soros) gave money to fund the publication of textbooks and magazines.

THE LESSON TAUGHT

A people in struggle are likely to use their schools to inculcate a collective ethos. Supporters present this as consciousness of their culture and a sense of solidarity, while critics perceive a type of nationalist indoctrination, urging sacrifice in the struggle, with an ethnic version of history and geography. So it was in Kosovo for both Serbs and Albanians. The parallel schools aimed more to strengthen national consciousness than to open minds.

One *Koha* writer complained not just at the authoritarianism of an announcement in December 1994 that only one children's magazine, *Pionieri*, was authorised for distribution in school, but also at its content. 'Instead of games, colors, aphorisms, humoresques, etc. children are served war, blood, death and sado-masochist verses.'[41] The teaching methodology in schools was also, to say the least, conservative, pupils learning by rote rather than by enquiry. The head of one international relief agency bemoaned 'the waste of children's lives' in this political cause.[42] Some visitors were even more damning, suggesting that parallel education could only deepen the hatred between the two communities. Certainly, the segregation of education cemented prejudice between Serbs and Albanians. However, the parallel system was not the cause of this segregation but rather a response to Serbian-imposed segregation and the subsequent Serbian domination of the curriculum.

In 1993, one woman told me, 'I don't want my son to grow up hating Serbs'. As it turns out, he hasn't, largely I think thanks to family influence. The parallel schools did try to instil values, urging patience, promoting the idea that 'the pencil is mightier than the sword' and affirming the value of education. But they could do little to counter youngsters' primary experience of Serbs as people who maltreat Albanians, or who at best sit in half-empty but properly equipped and heated classrooms while Albanians make do. They could offer few opportunities to show anything different.[43]

Maliqi offers a positive evaluation of the system:

The parallel school system has successfully preserved and improved its function of socialisation of generations of pupils and students who have experienced a series of enormous political and social shocks. ... This several-years' long experience of such schooling which itself is the result of repression (children in lower grades in fact do not even know what 'normal school' is) must have become a unique life school of resistance. The quality of knowledge acquired is less significant than the accelerated maturing of character that occurs as a result of the need to constantly defend personal dignity and threatened national and human values. These will not, after all, be 'lost generations'.[44]

Masha Gessen, visiting in 1994, noted 'the delicate art of becoming invisible is now one of the most important elements of a Kosovo Albanian's education',[45] what one of my student friends called 'the daily hide and seek of getting home without police catching me with my notebook'. However, Gessen also noted the self-respect gained through the parallel education system. After questioning the effort to obtain university diplomas that nobody else recognises, she concluded: 'Kosovo Albanians not only recognize their university, they recognize themselves in it. Everywhere else they look – on TV, for example, where all the broadcasts are in Serbian – they see themselves as subhuman.'

Perhaps the achievement of the parallel school system is best evaluated by asking what would have happened without it. The *Koha* journalist Baton Haxhiu asked this question in 1995, and few would dispute his answer: there would have been increased emigration, political extremism and widespread criminality. The occasion for his article was that he was scandalised to learn of a gynaecologist breaching the convention that teachers should not be charged for medical attention. His polemic is representative of the high esteem in which teachers were held:

> Even being beaten and expelled from their premises, the teachers didn't give up, and in essence education is the only institution which Serbia could not take over ... From all that was promised and realised by the referendum [on independence in 1991], education remained the only bearer of the will of the people, while teachers were the ones carrying this will.[46]

MEDICAL CARE

Even before 1990, 80 per cent of deaths from contagious diseases in Yugoslavia occurred among Kosovo Albanians.[47] Despite its predominantly rural character, Kosovo had been the most densely populated part of Yugoslavia, yet some 30 per cent of households were not connected with a sewage treatment system and only 44 per cent of the population had piped water. The alleged poisoning episode of March 1990 exacerbated the existing fear that Serbian doctors would mislead Albanians or even carry out operations such as sterilisation without consent. For some time afterwards, many Albanian families would have no dealings whatsoever with 'Serbian medicine', preferring in emergencies to go to Zagreb, Ljubljana or Tirana. This suspicion, together with the Serbian emergency measures, compounded the existing poverty and underdevelopment to make the health situation in Kosovo even more precarious.

Polio, thought to have been eradicated only as late as 1983, reappeared in 1990.[48] Vaccination rates fell, while the incidence of dysentery, tetanus and TB grew, and more infants died from diarrhoea. Epidemics became more frequent, with a higher rate of fatality. An outbreak of entero-colitis in winter 1993–94 would not have been detected if emigrés in Switzerland had not contracted it during their holidays in Kosovo.[49] Despite appeals from the LDK-aligned *Bujku* in January 1993 not to boycott Serbian vaccination programmes, parents were simply too suspicious of Serbian plots to 'sterilise the nation' to bring their children.[50]

From August 1990 onwards, more than half of the medical staff of Kosovo were dismissed – beginning at the Gynaecological Clinic in the Medical Faculty. As elsewhere, any sign of disloyalty could be a reason for dismissal, including treating demonstrators, offering humanitarian aid to strikers or dismissed workers, or writing in Albanian – Serbo-Croatian was to be the language of treatment, even for Albanians. In the Medical Faculty, police dragged senior doctors from their offices. Clinics were shut down – 38 in Prishtina alone and many more in towns and villages. Few Albanian doctors, if any, withdrew from the State structures. Rather, they worked on trying to mitigate anti-Albanian policies, often engaging in voluntary activity outside their work.

Dismissed physicians responded to medical needs as best they could. Some set up in private practice, generally offering free treatment to certain categories of people (the families of sacked miners were honoured above all, then teachers). Activists responded to the emergency created by the mass sackings and suspension of child support payments by forming solidarity funds or launching food distribution schemes. Local branches of the LDK were central in this, collecting and administering the LDK Solidarity Fund and establishing distribution centres for flour and other essentials even in the days before the voluntary taxation system was in place.

The main collectively organised response to the emergency in health came from the humanitarian Mother Theresa Association (MTA), set up independently of any political party. Although it was named after Mother Theresa of Calcutta – herself an Albanian – this was not part of her organisation. Its first president was Anton Çetta, succeeded after his death by his colleague from the blood feud campaign, the Catholic priest Don Lush Gjergj. From 1990 onwards, they were involved in distributing food and other forms of humanitarian aid, especially in rural areas, but in so doing bringing medical needs to the attention of a list of doctors willing to donate their services. The first MTA clinic was opened in Prishtina on 30 March 1992, and the network expanded continuously until by the start of 1998 there were 91 clinics and some 7,000 volunteers were distributing humanitarian aid to perhaps 350,000 people.[51] All treatment was free, including medicines, for whoever needed it – whatever ethnic group. A maternity clinic opened in Prishtina in July 1996 capable of handling around 15 births a day.

Clearly, this was not a complete health service – people with serious illnesses or needing hospital treatment had to fall back on private practices, go abroad or turn to the state institutions. Yet it was a remarkable success story of self-organisation and solidarity. In establishing the first clinic, MTA relied entirely on the support of local businesspeople – for the premises and the equipment – while the staff donated their services. There were occasional incidents of police harassment, including police confiscating medical drugs and medical records.

In 1993, the French humanitarian agency Equilibre's first efforts to open an office working alongside MTA were blocked.[52] However, MTA's work expanded rapidly from 1994 onwards when Médecins sans Frontières and Catholic Relief Services began giving support. In 1994, after floods in the Suhareka and Rahovec area, there was a concerted campaign with some international organisations to prevent the spread of typhoid,[53] and as we shall in Chapter 6 there was later to be a major immunisation campaign against polio. With this international support, MTA clinics tended to be better stocked with medicines than their Serbian counterparts, and a growing number of Serbs began to come for treatment – a recognition that Albanian self-activity could be more effective than the regime in caring for people of all ethnic groups.[54]

Associations such as those for people with hearing and sight handicaps were closed down following the loss of autonomy, but not the Regional Association for Paraplegics and Polio. It incorporated as much of their work as it could and maintained 24 active branches throughout Kosovo. Otherwise, it was up to small, usually voluntary groups to set up in order to respond to specific needs. Thus Mens Sana, founded in 1994, concentrated on mental health and counselling and later produced an educational magazine *Shëndeti* (Health) circulated throughout the school system.

THE MEDIA

Any social struggle needs information media. Kosovo's strong oral culture and the direct experience of police harassment or imprisonment in every extended family meant there was a strong level of basic awareness. It was not only rumours that spread quickly, but sayings, transmitted by word of mouth or in school. Media manipulators who coin sound-bites would envy the way key ideas in pithy phrases were repeated: 'We already have our Republic of Kosova.' 'Education is our light.' 'Our way is the force of logic against the logic of force.' 'To obtain independence, we organise ourselves.' In this situation, the role of the print and broadcast media was to cover events outside the experience of one's social circle or to introduce new ideas and analysis.

The initial response to the clampdown on *Rilindja* was to produce private newspapers registered in Slovenia and Croatia. This was rather short-lived. Beginning in January 1991, the tactic was to convert a specialist paper to serve wider purposes. Thus the agricultural weekly, *Bujku* (the Farmer), came out four times a week as a general newspaper and the youth paper *Zëri* (Voice) became a political weekly. From 1991–92 virtually every editor served a prison sentence, ranging from 15 to 60 days.[55] Shortage of paper limited the printrun of *Bujku* to about 8,000 during the period when sanctions were in force against FRY. The Amsterdam-based *Press Now*, supporting independent media in former Yugoslavia, in December 1995 profiled 15 other Albanian-language magazines, distributed in Kosovo at that time, including two sports fortnightlies. None approached a circulation as high as the children's *Pionieri* (30,000).[56]

In May 1993, Belgrade decided to merge the sales and distribution arms of the previous Albanian and Turkish publishing enterprises in Kosovo (*Rilindja* and *Tan*) into the Serbian enterprise Panorama. The first step was for Panorama to take over the *Rilindja* bank accounts, transferring the money into Panorama and so forcing the temporary closure of *Bujku*, *Zëri* and three other papers. On 24 May, Adem Demaçi and Blerim Shala bedded down in the *Rilindja* building and began a hunger strike 'until death' supported by 250 other journalists. Students and other trade unions wanted to join in but Demaçi preferred to confine the fast to journalists. The CSCE mission showed the value of an international presence. A physical reminder to the authorities of how it would look in preventing Albanian publishing, the mission mediated an agreement that stopped the Panorama takeover and ended the strike after 11 days. The papers had to register – which, according to Demaçi, the mission guaranteed would be successful (alas, the mission was in no position to guarantee anything – this was more or less its final public act in Kosovo). *Bujku* resumed almost immediately, *Zëri* before the end of the year, but at the price of having to subsidise the Kosovo Serb publication *Jedinstvo* by paying higher printing and paper prices and higher rent.[57]

In the official broadcast media, the only news content in languages other than Serbian was directly translated from Serbian bulletins. For any alternative view, until the spread of satellite TV, Kosovo Albanians had to depend on receiving the ten-minute Albanian bulletins from Radio Zagreb, or broadcasts from international radio stations, such as the BBC (which in 1993–94 employed Veton Surroi to set up an Albanian service), Voice of America, or Deutsche Welle. As satellite dishes became increasingly common, however, the Albanian TV news broadcast every evening became the most important news bulletin. With the LDK in control of the content of both *Bujku* and the Tirana broadcasts, it had a powerful means of presenting its version of reality, one designed to encourage Albanian perseverance, while magnifying any sign of international support.

The most important move against the LDK's media domination came in 1994 when Veton Surroi returned from London, and, with

funding from the Open Society Fund (Soros), re-opened the weekly
Koha (Time). His intention was to stimulate debate among Kosovo
Albanians and to break the LDK's and *Bujku's* silence over the
strategic problems faced by the movement. In March 1995, he noted
public indifference to news that excited him – namely that the UN
Commission on Human Rights had passed a resolution urging
'respect of the will of the inhabitants of Kosovo, allowing its
expression with democratic means, as the best way to stop the
escalation of the conflict there'. He editorialised:

> Public opinion has become numb to the non-differentiated
> information it receives. For years it is said that every part of the
> world is discussing about Kosova and that Kosova receives support
> from all sides of the world. It has become the same whether
> Kosova is supported by a Dutch village or by the foreign ministry
> of a Security Council member state. What's more [the public]
> doesn't trust the village nor the ministry. The public has seen too
> much Bosnia and Croatia on TV, and has listened to just too many
> words which were to prevent war ... After the initial euphoria,
> fully believing in the Albanian democratic movement, the phase
> of suspicion on what is read and written is developing. However
> dangerous this phase might seem, it is nevertheless an expression
> of an evolution in the political culture, going towards the creation
> of responsibility of the leader(s) towards the citizen.[58]

Some of its critics might suggest that *Koha's* purpose was to usher in
this 'phase of suspicion', trying to undermine Rugova's authority yet
without offering a clear alternative. For Surroi, however, the point
was to have frank political discussion involving a variety of
viewpoints – a rather fresh approach in Kosovo.

Another dimension of Kosovo journalism was informing the
outside world about the situation, something international press
could not be relied on to do. Their correspondents, if any, were
Belgrade-based and – with few exceptions – knew more about events
in Bosnia than Kosovo. For the diaspora and the international
solidarity network, the main source of information was the Prishtina
Kosova Information Centre (KIC), aligned with the LDK (indeed
including the LDK flag on the masthead of its daily bulletins). It
reported primarily on the activities of the LDK leadership and the
details of Serbian repression or plundering, reiterating the dominant
themes of the moment.[59]

Journalism was one of the rare areas where there was good cooperation between Kosovo's independent journalists and a section of the Serbian democratic opposition. As well as personal links made before the loss of autonomy, the main structural vehicle for this in the first half of the 1990s was *AIM* (*Alternativna Informativna Mreža*), a network of independent journalists. Founded in October 1992, this was a consistent source of information and interpretation. It had Albanian, Serbian and mixed correspondents in Kosovo, several of them also contributing to *Vreme* (Belgrade opposition weekly) and *Balkan War Report* (London).

As with almost every other area of self-organisation, the consolidation of their own media required dedication, perseverance and voluntary activity. However, if *Bujku*, KIC and the Tirana broadcasts helped maintain the unity of the Albanians in Kosovo, their perpetuation of wishful thinking about what Kosovo might expect from foreign powers ultimately did a disservice to their cause.

ARTS AND SPORT

Keeping alive Kosovo's artistic and sporting life was itself a form of resistance. The regime's offensive against the Albanian way of life included closing down various cultural bodies, forbidding the use of facilities and 'cleansing' Albanians from employment in state cultural or sporting institutions. There was a period without performance or display spaces. From 1993 onwards, certain restaurants or cafés displayed paintings by local artists and in the second half of the 1990s more performance spaces opened up. Students managed to hold exhibitions and concerts, in 1994 beginning a spring poetry festival.[60]

As the existence of two sports magazines shows, sport was as popular in Kosovo as in other areas of former Yugoslavia. All but three of the 112 Albanians working in sports facilities lost their jobs and members of the parallel football league were banned from using publicly-owned stadiums. However, out of stadiums and on substandard pitches, the league continued, even though sports events were one more occasion for police harassment.[61] Indoor sports such as table tennis were occasionally disrupted, but less frequently. A particularly successful assocation was the Kosovo Karate Association.[62] It was popular with youths of both sexes (although in one or two places girls did not take part). It was promoted partly because its philosophy is based on self-discipline, it could be practised in relatively small private venues, and – most important – Kosovo Albanians managed to take part in international competitions. This served both as a reminder to other countries of Kosovo's existence and as a source of self-esteem for the Kosovars – especially in a Budapest youth tournament where Kosovo girls gained a gold and two bronze medals.[63]

Apart from receiving DM 70,000 from the funds of the Republic of Kosova for international travel, the Kosova Karate Association depended on its own fundraising. On the basis of its success, its chair – Besim Hasani – was elected chair of the Kosova Olympic Committee in 1996, having dared to stand against an LDK candidate. The goal of this committee was in theory to obtain recognition for Kosovo from the International Olympic Committee; in practice it was to raise Kosovo's profile and to create international sporting opportunities for Kosovo Albanians.

ECONOMIC SURVIVAL[64]

Whatever else the Serbian Programme PPLEDP (see Chapter 4) might have brought, it did not bring prosperity. Far from a Serbian economic revival in Kosovo, levels of production slumped to what they had been 30 years earlier. Predictably, the projected immigration or return of Serbs and Montenegrins did not materialise: rather, emigration continued. The only achievement the Programme could claim was to reduce the level of unemployment among Kosovo Serbs. Kosovo remained a financial burden to FRY, even if the regime had saved the wages of 33,561 Albanians previously employed under the federal budget and payments of allowances for 247,000 children. The taxes levied on Kosovo – DM 414.7 million a year – did not cover the cost even of policing.

The Serbian economy, however, did benefit from asset stripping, what Miranda Vickers has called 'a form of legalised looting' of Kosovo industry.[65] Twelve public enterprises in Kosovo were taken into state ownership, while another 238 enterprises were absorbed into their counterparts in Serbia and Vojvodina, their production in Kosovo either halted or reduced, and their assets and materials either sold off cheaply (a tractor for DM 1,000) or transferred to Serbia. Some Serb managers brought in to run Kosovo companies succeeded in accumulating large shareholdings for themselves and their families. The only bank in former Yugoslavia to be liquidated was Kosovo Bank, although its assets still covered its liabilities. The losers were the 66,000 individuals whose hard currency accounts were simply confiscated by Jugobanka.

In response to the mass dismissals, the Albanians showed enormous resilience. There were four basic survival strategies:

– for those in a desperate situation, various forms of social solidarity were mobilised, most significantly, as we have seen, the funds organised by trade unions, the LDK and the Mother Theresa Association;

– almost every family had at least one member in another country: if they were employed, they would send what they could back to the family. The most common figure is that the number in exile rose above 350,000;

– families cut back, some gardening, some baking more at home, few spending so much on weddings and other ceremonies and

– thousands of new small trading businesses started up spontaneously.

It is impossible to know how much hard currency was sent back to Kosovo by people living abroad. An EU study in 1996 showed that only 15 per cent of Kosovo asylum seekers had jobs,[66] and the large number of families requiring humanitarian aid from solidarity funds advises caution in estimating the ingress of funds. Paring down spending on village ceremonies – above all the three-day wedding extravaganzas – 'came as a relief to many families whose desires to depart from traditions of the past were [previously] thwarted by a perceived need to conform', suggests Reineck. She sees this as 'the familism of the past ... [giving] way to an expression of social unity in the struggle for economic and political survival.'[67]

Nevertheless, during sanctions against FRY – although Kosovo Albanians would always say they were victims of double sanctions – Kosovo was much better supplied than Serbia, its multitude of mini-markets more fully stocked than their counterparts in Belgrade. *Vreme* journalist Perica Vucinić suggested 'the ethnic Albanians' financial superiority can be seen by the number of luxury cars, restaurants, shops and satellite antennas.'[68] By 1994, there was even talk that the performance of the Kosovo traders was one of the arguments against Serbia waging war in Kosovo.

The Serb-controlled state economy was in ruins – a victim of a combination of criminality and corruption, mismanagement and obsolete technology, all compounded by sanctions. Yet Kosovo's

Albanian-controlled private business sector was apparently thriving. In 1995 there were 18,534 small firms registered in Kosovo, compared with only 1,733 in 1987.[69] This enormous growth is primarily attributable to the Albanian response to mass dismissals. The best smugglers in old Yugoslavia, Albanians in Kosovo with help from those in Macedonia were still displaying their entrepreneurial acumen.[70] In trade, as in the payment of teachers and provision of medicines, the oppressed Kosovo Albanians seemed again to be out-performing Serbs.

The shops and small businesses played a vital role in the life of the community. They contributed the bulk of the voluntary taxes levied, provided essential goods and were central to the personal survival strategies of many families. They spread spontaneously and through the power of example, although small businesses too faced their share of police harassment. However, there was a strategic vacuum, without even a guiding idea of what economic developments would most benefit Kosovo Albanians.

Politically the prescribed attitude was boycott. Economically this proved unsustainable. BSPK and its member unions had at first asked people hiring private premises not to rent from enterprises under emergency measures – nothing should obstruct their members from regaining their former jobs. When they had to modify this stance, neither they nor anybody else offered a strategic alternative to the boycott. *Laissez-faire* ruled. While the Albanian population was keeping its political distance from Serbia, the question of economic relationships was left to the 'invisible hand' of the market.

Lack of coordination produced problems. By 1995 perhaps only a third of the registered businesses were really functioning, nearly all of them family businesses with few employees – together they employed an estimated total of 20,000. Most were trade or services; there was virtually no production. Did Kosovo really need so many pizzerias, small petrol stations, or mini-markets? The result was a heavy dependence on imports of essentials from Serbia – flour, sugar, cooking oil and salt. In 1997 Riinvest estimated that total Serbian food product sales in Kosovo were DM 400 million a year (roughly US$1 million per day) – *Koha* reported DM 5–6 million spent on ice cream alone!

Kosovo grew three-quarters of the wheat needed, yet because of a lack of coordinated distribution, it imported over half its needs from Serbia at a cost of DM 60 million. It produced more milk than it consumed, yet – because 22 Kosovo dairies had been swallowed up by a Belgrade diary – it imported nearly a third of the milk it consumed. It was not until 1997 that anybody invested in a type of mini-dairy developed in Israel for units the size of kibbutzim.

A small Prishtina-based group called Home Economics helped some people – including the wives of migrant workers – develop small income-generating projects. More people took up gardening to grow their own vegetables. However, many fields and vineyards lay neglected and farmers produced primarily for their own families. There were enough stories of police (or private Serb) vandalism of crops, vineyards and orchards to discourage farmers from risking investment or trying to expand, but the main problem in economic development was the lack of clear objectives. Police harassment played its part here: in 1994 three people were sentenced to two and a half years' imprisonment for founding a Chamber of Commerce.[71]

While migrant workers sent enough hard currency home to keep the economy going, there was a continuous flow from Kosovo into Serbia – taxes (or fines, or bribes) from businesses, plus all the imports. Private enterprise had brought a form of stability, a *modus vivendi* without war, but could not define what economic strategies would serve the goal of self-determination, what economic relations with Serbia would best serve to undermine the regime's domination of Kosovo and what economic programmes would best serve Kosovo's own development. This is a striking contrast to the struggle of the Palestinians during the *intifada*, with its call to buy Palestinian and the willed stimulation of the home economy,[73] and of Gandhi's programme of *swadeshi* – local production and the use of home produced articles, an essential part of his 'constructive programme'.

POLITICS 'AS IF'

> Oppressed, but organised ... This is the first time that [Kosovo Albanians] feel that they have a power ... that they feel citizens, despite the occupation ... With our organisation, we are active, not for war but for something else. We have this internal, psychological freedom, and these are the first steps towards physical freedom and, one day, collective freedom.[73]

There was a growing discrepancy between these words and the lived experience of Kosovo Albanians. In 1993, perhaps Rugova was right that there was some sense of empowerment. 'We are going to suffer, and we are going to win' was a fairly widespread refrain in the early days of nonviolent struggle. However, far from being renewed by the population's sense of achievement, people's conviction that they were shaping their own destiny attenuated over time. Doubts grew about how anything was going to change, and – despite the bland assurances coming from LDK-controlled media – gaps in the logic of the struggle became evident.

If the main lines of Kosovo Albanian strategy were clear – refusal to be provoked, contesting political legitimacy, building or maintaining 'parallel' structures and mobilising international support – progress was slow. The LDK's watchwords were prudence, patience, endurance. The strategy of 'political as if'[74] required Kosovo Albanians to persist in behaving as if the Republic of Kosova existed until others – and they primarily had international centres of power in mind – recognised the emerging 'reality' that Kosovo was indeed not part of Serbia. If the Republic of Kosova was a fiction, so too was Belgrade's claim to control 'Kosovo and Metohija' – and by extension so too was the international compliance with Belgrade's claim.

Ibrahim Rugova, as a literary historian and semiologist who studied with Roland Barthes in Paris in 1976–77, is fascinated by the theory of power. In his view, Kosovo Albanians were now defining a new reality against Serb domination and so undermining it. The contest itself had an element of theatre, as recognised by two critics from diametrically opposed viewpoints. The Serbian oppositionist Dušan Janjić wrote of a 'Balkan fairy tale, with both sides convincing themselves that they did not need to engage in dialogue with the other'.[75] From the standpoint of pan-Albanian nationalism, Rexhep Qosja denounced the Kosovo Albanian strategy as a 'tragicomedy designed to smother active resistance'.[76] For Janjić and Qosja, the plot was lacking the essential element – be it 'dialogue' or 'active resistance' – to achieve either of the contradictory resolutions they desired. For the LDK leadership, that essential element was 'the international factor' – Western magic bringing a happy ending to the fairy tale, a latterday *deus ex machina* resolving the tragedy.

Persevering with a strategy of acting 'as if' requires some kind of conviction, perhaps based rationally on the credibility of the strategy, perhaps more a matter of faith, or perhaps validated experientially by its successes. In Kosovo, this conviction was initially sustained by a combination. The rational level was that 'the alternative would be a catastrophe' – and the wars elsewhere provided a bleak reminder of what could happen. Faith was not a matter of religion but rather a trust in Rugova personally from an overwhelming majority of people – this wise, brave and careful man knew what was best – and beyond that a hope, not a trust, that the USA would fulfil the promises from Bush and Clinton that they would not allow Kosovo to become another Bosnia. At the experiential level, the early accomplishments were certainly empowering. People's eyes would light up when they talked about how their generation had ended the blood feuding that had blighted their society for centuries. Parallel schooling might mean that pupils or students were sometimes sitting on floors, but it was also a sign of the strength of the people's will. The referendum of September 1991 and the parallel elections of May 1992 were events in which virtually the whole Albanian population participated – great symbolic moments.

However, instead of building on this, the movement stood still. Voting in parallel elections loses its meaning if there is no serious attempt to make the parliament function. After two or three years, the pride in stopgap schools began to wear thin. The longer they existed the more they gained a paradoxical character. As Denisa Kostovičová suggests, the parallel education system 'became a metaphor of prison and freedom at one and the same time'.[77] On the one hand, it demonstrated the Kosovo Albanians ability to organise themselves in adversity. On the other, pupils' and students' daily experience in such constrained conditions confirmed their sense of deprivation. Unless there was a sense of renewal in the struggle, politics 'as if' became reduced to a test of endurance – better than war, but a strategy of waiting rather than empowerment.

A STATE-IN-EMBRYO

The Republic of Kosova was a 'state-in-embryo', to which its people owed allegiance and paid taxes. While the structures were brought into existence and crucially depended on voluntary activity, at the same time they had a traditional hierarchy: command structures and other features of the old one-party style mixed with pre-communist authority patterns. As the 1990s progressed, there was increasing criticism of the LDK 'monopolisation' of political space and of the growing remoteness of Ibrahim Rugova. The 'president' rarely deigned to answer criticism. This may have infuriated his critics, yet the population esteemed him for being 'above' the hurly burly of political debate. He 'presided' rather than showed the way, and increasingly tried to play the role of 'head of state' rather than leader of a movement in struggle.

After the presidential and parliamentarian elections of May 1992, the LDK behaved as the only true representative of the national interest of Kosovo – as much at a village level as at the international level – while its decision-making and debates grew ever more opaque. The lack of democracy was partly to limit the influence of former political prisoners inside the LDK; their network seemed to constitute a faction, suspicious of anything sounding like compromise and pressing for greater militancy. Therefore a tight circle around Rugova took a firm grip on decisions that mattered. If the necessity for self-restraint and refusal to be provoked offered some rationale for this concentration of control, the democratic alternative of resolving issues through open debate would surely have been healthier. Later some people would poke fun at the LDK dinosaur, with its huge body and small brain.

In 1994 in the lead-up to the scheduled LDK Assembly – only its second – both Adem Demaçi and Rexhep Qosja launched attacks on the LDK. 'Its political organism is petrified and based on clichés, so that all criticism is regarded as destructive', declared Demaçi,[78] while Qosja lambasted 'the movement of stagnation'.[79] Maliqi commented at the time that Demaçi and Qosja's criticisms found no public echo. As 'they did not offer any other political platform', they were seen as speaking out of frustrated personal ambition, jealous of Rugova's popular support.[80]

In 1994, a split also surfaced between the LDK leadership and the government-in-exile, epitomised by a brawl inside the Republic of Kosova Embassy to Tirana when both president Rugova and prime-minister-in-exile Bukoshi appointed different ambassadors to Albania. On a visit to the USA in March 1994, Bukoshi told reporters that the 'Kosova government's pacifist approach was losing credibility within the population. "Meanwhile this nonviolent attitude is viewed by Belgrade as an invitation to increase oppression, and seen by the international community as an excuse to ignore the situation."'[81] Having himself been reported as being willing to concede the demand for independence and accept autonomy, he redoubled his advocacy of independence and denounced those willing to accept anything less.

When the LDK Assembly eventually took place in July 1994, it was just a one-day affair and avoided analysing the situation beyond repeating that the nonviolent strategy was succeeding in averting war and that the level of international understanding was increasing. Rugova insulated himself even more from the rank and file and personally appointed three Board members. In September that year, his vice-presidents Fehmi Agani and Edita Tahiri resigned, but Rugova prevailed on them to return. Agani was especially important as a negotiator and for his willingness to join debate with Rugova's critics. For some – including some parliamentarians[82] – the lack of debate at the 1994 Assembly marked the turning point in the LDK's 'monopolisation' of political life in Kosovo, although it could equally be argued that the LDK was constructed to be the one voice.

At this stage, the policy of nonviolence was not in question. Seeing the war in Bosnia, most Kosovo Albanians would settle for putting up with Serbian policing. Moreover, the policies of the Berisha government in Albania (1992–97) were reinforcing the Kosovo stance of nonviolence. However, there was a growing pressure for some 'radicalisation' of the LDK programme – primarily towards more confrontational forms of action. To the extent that the 1994 LDK Assembly was an exercise in consolidating central control over the movement, it was exactly the opposite of what was needed to re-invigorate the struggle: namely, more rather than fewer sources of initiative; more rather than less discussion of what kind of strategy could achieve what kind of goals. A re-evaluation of grand strategy was overdue: from objectives through forms of organisation down to what untapped potentials now existed and what tactical innovations might be possible.

Two small parties – the Parliamentary Party (PPK) and one wing of the recently split Social Democratic Party – proposed an all-party symposium in 1994 to discuss the problems, situation and prospects for the Albanian movement in Kosovo. The proposal fell, but what would such a symposium have found?

A Stocktaking in 1994

Serbia: Despite the damage inflicted on Kosovo Albanian society, the primary policy objective outlined by Serb nationalists – permanently to change the demographic balance – was no nearer achievement now than in 1989. However, there were few forms of pressure on the

regime. Many in the Kosovo Albanian movement saw an incompatibility between non-cooperation and dialogue, rather than seeing
that they could strengthen each other, and efforts to find a basis for
common action with democrats in Serbia were confined to a few
'personalities'. Those few Serbs willing to speak up for Kosovo
Albanians remained marginal.

The efforts of the CDBRF and LDK branches efforts to document
repression had not muted it significantly, but had brought
widespread condemnation on Serbia. Many observers noted an
increase in repression upon the withdrawal of the CSCE mission.

Internationalising the issue: International pressure remained the
main hope. The main ally, President Berisha of Albania, was more
active than his predecessors, but Albania's capacity to influence the
situation was limited by its dependence on international support
for reconstruction. Some steps towards internationalisation had
been achieved during 'the Panić Interlude' – the CSCE mission and
international mediation for the education talks, but Kosovo was
overshadowed by war elsewhere. Kosovo international lobbying was
successful at the level of gaining resolutions condemning human
rights violations, but was making little headway towards a change
of status. Despite any guarantees the Kosovo Albanian leadership
were willing to make for the rights of Serbs and other ethnic groups
in Kosovo, or their espousal of neutrality, demilitarisation and open
borders with FRY, Macedonia and Albania, both the USA and the
EU had adopted the position that Kosovo must remain inside FRY.
On that basis they ruled out Rugova's proposals both for a
preventive deployment of troops, as in Macedonia, and for an international protectorate.

The situation inside Kosovo: The principal functioning structure of
the Republic of Kosova was the educational system. However, the
improvised school premises were far from adequate. While the
voluntary taxation system succeeded in paying teachers, in most
areas payments were behind schedule. The health situation also
remained grave, despite the efforts of the Mother Theresa Association
with local business support. However, international charities were
ready to step up their support. Many families were in need of
humanitarian assistance. Nevertheless, considering the mass
dismissals and the loss of productive capacity in Kosovo, the Kosovo
Albanian economy was in a better condition than anyone would
have dared hope in 1991 – largely thanks to money sent home from
family members forced to leave and to the efforts of traders. At the

same time, problems in producing and distributing essential foodstocks in Kosovo led to a disturbing level of imports from Serbia, and there was a lack of coordination of economic strategy.

The organisation of the movement: Actions such as the referendum and the parallel elections along with the electoral boycott succeeded in denying legitimacy to Serbian rule. However, alternative political institutions were not properly functioning in view of the failure to convene the Parliament and the irrelevance of the Coordinating Council of Political Parties. There was substantial unity among Kosovo Albanians. However, in shedding its initial pluralism, their movement began to lose the capacity for harnessing a diversity of interests and talents in a concerted strategy. Through its persistence in the face of repression, the movement gained more space for organising but did not use it. There had been no public demonstrations since October 1992. Women and youth, each of which constituted more than half the population, were not only under-represented but their perspectives and concerns were not adequately reflected within the leadership. The enthusiasm of people's participation in the referendum and the blood feud campaign had waned, as had the spirit of voluntary solidarity when people first gave their homes for use as schools or student accommodation and created a net of social security. There were some voices of frustration, but a stronger tendency was resignation and a tendency to exaggerate the regime's power to prevent Kosovo Albanians from improving their own lives. The years of struggle to 1994 had laid a base, but a nonviolent strategy needed further development to animate people once more in the shaping of their own lives.

6
Pointers for an Alternative Strategy

The Kosovo Albanian movement was a movement for survival against assimilation or expulsion and for self-determination. Initially, it was also partly a movement for change in Kosovo – away from communism and from burdensome customs and towards democracy and pluralism. As the regime showed the degree of repression to which it would resort, the defensive assumed more importance than the transformative aspects of the movement. However, by the time of the Dayton Accords, November 1995, Kosovo Albanians had gained more space and more money was available to support social initiatives – either from the Open Society Fund/Soros or international donors. Hopes rose that Dayton would quickly be followed by a move on Kosovo. While criticism spread of the passivity of the LDK leadership, Ibrahim Rugova as a personality and the LDK as an organisation continued to command overwhelming popular support.

Dealing with the period between Dayton and the Drenica massacres, this chapter looks at a range of alternatives that could have become components of a revised nonviolent strategy. It begins with the political debate, moving on to suggest a possible strategic framework – often with reference to Gandhi[1] – and then illustrating how certain projects brought new enthusiasm. The chapter concludes with an account of the most substantial experience of 'active nonviolence' – the students movement of autumn 1997. This went some way to showing that a strategic re-orientation was possible without fatal divisions in the movement. Whether such a re-orientation would have succeeded in achieving the movement's goals is now, unfortunately, only a matter of conjecture.

THE DAYTON EFFECT

In November 1995, the USA and the EU brokered the Dayton Peace Accords on Bosnia-Herzegovina. Dayton also ended the sanctions against FRY – apart from an 'outer wall' which, it was understood, would stay in place until there was progress on Kosovo. (See Chapter 7.) Surely, most Kosovo Albanians felt, now international attention would finally turn to Kosovo. The USA announcement in January that it would open an Information Office in Kosovo confirmed the growing expectation of a breakthrough. There were even rumours of a secret addendum to Dayton. At the same time, the EU, especially Germany, began to behave as if the situation was already resolved – the EU granting diplomatic recognition to FRY while Germany decided to 'repatriate' refugees from former Yugoslavia, including 130,000 Kosovo Albanians. From Belgrade came one concession in March, the abolition of exit visas to Albania.[2]

With no new initiative forthcoming from Rugova and the LDK, their Albanian rivals were restless. The PPK convened a meeting on 15 January 1996 apparently wanting an inquest into Rugova's leadership, but when Rugova himself would not come, neither would several other leading figures. Rexhep Qosja repeated familiar attacks on Rugova and Berisha, declaring Dayton the end of the illusion that 'the international community' would heed Kosovo's call for independence.[3] Adem Demaçi, who as chair of the CDHRF had stayed out of party politics, was edging towards standing openly against Rugova. He argued for a more 'realistic' demand – such as to be an equal republic rather than fully independent – and that, in the present situation of de-mobilisation, 'tactics would be more important than strategy'.[4]

In general, criticisms of Rugova came along four axes: his undemocratic style; his opposition to any form of confrontation, including nonviolent protest; his negotiating position (some calling him too rigid, others accusing him of preparing a 'sell-out' for autonomy); and – from those more flexible about negotiations – his stance of 'indifference' towards the democratisation of FRY. Rugova seemed content for others to take non-confrontational initiatives, while he remained the figurehead. However, if the LDK was standing still, events were not.

At 3 a.m. on 21 April 1996, a Kosovo Albanian student Armend Daçi was shot by a Serb civilian sniper in Sunny Hill, Prishtina. Daçi was not the first Albanian to be killed by a civilian, but his death brought two reactions. In Prishtina, women – contrary to advice from the LDK – demonstrated. Also, in different parts of Kosovo, four almost synchronised attacks took place within two hours of each other, killing three Serb civilians and two policemen and wounding three other policemen. In a letter to the BBC World Service, responsibility was claimed by the Kosova Liberation Army (UÇK).[5]

At the time, many expressed scepticism that UÇK existed – including some who later aligned with it. However, regardless of speculation about police provocation, one would have expected the leadership of a nonviolent movement to try to regain the initiative and to step up its own activities. Instead, the LDK Council, meeting on 21 May 1996, issued a statement as anodyne as ever and two days later – the day before the parliament's mandate was due to expire – a 'presidential decree' signed by Ibrahim Rugova extended this mandate another year, postponing parliamentary elections until 24 May 1997. There was not a word about convening parliament.

Openly and publicly convening this parliament would have been a classic 'dilemma demonstration'.[6] Either the regime would have had to allow it to meet, to be reported internationally and to function, or it would have to prevent any meeting, thereby forfeiting whatever credit it sought to gain by abolishing exit visas. With the US Information Office opening at the beginning of July, would this not have been the ideal way to mark Kosovo's 'Independence Day' – 2 July? If the parliament did not meet, why should anyone bother to vote in the next elections, would it not be a meaningless ritual?

The other demand – raised by the PPK as well as by students – was for demonstrations for the right to education at the start of the 1996 school year. Here and there some schools had quietly regained use of buildings, but there had been no concerted effort to dramatise this issue since October 1992. Again, the regime could permit protests or crush them and in either case the Albanians would have made their point. If Belgrade stuck to its policy, it could not win – its alternative, a complete reversal of policy, would have been the win-win solution of permitting the use of the buildings.

Some people asked 'Why restrict this thinking to students? How about sacked workers going back to demand their jobs?' An orchestrated campaign, highlighting different sectors at different times, could show that, if there was no war in Bosnia, there was still no peace in Kosovo – that the West in treating Milošević as a guarantor of the Dayton Accords was legitimising the person most to blame.

During 1996, such ideas came increasingly on to the agenda. 'Active nonviolence' could be an alternative to the 'passive nonviolence' of the past four years. However, to be carried out successfully, any campaign involving nonviolent confrontation needed a high degree of unity, hence approval and organisational support from the LDK. As the new school year approached, the PPK publicly proposed nonviolently re-occupying school or university buildings. Then events took a surprising turn. To general amazement, it was announced that Rugova and Milošević had signed an agreement on education. Was this the secret pay-off after Dayton? Was this what Rugova had up his sleeve during those months of apparent passivity?

It transpired that Serb officials and LDK negotiators had been meeting secretly, mediated by an Italian Catholic body, the Comunità di Sant'Egidio. On 1 September 1996, simultaneously in Belgrade and Prishtina, Milošević and Rugova signed an agreement announcing the return of Albanian students and teachers to schools, setting up a mixed group (three Serbs, three Albanians) to negotiate implementation.

First responses were cautious. However, there were three downright hostile reactions. Qosja opposed any process of step by step to negotiation: 'Serbia speaks about solutions of problems in Kosova, and not about the solution of the question of Kosova … Who in this world will deal with Kosova when the problems of Kosova are "solved"? Nobody.' Demaçi made the petty point that Rugova – by signing the agreement only as 'Dr. Ibrahim Rugova' when Milošević had used his full title, President of the Republic of Serbia – 'with his own signature gave up the mandate the people had given him … and is now even trying to sell his political defeat as a success.' University rector Statovci asserted that the return of pupils and students to their premises 'is essentially a question of a national and political right' and was not acceptable 'if it is done in order to be reintegrated into the occupiers' system and jurisdiction'.[7]

When student leaders went to Rugova to inform him of their intention to organise protests to re-open the university, he prevailed on them first to wait and see what had been achieved through negotiation. They deferred to him.

Three events towards the end of 1996 highlighted the impatience to end the LDK's political monopoly. First, Adem Demaçi chose this moment to enter explicitly the political arena, joining the PPK as its leader. He was the only Kosovo Albanian with the stature to offer an alternative to Rugova. Second, the daily pro-democracy protests in Belgrade after Milošević annulled local election results sparked some debate among Albanians. Third, 550 students addressed a petition to Rugova.

Demaçi's long-expected decision to throw his hat in the political ring coincided with president Sali Berisha becoming more active about the situation of Albanians outside Albania, perhaps a diversion tactic from the impending crisis over pyramid schemes inside Albania. Tirana TV gave long interviews to critics of Rugova – first prime-minister-in-exile Bukoshi, then Demaçi and immediately afterwards the Paris-based novelist Ishmail Kadare, all calling for a more active strategy in Kosovo.[8] Berisha himself indicated his support for convening the Kosovo parliament.[9]

When the Belgrade protests began, the LDK leadership displayed an 'exaggerated lack of interest'.[10] A number of Kosovo Albanians, mainly students acting out of curiosity, went to Belgrade on the quiet to see what was happening. *Bujku*, however, reported on the protests only briefly and then included them – as all events in FRY – in its 'World News' section (hence remote from Kosovo). In contrast, Berisha and Demaçi welcomed the pressure for democratisation, Demaçi sending a letter of support.[11] *Bujku* mocked Demaçi's letter for its fulsome 'friendliness' to the Serb oppressors, but this was true to his instincts, consistent both with his new call for 'active Gandhism'[12] and with his previous statements of fellow-feeling with Serb prisoners and the message of sympathy he sent Vuk Drašković in summer 1993 when the Serb oppositionist and his wife were publicly beaten up by Milošević's thugs and jailed. That kind of surprising action earned him respect and perhaps even a hearing among some Serbs.[13] In December 1996, Demaçi was not alone in thinking that 'Albanians should also offer support [to Belgrade demonstrators] for the sake of facilitating evolution and freeing of this movement of nationalistic burdens and myths, especially concerning the Albanians and Kosovo.'[14]

On 16 December, something previously unimaginable happened. A mass demonstration in Belgrade observed one minute's absolute silence, marking the death in police custody of a Kosovo Albanian teacher. Some of these demonstrators a couple of weeks earlier had called on police to go to Kosovo instead of beating them, but others now accepted the argument put by Nataša Kandić of the Humanitarian Law Centre at a roundtable in November 1996:

Human rights will not be respected in Belgrade as long as the terror in Kosovo lasts. It is the same police force. In Kosovo, it protects the regime by beating people. But this report [HLC *Spotlight Report* 26] shows that abuses akin to those in Kosovo exist everywhere, that beatings and use of force are becoming the norm in the relationship between the state and the individual.[15]

Rather than remark on the change of attitude represented by the minute's silence, Prishtina KIC chose to take offence that Vuk Drašković had referred to the teacher not as a Kosovar or a Kosovo Albanian but as a 'citizen of Serbia'.[16] LDK vice-president Fehmi Agani was, as usual, more intelligent. His initial argument was that the realities of power had somewhat tamed Milošević's extremism on Kosovo, forcing him into a more compromising attitude. Many in the Serbian opposition, however, still had dreams of re-Serbianising Kosovo.[17] As the demonstrations grew into a movement of civil resistance, both LDK vice-presidents – Agani and Hydajet Hyseni – spoke of how democratisation of Serbia was in Kosovo's interest, and that the test of how far that democratisation extended would be its treatment of the Kosovo issue.

The Prishtina student petition, also in December 1996, seemed to be taking a leaf out of the book of their Belgrade counterparts. The 550 students, without any public affiliation, began by calling on Rugova for the re-opening of school buildings. The petition then grew into a critique of the state of Kosovo Albanian politics. It demanded the convening of the parliament with Adem Demaçi as a member ('if that is not effectuated, all deputies should publicly submit their resignations and apologise to the people for having ... deceived them'), the abolition of censorship in the Kosovo Albanian media, that former political prisoners 'wake up from their dream', the normalisation of relationships between president Rugova and prime minister Bukoshi, the re-activation of the coordination between Albanian political parties in former Yugoslavia and 'an end once and for all to the policy of castes or introducing feudalism in Kosovo'.[18]

Students, a report in *AIM* suggested, might become 'a catalyst of everything accumulated among the Albanian population during years and everything that is currently cooking under the surface on the Albanian political scene.' It went on to report rumours that the second school term had been postponed not because of the stated shortage of heating fuel, but in fear of 'uncontrollable public protests' for implementation of the Education Agreement.[19]

There were no uncontrollable protests. Nor was there any progress in implementing the agreement, nor for convening the parliament. Instead a crisis in Albania brought down the Berisha government.

The Gheg sympathetic to the Kosovo cause had to make way for the less sympatethic Fatos Nano, a Tosk, while the chaos brought attacks on police armouries releasing a mass of AK47s into the volatile region. Rugova could now pose as a force for stability in the Albanian space. In May, he yet again extended the mandate of the parliament. Demaçi declared that he would convene it by collecting signatures from elected deputies. He tried, but failed to convince enough of them. Without Rugova's imprimatur, parliamentarians were not ready for this brand of dynamism.

In FRY, the *Zajedno* coalition that had led the winter protests never developed a policy for Kosovo, nor indeed a coherent platform within FRY, and broke up in squabbles.

A FRAMEWORK FOR 'ACTIVE NONVIOLENCE'

Under the leadership of the LDK, with persistence and patience, the Kosovo Albanians had followed a policy of refusing to be provoked and maintaining their own structures at home while lobbying for international support. This had succeeded in limiting Serbian aggression and averting war, in keeping the population together and its social structures functioning, and in bringing repeated international condemnation on Serbia for human rights violations.

1. Refusing to be provoked denied the regime a pretext to unleash its full force, and gave Kosovo Albanians the moral upper hand, hence strengthening their claim on third party – especially international – support. However, if self-restraint and active monitoring inhibited the escalation of police violence, and if Kosovo Albanians derived some satisfaction from their nonviolent identity, nonviolence could not be sustained without some change in the situation.
2. Maintaining parallel structures demonstrated a capacity for self-organisation and fulfilled two essential but defensive objectives – maintaining Albanian life in Kosovo and denying the regime's objective of dispersing the Albanian population. They relied primarily on the Albanian community and diaspora, on voluntary activity and the organisation of social solidarity. However, if in adverse conditions these structures served as a carrier of values – including national unity and self-sacrifice – they lacked the capacity to generate or sustain enthusiasm.

3. International support meant that, unlike in 1989, Kosovo was no longer seen as an 'internal affair' of Serbia. However, the West remained more interested in influencing Kosovo Albanian policy in the direction of integration into FRY and away from independence. Mere lobbying could not create the pressure that might be exerted through more dramatic actions. The foreign governmental support on which so much was staked was contingent on too many factors outside the control of Kosovo Albanians – not least that, after Dayton, Western willingness to act against Milošević was limited by accepting him as the guarantor of peace in Bosnia.

Apart from the international support, the only strategy for changing Serbian policy seemed to be through some kind of attrition. Not only was Serbia failing to alter the ethnic balance in Kosovo, but its administration was managing less well in many respects than the parallel system. A number of people shared the analysis that the elite in Belgrade was preparing to resign itself to the 'loss' of Kosovo – as evidenced by proposals coming from nationalists ranging from the Orthodox Church to SANU for either cantonisation or partition of Kosovo. However, this strategy of eroding the Serbian will was slow and long term and itself subject to the attrition of the frustration of everyday life and the humiliations experienced under 'occupation'. Progress towards ending the Serbian oppression was too slow, and progress in improving the quality of life for Kosovo Albanians too little.

Hence the call for 'active nonviolence' – coming from people both inside and outside the LDK – as a response to a 'loss of hope'. Demaçi was the most prominent of those who called for greater activity for less ambitious demands as a way of dynamising the struggle. He was echoed by the leading voice of political prisoners inside the LDK, vice-president Hydajet Hyseni, who saw a need to 'maximise the potentials within our society'.[20] Some suggestions had the character of action for action's sake, smacking of desperation. Refusal to pay electricity bills or tax resistance[21] would have been pointless unless accompanied by a campaign to redefine economic relations, to reduce dependence on imports from Serbia and strengthen home production. Otherwise, they would make little impact either on the regime or on the morale of the Kosovo Albanian population. Ideas for 'active nonviolence' needed to cohere with a 'grand strategy'.

Going back to Clausewitz's analysis of conflict, Robert Burrowes has argued that – as in war so in nonviolent struggle – the centre of gravity is the battle of wills. 'The strategic aim of the defence', it then follows, 'is to consolidate the power and will of the defending population to resist the aggression. The strategic aim of the counter-offensive is to *alter* the will of the opponent elite to conduct the aggression'.[22]

The distinction between altering the *will* and undermining the *power* of the opponent elite is especially noteworthy in this case, where Kosovo Albanians had little direct leverage on the Serbian elite. They could not themselves undermine its power, but rather had to look to others – either at the international level or in the Serbian population. This was one reason they invested undue hope in international support: their own non-cooperation served mainly to strengthen their own morale and to demonstrate their dissent to others.

Consolidating the will of the defence required empowerment, an effort to make the population feel more in control of their own lives. The existing strategy needed to be augmented by greater willingness to risk confrontation on the one hand and for a stronger constructive element on the other – in general, greater coordination in realising the potential within their own population. Persistence is one of the most important qualities of a protracted struggle.[23] However, a movement needs more than exhortations to sustain this persistence.

Altering the will of the opponent takes place, according to Gene Sharp, through four broad mechanisms, or their interaction: conversion (the opponent has a change of heart), accommodation (a compromise is reached), coercion (the opponent backs down) or dis-integration (the regime collapses).[24] The 'counter-offensive' in civil resistance is not directed just towards the regime but also – and usually mainly – towards those on whom the regime depends. A change will come when it cannot rely on its security forces or when its power base withdraws their support.

The Albanians of Kosovo – the first people against whom the regime mobilised opinion – tended to be resigned to their lack of influence in FRY. Attitudinal surveys invariably showed deep hostility towards Albanians.[25] The LDK therefore paid less attention to making allies in FRY or using divisions between the population and the regime, than to appealing to the greater power of interna-tional force. This reflected an exclusivist impulse that did not serve them well in terms of building a strategy.

Serbia claimed to rule Kosovo; tomorrow it would be at least a neighbour, and Serbs living in Kosovo gave their allegiance to Belgrade. A low level of interaction with FRY may have served to allow some calming of hostility, and given Milošević time to adjust to the limits of his power, but it did nothing to reassure Serbs about future inter-ethnic relations in Kosovo or the safety of monasteries. Moreover, an apparent preference for ethnic separation among many Albanians did nothing to maximise what interest there was from any part of FRY or from any other ethnic group in making common cause, let alone encouraging those who wanted to negotiate some solution. Finding points of contact with Serbs warranted effort alongside the effort to persuade the governments of the world to accept what they saw as 'separatism'. A more democratic FRY – without the regime's control of the media, with a stronger human rights culture, with a smaller and less politicised (and less criminal) police force, giving a full voice to ethnic groups such as Vojvodinans, Sandžak Muslims and Montenegrins – would still not have given its blessing to Kosovo's independence. However, it would have been more willing to negotiate and less ruthless in its treatment of Albanians.

More fundamental than any strategic calculation about what might be gained from greater communication with Serbs, however, was the question of the future of Kosovo. 'Indifference' to the concerns of Serbs – both in Kosovo and in FRY – would prejudice the long-term possibility of inter-ethnic coexistence in Kosovo. Civil resistance cannot solely be concerned with the defence of territory, but rather seeks to uphold the values of civil society – and this extends to the methods directed towards the regime and its population. If a struggle needs a degree of unity, an ethnic population also needs some openness to ethnic outsiders. In this chapter 'strengthening the values of coexistence and dialogue' is also included among the elements of a strategy of empowerment.

A STRATEGY OF EMPOWERMENT

Social empowerment is not about domination or 'power-over', but rather about the power-to-be and the power-to-do. It can be analysed on three interconnected planes – *power-within*, *power-with* and *power-in-relation-to*. 'Power-within' is personal power, the sense that each person can do something to improve a situation, that in our own lives we can be more than victims or spectators. 'Power-with' comes from combining with others and ideally will in turn strengthen 'power-within'. This collective sense can begin with an immediate social circle, can spread to a whole identity group, can build up through the growth of a movement and extend to making strategic alliances on points where other groups share a common purpose or interest. 'Power-in-relation-to' recognises that a person and a movement's power is limited by external factors, especially in a situation of conflict. It requires a judgement about what goals can be achieved and a strategy towards those who oppose those goals.[26] After Dayton, the Kosovo Albanian movement needed a phase of remobilisation, developing and using its full potential.

Renewed Mobilisation

Experimenting to widen the range of tactics: The movement began by using a variety of tactics involving different social groups and levels of risk. Then it settled down. Life was never actually routine in Kosovo in the 1990s, but there was a sense of routinisation about the resistance. There was enormous scope to experiment with new tactics. Some were controversial, such as sending deputies to the FRY assembly or voting in local elections. Most were risky. But some tactical innovation was called for after Dayton as a recognition of having reached a new phase. Innovations could have been introduced through small-scale tester actions or local experiments, somewhat breaking with the norm of 'everybody do such and such'. The recent example of small groups in Eastern Europe could have stimulated ideas.

Nonviolent confrontation: The refusal to be provoked was vital, but prudence became associated with an unwillingness to risk Serbian violence. Instead of refraining from nonviolent confrontation, a more assertive approach would have planned carefully, taking limited risks for specific strategic purposes. In many ways, convening the 1992 parliament and trying to re-open the schools offered the ideal opportunities. With the parliament, the primary risk would have been carried by just 130 people, a highly committed group, few of whom were doing essential work to maintain the parallel structures and all of whom could be relied on to abide by group discipline. It is hard to see how the international advice against this could serve the interests of Kosovo Albanians – either in terms of their internal democracy or in terms of the conflict with Belgrade. By ensuring good media coverage of any attempt to suppress the parliament, Rugova had it in his power to shift the diplomatic discourse from *realpolitik* to their avowed concern for 'democracy'.[27] As we shall see, in October 1997 the students, against the advice of international diplomats, confirmed the potential of nonviolent confrontation for dramatising their situation, putting pressure on international actors as well as attracting Serbian support. Joint actions with short-term international visitors, if properly conceived and strategised, could have had a dramatic impact.

Making news: One side of this was simple public relations. Among Kosovo-watchers, the *KIC* bulletins were an essential source of information, but their typical lead item 'Today President Rugova saw ...' was a standing joke. It was hard to put resources into public relations when there were so many humanitarian needs unmet. Also Kosovo offices in the diaspora were often dominated – especially after Dayton – by the danger of asylum-seekers being repatriated. However, investing in educating international opinion would bring new resources – and meet a key strategic need. The other side was to organise activities that dramatised issues from Kosovo, providing images both for the media and for international supporters. The women's demonstrations were especially skilled at this – but only *after* Drenica.

Organisation: A protracted struggle needs to have forums where activists feel their voices are heard, where ideas for initiatives can be tested in debate, and where it is possible to identify the centre of gravity of opinion for what can be negotiated – what people now feel is at stake. In view of the growing gap between the leadership and their activist base, the lack of democracy in the LDK was a long-term problem. The LDK began to seem more interested in running Kosovo as a state than in waging a struggle, and even at times in controlling rather than facilitating activity. Its own undemocratic structure – and its neglect of structures such as the Coordinating Council for Political Parties, the parliament itself or the parliamentary commissions – put the leadership out of touch, less likely to have suggestions for channelling discontent than justifications for blocking initiative. The dominant organisational concept in the male-dominated political scene was of 'mass struggle' hierarchically controlled. Their mode of thinking focused on what the leadership should do, rather than looking at encouraging centres for more modest initiatives. The 1980s experience with 'cells' and the existence (albeit unacknowledged) of conspiratorial groups preparing for armed revolt seemed to inhibit the possibilities for gingering up the nonviolent movement by giving rein to the creativity and imagination of small nonviolent action groups.[28]

The kind of mobilisation discussed here carried dangers. Nonviolent confrontation and greater assertiveness by raising expectations and reducing patience could have been disastrously de-stabilising. Here specifically Gandhi had pointers to offer.

First, in order to judge when to embark on major civil disobedience, Gandhi developed:

> ... a method of 'testing' by observing the conduct of public demonstrations, especially *hartals* [closing of shops/suspension of work], or the take-up of his campaigns of constructive work, or the number of signatures to a pledge, or contributors to a fund.[29]

A number of activities in the 1990–91 period – most notably the petition *For Democracy, Against Violence*, and the 'homages' – had offered such indicators. However, nothing comparable was organised in the period after the October 1992 demonstrations, leaving everything to the prevailing caution of Rugova.

Second, Gandhi saw a vital relationship between civil disobedience and constructive programme. The Gandhian scholar Bob Overy offers this insight:

> Gandhi's successes as an organiser cannot be understood unless it is recognised that at the base of every campaign of civil disobedience – especially at the national level – was a programme of constructive work ... Constructive work was designed to discipline the people prior to civil disobedience. It was to provide tasks which could be taken up by the poorest peasants and give them a place in the national movement. It was designed to provide a link between the national political elite and the peasantry and to take active nationalists out of the legislatures to the 'real' politics of India, tackling poverty in the villages. [Because of the problem of mass all-India civil resistance campaigns getting out of hand if the leaders moved too quickly to aggressive con-frontation,] it was used not only as a preparation for civil disobedience but also as a delaying tactic: until the targets were reached and the 'capacity' of the nation demonstrated, civil disobedience could not be launched.[30]

Constructive Programme

Self-activity: 'Victim' behaviour is evident throughout the warring nations of former Yugoslavia, indeed in many forms of exclusive nationalism – each cultivating its own sense of grievance, and thereby strengthening its national cohesion as defined against the Other. In the case of Kosovo Albanians, there sometimes seemed more willingness to suffer than to change. Victim behaviour blocked efforts at self-improvement by preferring to blame 'the Serbs' rather than looking at what could be achieved 'without the Serbs' through self-organisation. The heaps of rubbish in the streets of Kosovo cities provided a visual image of this. Whereas Gandhi said: 'If we impute all our weaknesses to the present government, we shall never shed them',[31] Kosovo Albanians sometimes seemed to think 'the more we suffer, the worse the Serbs look, the better for us'. Certain groups emerged – especially among women, youth and medical workers – that took the attitude, 'Let's make what we can, let's change what's near to us'.

Improving daily life: It is harsh to criticise the parallel educational system in view of the countless small acts of resistance it required. Yet small youth groups, feminist groups, literacy projects and organisations for people with disabilities showed that it was possible to do much more to stimulate initiative and to value pluralism. Nonviolent struggle depends on being able to regenerate itself, for instance by giving people a taste for self-organisation, changing the quality of daily life in a way that encourages a higher level of engagement, and creating opportunities for new initiatives. The LDK, on the other hand, asked people to wait for international pressure without promoting activities that could retain and renew the momentum of the struggle.

An economic strategy: This could have two aspects, both more to do with community morale than leverage on the Serbian economy. First, as a complete boycott of imports was impossible, a specific type of Serbian import could have been boycotted – as with Gandhi's decision to boycott foreign cloth. This would have been especially effective if the item could be home produced instead (Gandhi's concept of *swadeshi*, favouring local produce). Second, economic revival could have been an important goal, reducing dependence on imports from Serbia, instilling self-respect and even the hope of employment. This could have begun by regenerating the 'household economy', as during the Palestinian *Intifada*,[32] and gone on to develop a range of small 'incubator enterprises'. A former federal economist proposed such a scheme in 1995. Each business would require small levels of capital, maintain low cash levels to reduce police harassment and aim only for a modest profit. The point would be 'to build self-confidence and the courage to make someone able to decide their own destiny'. Three years later, he had concluded that 'people here are not interested in economic success': he had received no public criticism yet there was no enthusiasm to act on his suggestions.[33] Even in a climate of harassment, such opportunities existed. However, without a coordinated programme for small-scale economic development, people tended to indulge in pipedreams about the future wealth of Kosovo once Albanians gained control of the heavy industry and the mines.

Strengthening the values of coexistence and dialogue: Seeking to include the opponent in the search for solutions is one of the hardest demands Gandhian nonviolence makes of an oppressed group. Just as any Serb leader felt s/he would be committing 'political suicide' to offer concessions on Kosovo, so there were restraints on what was possible within the Albanian community. Yet even in this situation where pragmatism – and not Gandhian principle – ruled, a basis needed to be laid for future coexistence. While economically there was no boycott, politically and socially the prevailing attitude towards Serbs in public was shunning them[34] – without a strategic rationale. No gesture of the leadership would end inter-ethnic hostility at a stroke. 'Learning sites'[35] were needed, meeting places where Serbs (from Kosovo or FRY) and Albanians – and other ethnic groups – could have or revive a different experience of each other. Beginning with media reporting that showed the variety of Serbian attitudes and welcomed inter-ethnic cooperation, and spreading to practical cross-ethnic projects that would meet basic human needs in villages – water supply being the most obvious – there needed to be measures that would build confidence between the communities of Kosovo. The majority had to learn not to ignore the concerns of the civilians in the minority.

Re-shaping goals in terms of a process of expanding self-determination and of universal human rights: Having asserted and practised the right to organise their own lives, the Kosovo Albanians needed to regularise this through negotiations. Kosovo's unilateral declaration of independence in 1991 – in response to Serbia's unilateral annulment of Kosovo's autonomy – presented Serbs, Serbia, FRY and foreign governments with the most difficult Kosovo Albanian demand to accept. The goal of independence could not have been abandoned without fatal divisions in the movement, yet without international intervention, the key to achieving it lay in taking a long-term view and finding some way of 'helping' Serbs to let go of Kosovo. This suggests a need to re-cast goals, focusing on transitional possibilities open either to independence or to some form of federation. These might include a type of cantonisation or system with spheres of 'personal autonomy' for each ethnic group (for instance, on education and culture). On the Albanian side, the need was for a switch from the idea of being 'masters of Kosovo' – breaking with the old cycles of ethnic domination – to an idea such as Gandhi's *swaraj* (self-rule), control over one's own life beginning at a personal level, extending through the local to the regional and national. The other part of Gandhi's notion of *swaraj* is that independence is not an exclusive notion, but links with interdependence. A practical constitutional interpretation of such an attitude might propose a system with distinct levels of territorial and political self-determination.

Building a new society: Gandhi had a vision of a 'constructive programme' – self-organised efforts at transforming one's own society – and *swaraj*, a rich concept connecting personal self-realisation through various levels of decentralised self-government up to the national goal.

> Imagine all the forty crores of people busying themselves with the whole of the constructive programme which is designed to build up the nation from the very bottom upward. Can anybody dispute the proposition that it must mean complete Independence in every sense of the expression, including the ousting of foreign domination?[36]

Gandhi's Constructive Programme began in the 1920s as a Triple Programme – hand-spinning and wearing handspun cloth, working for Hindu-Muslim unity and seeking the removal of 'untouchability'. By 1941, the programme had 18 points, including education about health and hygiene and the removal of various social evils.

In Kosovo, the campaign to remove blood feuds was a powerful example of Constructive Programme (see Chapter 3). On a smaller scale a similar spirit could be found in the longer-term work of the Rural Women's Network (see below) and more widely and briefly in the 1996 polio vaccinations drive (see Chapter 7). The LDK itself, however, was more like the Congress Party of India before and without Gandhi, lacking this kind of spirit. There was no concerted attempt to mobilise resources for the social development desperately necessary, indeed that was needed even in the days of autonomy, nor to foster a different vision for what self-determination might bring to Kosovo. The parallel structures tended to patch up gaps rather than prefigure how life could be. After the blood feud campaign, the need for self-reform dropped off the national agenda. The politics 'as if' would have benefitted from an injection of utopianism (in the proper sense of the word), not just acting 'as if' Serbia did not rule Kosovo but throwing off the mental limits of what existed, and trying to 'live the future now'.

Any re-orientation in Kosovo would have carried risks, especially a re-mobilisation. It could not have been simply ordained from on high, but would rather have had to evolve as a new national consensus. At every point it would need framing in terms of enhancing the capacity for self-determination and in terms of the new Kosovo Albanian identity. The points of discord and division that might surface within families, within villages as well as within the movement as a whole would need to be negotiated with care. However, 'Gandhism' in Kosovo became interpreted as 'waiting'. Instead of the idea being of a progressive reclaiming of self-determined space, the hope was that someone outside would intervene. The alternative framework would therefore have been a renewal of pressure matched by a strengthening of essentially long-term work with two aspects:

  i) reconstructing Kosovo Albanian society and
  ii) giving more substance to the commitment to inter-ethnic co-existence by greater openness towards meeting the concerns of Serbian neighbours, engaging in confidence-building and focusing mainly on transition questions in negotiations.

ALTERING SERBIAN WILL

Strategic thinking about civil resistance remains at the developmental stage. The key strategic insight has been that regimes ultimately depend on the acquiescence or cooperation of the people they rule. The main strategic goal then becomes to deprive a regime of this base by the intelligent combination of nonviolent methods. However, in some situations – Palestine and Tibet are examples in addition to Kosovo – far from depending on the oppressed population, the regime would rather expel it. In such conditions, the defending population has to rely on its will and strength to stay put, and to find the means to affect the will of the aggressor. These means can aim to persuade the aggressor that there is a more desirable, peaceful alternative; they can aim to undermine the regime's apparatus of repression or to separate the regime from its power base; they can seek allies with the power to put pressure on the regime; and/or they can aim to weaken international support for regime. The Kosovo Albanians' main goal was to coerce Belgrade through international pressure. Chapter 7 looks at the international dimension. Here, we consider relations between Kosovo Albanians and the population and regime of FRY (including Serbs in Kosovo).

As we saw in Chapter 1, the rising force of Serbian ultra-nationalism spread from Kosovo Serbs and the Church to intellectuals and then to the media and the apparatus of state. In the course of the 1980s it grew to be a strong enough force to bring down the temple of Tito's Yugoslavia. In 1996 Serbs continued to leave Kosovo while those staying felt like the biggest losers in the situation. The Church was now disillusioned with Milošević: the Patriarch had opposed war in Bosnia and the church leadership inside Kosovo – although not yet the Patriarchate itself – was beginning to look for a *modus vivendi* that did not depend on force. Meanwhile, leading intellectuals inside SANU had realised that 'reclaiming' Kosovo was an illusion and in 1996 SANU's president, Aleksandar Despić, went so far as to discuss means for the 'peaceful secession' of Kosovo – in effect its partition from Serbia retaining the mines in the north, and the monasteries around Peć/Peja being incorporated into Montenegro.[37]

If the regime continued to control the media and the state apparatus, above all the police and the mint, with the paramilitaries ready to do its bidding, there was nonetheless a substantial change in the will of the elite in Serbia – brought about by the toll of other events. Serbia had been defeated in war, isolated internationally and its ruined economy was now burdened with refugees from Bosnia and the Krajina and soon from Eastern Slavonia. Its plans for Kosovo – to disperse the Albanians and settle Serbs and Montenegrins – were as derelict as any of the unfinished buildings along the road from Belgrade to Prishtina.

The Kosovo role in this had been primarily to stand their own ground. Nonviolent struggle, comments Sharp, rarely produces change through conversion of a regime.

Far more often, nonviolent struggle operates by changing the conflict situation and the society so that the opponents simply cannot do as they like. It is this change which produces the other three mechanisms: accommodation, nonviolent coercion and disintegration.[38]

By not posing a threat but instead concentrating on their own survival, Kosovo Albanians had allowed the frenzy of 1989–90 to subside somewhat. However, the regime remained armed, the Serbian population predominantly hostile. If there were now fewer volunteers in FRY wanting to go and fight in Kosovo, discontent could just as easily rally behind an ultra-nationalist as behind someone committed to democratisation and human rights. What room for manoeuvre did Kosovo Albanians have?

First, let us consider the forces – the regime's instruments of repression. The means employed by Kosovo Albanians to reduce violence were non-retaliation, human rights monitoring and international exposure. They had a few allies, especially among the principled anti-war groups in FRY, various sectors in Vojvodina and eventually in Montenegro.[39] Serbian forces were increasingly war weary as the 1990s went on. In 1998 parents' protests stopped the deployment of new recruits to Kosovo,[40] while in 1999 many refused the draft or deserted, especially high proportions among Montenegrins and Vojvodinans.[41] In 1999, there were accounts that regular soldiers gave refugees water, food and milk for babies that helped them to survive.[42] There were also reports of local police acting to save Albanians. While army heavy artillery was used in Kosovo in both 1998 and 1999, the core of those carrying out the ethnic cleansing were not army units, but hardened special police units, augmented if need be by paramilitaries – some driven by greed and some by ultra-nationalism. Prospects of causing disaffection among these were minimal and almost non-existent after the emergence of UÇK.

Second, the regime's support base, the domestic population. The classic civil resistance strategy aims to detach the population from the regime – and in this case also from the equally hostile alternatives. This is less likely to be achieved through threats than through persuasion by word and deed. Few Kosovo Albanians were interested in such an approach. From the leadership down, they were more interested in 'overruling' the Serbian will than 'altering' it, more interested in presenting a *fait accompli* than negotiating.

Kosovo Albanians had plenty of reasons to be sceptical of Serbian politicians. What most Serbs – and therefore most Serbian politicians – desired for Kosovo was that it should be part of Serbia. No political leader said anything different in public. Any criticism of Milošević's policy on Kosovo was more likely to be on the grounds that it was 'losing' Kosovo than that it was immoral or unrealistic – only the Civic Alliance leader Vesna Pešić consistently condemned disregard for international human rights standards. Besides not having direct leverage on Serbian political decisions, Kosovo Albanians therefore feared triggering a renewed backlash.

Another consideration was that the Serbian ultra-nationalism described in Chapter 1 was not only profoundly non-rational, but at times bordered on the psychotic. One Kosovo Albanian analysis was that Milošević's extremism had been tempered by the realities of power – including that of feeling their will against his – making him a less extreme opponent than rivals or colleagues without such experience. People also saw Milošević's patterns: responding to one crisis by creating another, waging war not to win but to punish (as in Croatia) and in general manipulating events for his own advantage without consideration of long-term damage. As cunning and ruthless as he is, he did not try to mount an effective strategy of divide-and-rule against Kosovo Albanians. Rather he preferred to be seen opposing Kosovo Albanians *en bloc*.

Such factors encouraged passivity towards FRY and avoided provocations such as voting in 'their' elections. There was, however, an alternative to inactivity, with three main components:
 – strengthening connections with the anti-war, human rights, pro-democracy and independent media groups;
 – confidence-building through projects addressing needs and interests that crossed ethnic boundaries; and
 – greater communication in general with the peoples of FRY to dispel the ignorant stereotypical images of Albanians.

This was long-term work and with modest objectives – creating conditions more conducive to future inter-ethnic coexistence and reducing obstructions to change.

'The Great Chain of Nonviolence'[43]

One strategic objective for an oppressed people on whom a regime does not depend is to build a 'chain of nonviolence'. Initially, it may only seem to be 'marginal' groups that are willing to make such a link, but the ultimate aim is to connect with either enough of the opponent elite's support base or sufficiently central sources of influence in the opponent's society to change policy. In Israel-Palestine one can trace the process from initial contacts between Palestinians and virtually 'outlaw' anti-Zionist Israelis in the 1970s, then bringing in 'anti-Occupation' peace and justice groups in the 1980s and leading onto the mainstream Peace Now movement by the time of the *Intifada*.[44] The LDK – unlike the PLO – had never endorsed 'terrorism' and those talking with it were not breaking any 'anti-terrorist law'. Over Kosovo the barriers were those of ethnic discipline. Several Belgrade groups valued links with Kosovo Albanians and spoke out. The most evident were the Humanitarian Law Centre, with its detailed reports on human rights violations, the Helsinki Committee and Women in Black who, after Dayton, switched the focus of their weekly vigil from Bosnia to Kosovo. The Balkan Peace Team (BPT) – a small international project – had the remit of facilitating contacts and visiting the growing number of NGOs in FRY to find out what interest they might have in cooperating with Albanians and what support they might need. There were various other internationally mediated attempts to stimulate connections between Serbs and Kosovo Albanians. The Italian Campagna Kossovo tried to develop 'triangular' cooperation (Albanian-Italian-Serbian) in educational projects, and to create a meeting space in Prishtina through events such as 'pasta evenings'. Pax Christi Flanders and Netherlands organised a series of meetings primarily for youth activists or organisers, a grass-roots level of leadership, often providing introductions between the communities and helping to raise consciousness of the other's point of view. The Norwegian Nansen Peace Academy had both Serbs and Kosovo Albanians on its ten week courses, following them up with workshops.

Every attempt at dialogue 'for dialogue's sake' was liable to mis-interpretation primarily by members of their own ethnic community. Inside Kosovo, there was one attempt in the mid-1990s to found a Kosov@[45] Peace Group in Prishtina, bringing together Serbs and Albanians. Simply cutting across the dominant community feelings in this way was hard to sustain. Another attempt was made in 1998 by participants in the Nansen courses, with outside support including renting an office to serve as a safe space and employing coordinators. It continued to function throughout the hostilities of 1998 until both communities were dispersed in 1999. Less ambitiously, the health group Mens Sana organised periodic roundtables with participants from both communities.

At a more formal level, there were repeated attempts at public dialogue meetings, often emanating from people who had been involved in UJDI (for instance, those involved in the Open Society Fund/Soros and related circles). Certain meetings – such as those between Kosovo Albanian and FRY political parties in 1992 – tried to see if any kind of tactical alliance might be possible. Others took place in the framework of human rights (for instance, meetings involving the Belgrade and Prishtina Helsinki Committees and the CDHRF), or as part of a pre-negotiation process. In general, the Kosovo Albanian participants were more prominent in their own community than their Serb interlocutors, and Kosovo Serbs were not themselves represented. Such meetings often served to reconnect people who knew each other from the days of Yugoslavia and were especially useful for those interested in testing out new ideas. In the period after Dayton, a number of international NGOs tried to facilitate 'Track Two' meetings,[46] less in the perspective of creating links between participants than to prepare the way for negotiations.

While LDK vice-president Fehmi Agani was particularly active in dialogue work, and while the LDK Youth were very open to contacts with Serbs,[47] the LDK leadership as a whole simply did not project the concept of connections with Serbs or other groups in FRY as any part of its strategy.

Crossing Ethnic Boundaries to Address Needs

This common approach to conflict resolution through negotiation is also a practical reality on the ground. The lack of any independent voluntary bodies or civil society organisations in the Kosovo Serb community reduced the possibility for bilateral partnerships to address mutual problems. Dialogue-minded groups from Belgrade were more likely to find partners in Kosovo among Albanians than their fellow Serbs, and while the group Most (Bridge) from Belgrade visited Prishtina to give an organisational workshop to the CDHRF, I know of no parallel activity between a Belgrade civil society group and Kosovo Serbs at that time.

One also cannot overlook the question of resources. Kosovo Albanians gained access to the resources to engage in confidence-building projects once international funding became available. A number of international bodies had this approach (see Chapter 7) and in general had little problem with the LDK – although the LDK did not take the initiative or suggest possibilities. At the level of public opinion, however, there was resistance. One pioneer in promoting inter-ethnic cooperation by responding to human needs was the International Confederation of the Red Cross, operating in Kosovo from 1994 onwards. An early scheme was for humanitarian relief to Serbs and Albanians including many Trepça miners. ICRC had cleared this with both the top LDK leadership and the Serbian authorities, when *Bujku* and the Kosovo Serb newspaper *Jedinstvo* got wind of the 'story'. They began scoring inter-ethnic points off each other, *Jedinstvo* reporting on Serb 'generosity' to Albanians, *Bujku* finally objecting to the degradation of the heroic Trepça miners through this project. It had to be scrapped. In future, the ICRC decided to concentrate on local agreements, as far as possible by-passing central structures.[48] Other international bodies had to learn how to negotiate such blocks, the most spectacular success being the 1996 polio immunisation drive (see Chapter 7).

In view of the repression by Serbs and mutual inter-ethnic suspicion, the LDK leadership made no serious effort to convince Serbs that they had a future in an independent Kosovo beyond formal measures such as reserving seats for them in the parallel parliament.

Greater Communication with the Public in FRY

In August 1994 Ibrahim Rugova proposed opening a Kosovo bureau in Belgrade.[49] It is unfortunate that he did not carry this out. There were consistently voices from Kosovo willing to give interviews or write articles for magazines or newspapers in FRY and even some willing to go and speak at meetings. There were also groups in Belgrade and other cities in FRY eager to hear from Kosovo Albanians – the most prominent such group in Belgrade being the opposition-ist intellectual Belgrade Circle.

The Belgrade demonstrations of winter 1996–97 offered an opportunity that was spurned. A first step as simple as a press conference calling on *Zajedno* to extend their concern for democra-tisation to Kosovo could have tested the waters. At the least it would have educated a few of the foreign press corps who had arrived to cover the protests, and it would have encouraged many of the rank and file protesters – above all, students – who went on to take a serious interest in Kosovo.

Independent media cooperated, as noted in Chapter 5, increasingly so as the 1990s progressed, to take advantage of the possibilities offered by broadcasting privatisation and the development of the internet. For instance, in 1997–98 the Women's Media Project/Radio 21 in Prishtina produced a series of twelve videos 'Kosovo: A view from the Inside' that were broadcast on eleven stations in Serbia, while BETA and ARTA in Belgrade cooperated with *Koha Ditore* in Prishtina in producing web pages.

A more general attitude, however, was to avoid communication in public. Two illustrations come from the students' union, UPSUP, which had previously shown its willingness to engage in dialogue. In January 1998, the Belgrade daily *Naša Borba* awarded UPSUP its prize for tolerance[50] – both a sign of the latent support for Albanian rights in Serbia and an opportunity. They did not even consider appearing to collect it. Again in May 1998, two members of the newly-formed Anti-War Campaign from Belgrade came to Prishtina to talk about possible cooperation with UPSUP – including the idea that some Albanian students might join them in going to speak at universities in FRY about the situation. So strongly had Albanians internalised the attitude that they were hated throughout Serbia that several students felt that such a visit would only harm the Anti-War Campaign.[51] In general, the main reason such activities were 'unthinkable', however, was conformity with a 'social circle'. Again, processes of testing were needed to see what was possible in FRY and to prepare the change of opinion in Kosovo.

EMPOWERMENT: WOMEN

Some writers have referred to the role of women in the movement in the early period, 1989–91.[52] On my visit to Prishtina in January 1992, I carried three letters from Staša Zajović of Belgrade's Women in Black for members of a small feminist group. One of these was Flaka Surroi, who told me that the movement was changing things for women – for instance, Muslim women had begun to participate in public mourning and to speak in public without first asking permission of the male heads of family.

On my second visit, in February 1993, I found a change. The feminist group had dissolved. Another member told me that now the national question came first, this was not the time to talk about contraception or such issues. Meeting leaders of the League of Albanian Women, I heard that the priority was Serbian violence, which did include violence against women but was mainly directed against men.

Vjosa Dobruna, looking back in 1996, wrote:

At the start of the 'alternative movement' or 'parallel system', women were very active and involved in large numbers but as the system grew to an entrenched way of living, women's involvement in decision-making positions in the movement has declined. Women represent half the work in the education system, more than half of the alternative health system, and the majority of social services, but work more or less in subservient roles rather than having an active voice in the development of society. The mentality has become that gender or individual freedom can be perceived only through the overriding philosophy of national freedom.[53]

As co-director of the Centre for the Protection of Women and Children, Dobruna was concerned about decision-making at every level – from the leadership of the movement down to the family.

Some talked about a re-traditionalisation (including a re-patri-archialisation) of Albanian life during the 1990s with families pushed by the emergency to regroup into the larger extended family units of previous times, where women are invariably pushed into service roles. Also there were reports of a turn towards Muslim schools and hence traditions. At the same time, there are stories of women – in common with other war situations of civil strife – taking on higher status roles in the absence of their husband. In a situation of flux, where great differences exist between remote rural areas and cities, there can be no simple generalisation. A point emerging clearly in conversations with younger women from Prishtina is that they found a range of non-traditional role models among women activists from the early days of the civil resistance. This partly explains why the Prishtina Women's Network and the Rural Women's Network became two of the most innovative circles in the period 1996–98.

The group Motrat Qiriazi[54] was for a time the only feminist project in Kosovo. Its founders – the sisters Igballe and Safete Rogova – named it after the Qiriazi sisters who in 1891 founded the first Albanian girls' school in Korça, Albania. The group began in 1990 primarily as a literacy project for rural women. By 1992, about 300 women had learnt to read and write with Motrat Qiriazi's support. Then, however, they suspended their activities. In Mertus's words, 'the group had not negotiated the relationship between gender and nation well'. Bluntly, local male leaders dissuaded women from attending classes that they felt emphasised gender identity *above* national identity.

The project was relaunched in 1995, primarily concentrating on villages in the remote region of Has (near the Albanian border, between Gjakova and Prizren). This may be the most traditional area of Kosovo – an area of widespread illiteracy where few girls attend high school and most are promised in marriage by the age of 13. Because Has is remote and does not have a mixed population, Motrat Qiriazi had the freedom to work in 13 villages, each with its own local organiser – once, that is, they had managed to establish their credentials. To do this they had to demonstrate to both men and women that the education of women strengthened the nation. Apparently, once word spread that women in some villages of Has were getting special attention that would benefit the entire nation, men in villages not yet visited became angry, demanding 'why haven't you come to see our women?'[55]

Mertus' analysis convincingly shows 'nationalism becom[ing] a powerful legitimizing force for organising women as women', a legitimacy needed by women themselves as much as by men:

They needed to find an identity for themselves within the nation first, and only then could they begin to explore their identity as women. When the group leader told them, 'Improving the lives of women improves the whole nation,' she gave them permission to think about themselves – a necessary pre-requisite to work with women as women. In other words, she helped them reconcile their national identity with a broader, potentially transformative gender identity.[56]

In collaboration with the Prishtina Group 'Home Economics', they began a sewing course leading to some income-generating activities. Health education was also included – from hygiene to the treatment of water-borne diseases and including contraception. The local paper agreed to include a four-page women's section. Having written stories about their lives, women then made these into audiotapes that were distributed as tapes to homes in Has and even played on the local buses. As well as showing girls how to play volleyball and organising a tournament, the group raised funds for seven village libraries and three schools. What might be called 'consciousness-raising groups' even began to meet every week.

The power of example was infectious. Similar groups began work in other rural areas – Legjenda around Viti and Aureola around Obilić. Together they formed the Rural Women's Network, meeting monthly for mutual support, training and networking. The League of Albanian Women began distributing wool to rural women, half to be used for their own families, half for income generation.

In Prishtina, as well as the League of Albanian Women, the LDK and the PPK had their own Women's Forums. Around about 1995, the Prishtina Women's Network began to function and new projects emerged such as the Centre for the Protection of Women and Children and the Women's Media Project (see Empowerment: Youth, below).

Until the Drenica massacres in 1998,[57] the Centre had a broad remit, serving as a coordination point as well as organising its own activities. With a network of volunteer specialists in support, the Centre's shopfront soon became a landmark. Its education work ranged from human rights to health education, from legal issues to literacy support, while it also offered counselling. In 1997, it began research into the problem of girls not completing elementary school, including visiting headteachers to discuss the issue with them. That summer the women's groups began to cooperate in a campaign for secondary education for girls, 'Let's Invest in Today's Girls, Tomorrow's Women'.

Co-director Sevdie Ahmeti was one of those frustrated with the passivity of the leadership, appealing to women 'it is our duty to change the mentality, to get out of the stagnation that has captured us'.[58] It was women who became the first group to disregard Rugova and the LDK leadership's warnings against 'provocateurs' when, in April 1996, they demonstrated at the killing of unarmed student Armend Daçi. From the Centre, from the League of Albanian Women, even from the LDK's own Women's Forum – a reported 10,000 women gathered with candles and flowers at the place where Daçi was shot.[59]

Feminists seek not to behave as accomplices in their own victim-isation. For Albanian women in Kosovo, this has had to be both as women and as Albanians. Not everything could be blamed on the Serbs. Vjosa Dobruna speaks of a woman coming to the Centre whose unemployed husband had been beating her for five years. She 'thinks that the problem will be solved if the problem of employment is solved, so keeps it quiet and sacrifices herself.'[60] Domestic violence, Dobruna believed, was on the increase,[61] countering Rugova's projection of 'interior freedom'. Interrupting women's victim behaviour also raised questions about the victim attitude set deep into the outlook of the nation. Instead of merely blaming 'the Serbs' for blocking any attempts to improve life in Kosovo, one could try to surmount the obstacles.

Other women's NGOs formed in Prishtina. In 1997, a former worker with the CDHRF Nazlie Bala founded 'Elena', a group specialising in human rights violations against women, while in 1998 'Norma', the Society of Women Legal Professionals, was set up.

EMPOWERMENT: YOUTH

Although the majority of the Albanian population of Kosovo are under 21 years old, the society's traditions instil a respect for age amounting to deference. In 1996, the LDK Youth (maximum age 30, average age 24) politely suggested that they should have a seat on the Presidency of the LDK. As a responsible party body, in touch with a significant constituency of the population, with branches in every municipality, it seemed a reasonable request. For two years, it was said to be 'under consideration' and was only resolved after the LDK lost its monopoly on legitimacy with the mass defections of 1998. The LDK leadership primarily seemed willing to treat its Youth Forum as a 'youth auxiliary', doing good works, organising transport vouchers for students, campaigning against drugs, but not entitled to represent the feelings of youth at a decision-making level.

In general, between the days of the Youth Parliament and the student protests of autumn 1997, youth did not intervene directly in the political debate. Yet there were a number of small projects that showed a different potential.

The trailblazers were the Post-Pessimists.[62] This was part of a network, initiated by an inter-ethnic meeting in 1993 in Norway, that by 1997 had groups in Belgrade, Subotica, Sarajevo, Tuzla,

Zagreb and among exiles in Oslo. Prishtina had the strongest group. Its founding generation built it up until by 1997, it had an office with powerful multi-media computers, produced two cultural magazines, organised concerts, a debating club, exhibitions, drama and video workshops and compiled a CD with the new talent in Prishtina. They organised some events in cooperation with youths from other towns in Kosovo and cooperated with a Gjilan youth magazine, but essentially this was a Prishtina initiative. Aged 16–21, there was a slight majority of young women in the group. What attracted especial attention, and made them beloved of international visitors – especially embassy staff – was that as well as their link with the other parts of former Yugoslavia, the group of about 25 included three or four Kosovo Serbs.

Yes, youths were oppressed in Kosovo and deprived, a woman from that first generation told me, 'but we're young, we want to make the good life now.' The conscious and deliberate openness to Serbs brought hostility, including press jibes against the 'Post-Pessimists *of Serbia*'. Therefore Rugova and Demaçi came to visit (separately) as a public sign that there was no treason here. If it took strength of character for Albanians to reach out to Serbs, the young Albanians felt that their Serbian friends had a much harder time – one Serb was even summoned to see the school principal. Indeed, when an upper age limit was set, it proved difficult to continue with Serbian participation.

A small group of young people, the most important impact of the Post-Pessimists was in pushing back the limits of what was possible in the present situation – not just for those who were members but also as an example to others. When Veton Surroi began recruiting and training young journalists to convert *Koha* from a weekly into a daily, the first place he looked was the Post-Pessimists. Ever mindful of the importance of youth, Surroi had already undertaken that *Koha* would distribute some issues of Post-Pessimist magazines (*Hapi Alternative* – Alternative Step) as a supplement. At the same time, there was bound to be envy of this English-speaking elite – feted by internationals eager to find a beacon of hope in benighted Kosovo.

The Women's Media Project also found itself the object of envy – especially of young men craving some of the skills it was teaching. It began in 1996 as a two-year course, two hours every weekday, for up to 24 young women, aged 17–24. This course taught not only media skills, but conflict resolution. The project co-leaders, Afërdita Saraçini-Kelmendi and Xheraldina Buçinca-Vula, had attended workshops using methodology derived from the practice of Western nonviolence and feminist groups.[63] 'I Know, I Want, I Can' was an assertion of women's self-esteem written on a wall inside the project's first premises in a flat hidden away in the Dardania estate of Prishtina. Alongside were photos of group sculptures around themes of personal empowerment.

Sacked from Radio Prishtina in 1990, Saraçini-Kelmendi was always one of those who was not going to wait for the situation to change but who would try to make things happen in the present. By 1998, the project was producing a regular magazine, had videos broadcast on various private TV stations in FRY and produced internet radio news bulletins.

The Pjetër Bogdani Club/Albanian Youth Action was a Catholic initiative, also producing a newsletter, organising meetings and social events, while in 1997 there began the group Alternativa, whose activities included educational campaigns against drugs and AIDS.

This spirit of self-activity was all in stark contrast to the response I got from the Minister of Health in the Bukoshi government, Adem Limani, the only Bukoshi minister based in Kosovo. Was it not possible, I suggested, to use the energy of medical students in health education campaigns around Kosovo? 'No, the Serbs would not permit it, and the students have to take care of their studies.'[64] Later I talked with some medical students, members of the Health Sub-Commission of UPSUP, who were in fact planning to begin first aid classes. 'He blockades us more than the Serbs', joked one of them. That was in November 1997. Six months later, after the Drenica massacres, eight members of UPSUP were arrested in Prizren for organising first aid classes, accused of 'preparing for war'. They were charged with membership of UÇK, the friend of one gave me an account of their hideous torture and in August they were sentenced to prison terms raging from one to seven and a half years.[65] In November, those students had been convinced that Limani's caution was excessive, indeed defeatist. I thought – and still think – they were right. However, by May 1998 the reaction to armed struggle had again closed down despite whatever space had existed.

THE STUDENT MOVEMENT OF 1997–98[66]

The presidency of the students' union (UPSUP) elected in 1997 wished to manifest an alternative to waiting. They set about building the necessary consensus and organisation for serious protests. While they paid Rugova the respect of seeking his approval and the LDK's organisational cooperation, UPSUP were determined to keep other parties and trade unions out of their action.[67] They would talk with all political parties, but did not want to be used. Their initial proposal was to call a 'test action' on 1 September, the start of the school year, a half-hour demonstration outside secondary schools, with pupils holding their books on their heads. On Rugova's advice, they did not pursue this – accepting that, as university students, they did not have the right to insist on an issue concerning secondary school students. However, they would not be dissuaded from proceeding with their own demonstration, scheduled for the start of the new academic year, 1 October.

As well as setting up organising committees in Prishtina and other towns with higher educational facilities, they decided to create 'an atmosphere of expectation'. The traditional daily *korzo* – the evening promenade in city centres – offered a means. In September, hundreds of students began to join the *korzo* from 8 p.m. to 9 p.m, groups holding hands and walking slowly. This move set the adrenalin running. In Prishtina police switched off the street lamps, stepped up their own presence and occasionally grabbed some participants for questioning – the most dangerous time was just after the *korzo*. Nevertheless, the numbers of students continued to swell, with critics of Rugova also joining in, such as Adem Demaçi and the staff of the daily paper *Koha Ditore*. On Wednesday 24 September, Prishtina police forced traffic to drive into the normally traffic-free *korzo* street, while on Sunday evening, 28 September, with loudspeakers blaring and banner aloft, a campaign vehicle for the ultra-nationalist Vojislav Šešelj – leader of the Serbian Radical Party leader and at the time campaigning for the presidency of Serbia – careered through the promenading crowd.[68] This incident highlighted exactly what worried the international diplomats: that a Serbian ultra-nationalist party would relish the opportunity of a large Albanian protest to stage a provocation as part of their election campaign.

With rumours and threats from various Serbian quarters, foreign embassies were warning against going ahead. Standing in for Rugova at the Friday press conference on 12 September, LDK vice-president Agani had welcomed the student protests, promising organisational back-up from the LDK.[69] However, at the press conference two weeks later – just five days before the protest – Rugova appealed to students to postpone the demonstrations until after the Serbian elections. UPSUP replied that they would not allow such 'political considerations' to interfere: they would demonstrate for their basic human right to study – a right more basic than politics. *Vreme* commented:

> Such an answer shook the Albanian political scene to its roots, where the patriarchal principle of subordination largely defines the rules of the games. The unthinkable happened: the father of nation called on the 'children' to listen, and they told him to mind his own business and to leave them be.

A few heads of faculty backed Rugova up, but UPSUP already had the university Senate behind them, above all rector Statovci who participated in the nine-person organisation committee – 'every meeting with him was like a workshop, we learnt such a lot', said Kurti. Some students circulated a petition for postponement, but quickly found they were an object of derision. ('How do we know that Elvis is dead?', asked a computer screensaver in the UPSUP office. 'Because he's joined the LDK.')

Rugova's warning clearly was at the behest of 'international opinion', that is, senior diplomats in Belgrade. The Monday before the protest, a dozen diplomats – including the US, British and Dutch ambassadors (at a time when the Dutch held the EU presidency), a Canadian and a Pole – came down to Prishtina to appeal directly to students to back down in this 'explosive' situation. This mainly served to strengthen the students' conviction that they were right to proceed. Already – before the demonstration – something momentous seemed to be happening in their community: civil disobedience first to their own leadership and now to the internationals Rugova had been courting so assiduously.

On the eve of the demonstration, students plastered posters around Prishtina and other cities, proclaiming 'University, Kosova, Students NOW – Tomorrow is Late'. At the same time, they recognised that it was vital to stay nonviolent whatever the police did. Their precautions were elaborate. They decided to march silently in faculty groups, five in each row, each wearing a white shirt and a university badge. Students wearing red armbands were stewards 'whose orders are compulsory for all', while those with blue armbands were observers from the organisational board. In case of police attack, 'everybody must sit down'. The public could stand by the side of their route and watch, but the march itself was confined to university students and staff. Although they concentrated on their own community, they also aimed to attract a strong press presence, especially of foreign journalists. Certain embassies sent staff to observe. As well as monitoring the demonstration itself, the BPT arranged for Serbian observers from the Centre for Peace, Nonviolence and Human Rights in Niš to attend, while in Belgrade the weekly vigil of Women in Black told passers-by about Kosovo.

All Albanian shops were closed on the day as the demonstration assembled in the area where 'parallel university' activities were most concentrated – about 15,000 students, with about 30,000 supportive onlookers. Before the front row had covered 500 metres – not reaching the city centre and not even within sight of the university buildings – they found their way blocked by police barriers, armoured personnel carriers (APCs), and police equipped for a riot. The rear of the demonstration had not even left the assembly point. For an hour, the procession stood facing the police cordon in silence, the front rows standing, those at the rear craning to watch.

At 11.50 a.m. the police attacked – 'quickly, brutally and efficiently' (*Vreme*). 'The first rows of protesters tried to sit down, but the APCs continued to drive forward' (BPT).

> With truncheons and teargas, including teargas grenades thrown from helicopters, they broke the demonstration into small groups, arrested the leaders, and then chased everybody else. Chaos ensued as protesters tried to escape the police violence. Meanwhile police tried to steer them into the city centre where further cordons were waiting. Natural sanctuaries – such as buildings where schools met – were blocked off. A three-storey building near the parallel university administration 'resembled a hospital' (*AIM*).

There were six simultaneous protests, the largest (both 10,000 strong) in Gjilan and Prizren and the most violently repressed in Gjakova and Peja. The Prishtina leaders were released later in the day with cuts and bruises, but for UPSUP the event had been an enormous success, a nonviolent demonstration of 'dignity and determination'. The US peace activist David Hartsough was deeply impressed:

> The contrast between the quiet, but powerful nonviolence of the students and the violence and brutal attack by the police was overwhelming. It reminded me of the march in Selma Alabama in 1965 where the police mercilessly attacked and beat up

nonviolent black marchers who were demanding the right to vote in the United States.

Now Rugova praised UPSUP, while Western diplomats beat a path to their door. The US government and several European officials condemned police brutality and called for Belgrade to engage in dialogue. Solidarity messages arrived from around Europe, from the USA and even from Belgrade. It was clear that the students had succeeded not only in expressing the frustration of Kosovo Albanian youth but also in dramatising the issue internationally. Indeed this was a rare instance when foreign governments saw explicitly *waging* strategic nonviolent conflict as a form of 'conflict prevention' in its own right and offered support.

UPSUP gave substance to the talk of 'active nonviolence'. Students showed that gaining international support was not just a matter of diplomatic lobbying but of mobilising one's own community and creating a pressure for action. To their own community, their placards said 'Breathe as we do', while internationally they appealed 'Europe: where are you?'. What was especially welcome for international diplomats, however, was that this took a 'non-political' posture: demands were not couched in terms of Kosovo's independence but instead invoked the universal human right to education.

Although they were not looking for allies in Serbia – indeed, while they had many placards in English, there was not one in Serbian – they found that police brutality was condemned inside Serbia. Students from Belgrade decided to make contact. Partly thanks to the bridging work of the BPT, the next UPSUP demonstration on 29 October was observed by a Belgrade student delegation. They had come down to Prishtina the day before – most for the first time – for two dialogue meetings, one with UPSUP and the other with local Serbian students. Later, one of these Belgrade groups successfully nominated UPSUP for the annual Prize for Tolerance of the Belgrade daily *Naša Borba*.

For the second student protest, UPSUP was just as attentive to nonviolent discipline. They drew up a detailed statement of principles and rules for the protest.[70] This time, they decided not to march but to have a short rally. About 15,000 people gathered to hear a speech and watch a short drama about education under repression and then the crowd dispersed. Police, meanwhile, had begun to advance up the hill in order to disperse the demonstration.

If this demonstration appeared somewhat anti-climactic to some participants, Kurti explained that the point was to get into 'a rhythm of protest'. Meanwhile the leadership of UPSUP was in demand with invitations coming for them to visit other countries.

The person in the limelight – Albin Kurti – spoke of nonviolence with an enthusiasm and idealism rarely heard in Kosovo. He started an UPSUP library on nonviolence. Indeed, when the US government invited him and UPSUP president Bujar Dugolli to the USA and asked them whom they would like to meet, top of Kurti's list was the leading scholar on nonviolence Gene Sharp. This personal commitment to nonviolence was not at all typical. Rather there was a spectrum of tendencies. The editor of the student monthly *Bota e Re*, for instance, was a romantic nationalist, a fan of Che Guevara, who devoted a large amount of the November 1997 issue to UÇK, with repeated images of a gun-cradling youth, claimed in an UÇK communiqué to be its first martyr and a confirmation of UÇK's existence from the information minister of the government-in-exile. Some people criticised the UPSUP leadership as 'Demaçi's children'. Some students active in other groups were critical that UPSUP had begun to see itself as a political player, while a few non-activist students simply did not want to demonstrate again – they had attended the first demonstration because it was expected of them and then were shocked at being attacked by police.

A third demonstration took place on 30 December. An estimated 15,000 students – each holding a declaration and a text book – tried to reach the city centre for a Protest Hour. Police violence now brought what was probably Patriarch Pavle's first public criticism of the Serbian authorities in Kosovo. However, a month earlier an event had happened that eclipsed the students and their active nonviolence. On 28 November, the Albanian national day, the Kosova Liberation Army made its first public appearance, at the funeral of teacher killed in a gunbattle. From now on, journalists by the score would speculate about this 'shadowy' force.

A further student demonstration was announced for 13 March 1998, but such plans were overtaken by events: the Drenica massacres. In the changed circumstances, the newly re-assembled Coordinating Council of Political Parties (including again representatives of the trade unions and now of the students' union) made this into one of the series of demonstrations 'For Peace, Against Violence, War and Serbian Terror'. At this point, UPSUP completely abandoned its non-political stance, aligning itself more firmly than ever with Rugova's opponents by joining the call for a boycott of the parallel parliamentary and presidential elections scheduled for 22 March.

At a time when issues of education were sidelined as public concerns, a flurry of international activity revived the education talks and on 23 March a schedule was agreed for re-opening university buildings. The first building, the Institute of Albanology – not actually part of the university – was to be re-opened on 31 March and it duly was. The first three faculties were to be re-opened on 30 April. The last UPSUP demonstration on education took place on that day. Hundreds of Albanian students assembled to enter the Mechanical Engineering Faculty, one of the three buildings agreed. The Serbian rector's opposition to the re-opening was well-known and a Serb student demonstration had even brandished the slogan 'Don't give them even pencils!' Now the Albanian students found their way blocked by police, while from student residences overhead, Serb students threw stones at them. For half an hour the Albanian students sat down and then they dispersed. In conditions like this, Kurti told me later,

> We can no longer guarantee that students won't fight back. It's one thing to stay nonviolent when we are being beaten by Serbian police, but it's something else when the police let Serbian students attack us – even though I know that those students are a minority among the Serbian students. Guys were telling me, 'Come on, there are enough of us, let's get them', and all I could say was 'If I call a demonstration, then it's nonviolent.'[71]

Even as late as June 1998, Albin Kurti was trying to organise a workshop 'Active Nonviolence as an Alternative to Armed Struggle'.[72] The problem was that the empowering dynamic engendered by the students demonstrations of autumn 1997 had been superseded by the excitement and then panic of UÇK's public 'arrival' and the Drenica massacres.

7
When the World Takes Notice

'Something must be done' was one of the dominant feelings of the 1990s when faced with media images from one ethnic conflict after another and victims crying out for international intervention. However, it is never enough to say 'the UN' (or whoever) should do 'something'. In the case of Kosovo, the Albanians had had the power to postpone war, but had relied on international action actually to prevent it. Kosovo Albanians, as we have seen, were quick to gain sympathy for the violation of their rights, but converting this into useful action was another question. For the sake of their own self-determination, they needed to set the agenda for what they wanted to happen in their society and the measures that would fit their strategy for altering the will of those who threatened them. Meanwhile, outsiders, foreigners – the misnamed 'international community' on behalf of which so many politicians and functionaries claim to speak – needed to be candid about what they could and could not commit to deliver, and on what terms.

Because Kosovo is in Europe, it enjoyed a higher international profile than a number of conflicts involving much larger populations and far more bloodshed. In the shadow of other events in former Yugoslavia, this was the most expected of all the wars. Thanks to the civil resistance, this was the war that international diplomacy had most opportunity to prevent. Many times Kosovo Albanians warned the West not to take their self-restraint for granted. Yet it wasn't until fighting broke out that serious concerted international action began.

PRINCIPLES AND INTERESTS

Not only was the disintegration of Yugoslavia itself complex, but European 'security architecture' was in disarray, re-orienting from the bi-polar Cold War era to a hoped-for era of 'our common European home'. As well as the different perceptions and interests between and within various groups of states, it was a time of institutional rivalries – between and within the EU, NATO, CSCE/OSCE, Western European Union and the UN and its agencies – as roles were being redefined.

The recognition of the sovereignty of Yugoslav republics and the Baltic states seemed to herald a new attitude to the right to self-determination. Falsely so, as in country after country, debates about Yugoslavia served as a metaphor for debates about the demands of nations or about inter-ethnic relations within their own polities. Many came to regret the recognition of Slovenia and Croatia as precipitate, giving heart to other separatists. This now prejudiced their view on Kosovo.

In 1993, International Alert – a conflict prevention NGO – proposed that the UN should establish a Commission on Self-Determination and so take this fraught issue out of the realm of power politics.[1] By clarifying criteria and providing a non-partisan framework to assess the validity of claims for self-determination, this would help channel conflict away from war and towards political processes and negotiation. Unfortunately, such a body does not exist and – in view of the number of states, including each of the 'permanent five' on the UN Security Council, with a vested interest in opposing specific claims to self-determination – perhaps it is destined to remain just another good idea.

Over the years, however, the theoretical criteria have become clearer. Five factors should be considered as crucial, according to one policy study: i) the conduct of the ruling group; ii) the choice of the people; iii) the conduct of the self-determination movement; iv) the potential for violent consequences; and v) the history.[2] Kosovo's claim plainly satisfied the first three criteria – much more convincingly than Croatia. On the fourth, the potential for violence, much would depend on process, while on the fifth, if historically Kosovo has never been independent, equally its federal status under the 1974 constitution should have precluded ceding it to FRY.[3] A study commissioned by the International Crisis Group set out the following premise:

> All self-identified groups with a coherent identity and connection to a defined territory are entitled to collectively determine their political destiny in a democratic fashion, and to be free from systematic persecution. In cases where self-identified groups are effectively denied their right to democratic self-government and are consequently subjected to gross violations of their human

rights, they are entitled to seek their own international status to ensure the protection of those rights.[4]

It went on to propose a status of 'intermediate sovereignty' for Kosovo – a transitional status during which there would be international safeguards for the rights of non-Albanians in Kosovo and monitoring to confirm the new authorities' fitness to govern.

Western diplomacy was not receptive to such thinking. Its prime aim in former Yugoslavia was to restore stability: sufficient stability to send back unwanted refugees and asylum-seekers in EU countries; sufficient, too, to return to 'business as usual'. Its tendency was to 'prescribe' solutions and, unfortunately, after the sabotage of the 'Carrington Plan',[5] this degenerated further into an inconsistent series of deals according to who was willing to make war, with what strength and for what purposes. There were differences of emphasis, but on Kosovo the USA and the EU converged in prescribing their solution – 'autonomy within FRY'.

For Kosovo Albanians, this prescription flew in the face of demography, history and rights. Yet the world's foreign ministers held to it as obdurately as they felt Rugova held to the goal of independence. A 'wrong move' on Kosovo, they feared, not only had the potential to de-stabilise Macedonia but even to make the Bosnia peace deal unravel. This fear offered a rationale for subordinating self-determination to the claim of FRY – a newly formed state that could best be described as 'Serbia-plus' – to 'territorial integrity'. Meanwhile, at Dayton, Milošević was made the Serbian 'guarantor of peace' in the region. The increasingly autocratic and corrupt Berisha regime was an Albanian counterpart.

The West – and even more, Russia – set its collective face against the notion that a population has the right to secede in self-defence in the face of state persecution. They thus excluded what could have been the toughest sanction against the Milošević regime, a political rather than an economic sanction: to suspend FRY's claim to Kosovo. If FRY was unfit to govern Kosovo, then its claim to sovereignty there could be suspended. Instead, the USA and the EU insisted on exactly the reverse – that Kosovo Albanians had to abandon their declared 'independence'. To enter negotiations on this condition was completely unacceptable to Kosovo Albanians and, even after negotiations, according to Fehmi Agani, any non-transitional settlement other than independence would have required another referendum.[6]

The alternative to 'prescription' was not immediate recognition of the Kosovo Albanian claim for independence and support for their cause – that could well have been a 'war option' – but rather some form of 'process'. Stefan Troebst offered this critique:

> The international community [sic] proved unable to develop a promising strategy of preventing the Kosovo conflict from escalating. To make things worse, it naively, yet unintentionally, contributed to such an escalation by prejudicing the outcome of Kosovo Albanian-Serbian negotiations on the future status of Kosovo, and by a rash condemnation of counter-violence to Belgrade's state terrorist-like oppression.[7]

Typical of an alternative approach were the November 1997 recommendations in the report *From Crisis to Permanent Solution*.[8] Calling for a common international policy and the appointment of a high-level special envoy, this report recommended support for democratisation in Serbia, immediate restoration of Kosovo Albanian civil and human rights, the cessation of advocating any specific option for permanent status, and the adoption of a 'strategy of sticks and carrots [to] ensure that the parties reach agreement on a permanent solution'. Mark Salter was one of a growing number of consultants who urged i) focusing on an open process and not trying to determine a final status, ii) confidence-building measures, humanitarian assistance and 'social reconnection' and iii) local capacity building for independent media and civil society groups.[9]

A *process* was essential. The point was to focus on transition, identifying and responding to the interests and concerns of the communities in Kosovo – Albanian, Serb, Turkish, Roma, Slav Muslim and Croat – and re-building inter-ethnic relationships and confidence in a way that could make this 'intractable' problem finally 'tractable'. Without such a process, no option for the future status of Kosovo would be viable unless it was imposed by force of arms. Several of the 'Track Two' meetings – that is, unofficial meetings mediated by international NGOs between Kosovo Albanian 'opinion leaders' and Serb counterparts – contained or developed useful suggestions.

Confidence-building had to begin with *immediate* issues: 'security' – ending police harassment, or after Drenica a real ceasefire; 'everyday' issues such as education and health tackled in a 'problem-solving' way without pre-conditions and without pre-judging the issue of final status. *Local capacity building* would identify not only voices for peace but projects that improved the quality of life. A key element in both confidence and capacity building could have been an *international civilian presence*, as urged by a range of governmental and non-governmental bodies. With sufficient staff (say an office in each municipality), with the ear of OSCE governments, deployed early enough – say, shortly after Dayton – perhaps this could have made a decisive difference. It could have combined human rights monitoring and peacebuilding wings.

No progress, however, could be achieved without *pressure* on Belgrade or *inducements*. The Education Agreement of September 1996 seemed a 'successful' example of internationally mediated private negotiations, without pre-conditions and without prejudging status issues. But it was not implemented. Indeed, there was no further progress for another 18 months, until March 1998 when FRY was under pressure to engage in 'confidence-building'.[10]

A negotiated *transition* was on the Kosovo Albanian agenda in Rugova's proposal for a UN Protectorate (although this was a step towards independence, not towards further negotiations) and discussed openly by chief negotiator Fehmi Agani. The Transnational Foundation for Peace and Future Research (TFF) in Lund, Sweden, proposed the framework of a United Nations Temporary Authority for a Negotiated Settlement (UNTANS).[11] Namely, for a three-year period, the UN would take over parts of the daily administration of Kosovo, including policing. The main incentives for FRY to join would be its full membership of the OSCE and that the leadership of UNTANS' 'permanent Professional Negotiation Facility' would be 'nations with no significant interests in the region'.

As to the *final status*, there were a number of responses to this challenge.[12] The 1991 Kosovo referendum left open the question of cooperation in a new post-Yugoslav federation – giving rise to Adem Demaçi's advocacy of 'Balkania' (initially a federation of three equal republics: Serbia, Montenegro and Kosovo). However, nothing could be agreed in advance of a process of confidence building.

In this process, it was better to include the voice of Kosovo Serbs (and of other non-Albanian ethnic groups) rather than simply to deal with their 'protectors' in Belgrade. Although that would have brought in more rancour, ultimately any peace made 'over their heads' would be unsustainable. Unfortunately, any signs of a shift in Kosovo Serbian opinion were limited to the Orthodox Church and those few Kosovo Serbs willing to participate in dialogue initiatives.

Had there been an international peace process, one essential point to communicate – and that partly underlay the mistaken prescription about a 'solution' within FRY – was that there was no option simply to 'overrule' Serbian opinions, interests and concerns. Rather they had to be taken into account and negotiated with. Even if it was ultimately recognised that Kosovo's right to self-determination entitled the territory to independence, that would be conditional on fair treatment for Serbs and other ethnic groups in Kosovo, and guarantees of their security and interests.

IN THE ABSENCE OF A PEACE PROCESS

If foreign governments neither accepted Kosovo's right to self-determination nor pushed for a peace process, at least Kosovo Albanians succeeded in persuading many that Kosovo was not 'an internal affair', that international monitoring of human rights standards was needed. From the exclusion of the CSCE mission in July 1993 until Dayton (November 1995), there were worthy resolutions but no significant governmental or intergovernmental initiatives on Kosovo. Bosnia was the main regional concern, and in this foreign states wanted Milošević's cooperation. The Kosovo Albanian leadership understood this, but Rugova dutifully kept making the rounds of foreign capitals to educate foreign diplomats about Kosovo, trying to make sure that Kosovo was on the agenda. This strengthened the US and EU predisposition to do 'something' to help resolve the situation and brought four specific tangible gains:

Support for an international presence in Kosovo: The ending of the CSCE mission in July 1993 left a gap. The mission had consisted of a mere 12 people divided between Kosovo, Sandžak and Vojvodina, yet its presence in Kosovo inhibited repression, as shown by the fierce wave of police brutality following their exclusion (including attacks on their former local staff). The UN High Commission for Refugees set up an office in Prishtina, a political decision as there were 20 times as many refugees in Vojvodina at this time, with no UNHCR office. The OSCE and the UN recognised that neither this, nor the increased visits from Belgrade embassy staff, nor the reports of the UN Human Rights rapporteurs, could be a substitute for a internationally-mandated permanent monitoring presence. In July 1996, Kosovo Albanians greeted the arrival of the US Information Office as a symbol of renewed international commitment, calling it the US Embassy. While the EU in the 1996–97 period repeatedly declared its intention to open an office in Prishtina, it failed to achieve this before the NATO bombings.

The 'outer wall of sanctions': On 11 July 1995, the US House of Representatives passed a bill barring any lifting of sanctions against FRY until 'the excessive Serbian control' over Kosovo had ended.[13] Hence, while Dayton ended most sanctions, an 'outer wall' stayed in place specifically to pressure FRY on Kosovo. It included denying FRY full diplomatic recognition, membership of various intergovernmental bodies and international financial institutions and not releasing contested assets. While the USA still preferred the 'stick' of withholding full diplomatic recognition from FRY, the EU was more inclined to think of incentives – especially Germany with its interest in returning refugees to FRY, including Kosovo. The EU offered renewed cooperation with FRY but it was 'conditional' on dialogue over Kosovo, respect for human rights and allowing the EU to set up an office. There was, again, little progress, and – having offered trade preferences in April 1997 – the EU 'temporarily' withdrew them in December.

International mediation of negotiations: Despite the EU and USA's position on final status, their continued willingness to mediate – and to encourage Track Two efforts by international NGOs – was reassuring for Kosovo Albanians.

Offers of development aid: The British, German and US Embassies were involved in funding the Riinvest research report, *Economic Activities and Democratic Development of Kosova*, on the revival of Kosovo's economy. The EU offered Belgrade funds to help finance implementation of the educational agreement and in general anything 'confidence building' or meeting the economic needs of both communities seemed fundable.

Tokens of international 'concern' also brought 'false promises' and 'bad advice'. The Bush-Clinton threat of unilateral air strikes in case of a Serbian crackdown seemed a gain. Yet, if Kosovo Albanians repeatedly reminded the USA of its promise that Kosovo should not become a second Bosnia, few saw this as a guarantee. Events in Bosnia gave plenty of grounds for doubt. Certainly it was far from the *besa* of Albanian tradition, a pledge as strong as life.

The West was also keen to give the Kosovo Albanians advice. Rugova did not need their warnings about the dangers of departing from the nonviolent policy – he knew that better than anybody. Some advice he rejected: 'Vote in the FRY/Serbian elections.' Some he accepted: 'Don't convene the parallel parliament.' Some he accepted but his people rejected: 'Delay the student demonstrations.'

To his own community, Rugova projected himself as the leader most capable of bringing international intervention. His welcome in Washington in April 1990, when he was already reportedly treated like 'a head of state',[14] and the subsequent Bush-Clinton promises were important sources of credibility in Kosovo. Therefore, instead of reporting international rejection of the demand for independence, Rugova and his spin-doctors filtered the image of international relationships. It would have served the cause much better to be frank about the problems and to appoint an advisory council for international relations.[15]

Whatever diversity of preferences existed within the movement at large, at the declaratory level there was consensus: the Kosovo Albanian movement was asserting Kosovo's right to self-determination, up to and including independence, while striving to avoid war and to guarantee the rights of all ethnic groups in Kosovo. As well as planning negotiating strategy – and therefore requiring representation from across the spectrum of the national consensus – the brief of such a group would be to give more focus to the diplomatic strategy and to address issues of how emerging (predominantly Western) governmental policies could fit into the Kosovo Albanian strategy, both as a lever on Belgrade, and for the strengthening of society in Kosovo.

Goodwill Gestures

There was more talk about what kind of pre-conditions Kosovo Albanians might require before negotiations, than about what gestures they might offer. This could be a delicate matter, raising divisions within their own population, but just as the Palestinians had to change their constitution to accept the existence of Israel and the Republic of Ireland had to renounce its constitutional claim to the North in the process of confidence building in negotiations, so some such gesture might have been required of Kosovo Albanians.

One gesture might have been to forswear unification with Albania for a number of years. Another, equally sensitive, might have been some more concrete reassurance about the treatment of ethnic groups. For instance, breaking a taboo from the past and showing good intent for the future, a proposal for post-Communist means of treating issues of ethnic quotas could stem from a frank and critical study of how the 'ethnic keys' system functioned – ideally carried out by a multi-ethnic team and based on social and economic, and not just ethnic, criteria.

Where to Focus Diplomacy?

The Kosovo Albanians sought to generate sympathy wherever they could, but above all with those whom they considered had power – primarily the governments of the West. This support came in the form not only of diplomatic pressure but sometimes of economic resources. As well as finding its own international allies, however, a civil resistance movement can try to weaken the aggressor's international support. The role of Russian and Finnish diplomacy in ending the 1999 war, and the earlier occasional interest of Greek and Romanian diplomats in playing a mediating role, should warn against the attitude 'my enemy's friend is my enemy too'. There was a need to identify states defending the Belgrade regime in international forums and see what influence their friendship with Serbia could exert. A historic ally of Serbia such as Russia would not convert into a supporter of the Kosovo Albanian cause. But with more understanding of their case and less suspicion of their intentions, Russia might have been less inclined to cry 'internal affair', readier to exercise some influence in support of international standards, more conscientious about abiding by international agreements such as the arms embargo on FRY and Serbian recruitment of mercenaries, or more willing to act as a broker. Or – if none of these things – at least the Kosovo Albanians would have laid a marker for problems other governments should take up with Russia.

As a movement wishing to avoid war, the Kosovo Albanians avoided alliances with out-and-out enemies of FRY. In addition to their spurning overtures from Islamic states or the approach from Croatia, they could have maximised their own stance of neutrality and demilitarisation by greater outreach among Yugoslavia's former allies in the 'Non-Aligned Movement'. In the scales of world power balances, these states are perhaps a low priority, but at least a better relationship would have counteracted some of the naïvety these states showed about Serbia and FRY in 1999.

How should the EU or USA Wield the 'Carrot and Stick' for Belgrade?

Sanctions against FRY over the Bosnian war had been something of a blunt instrument. Far from damaging the regime, they hurt the population, adding to the xenophobia in Serbia, while financially the regime looked after itself by printing more money. The 'outer wall' of sanctions were more regime-directed and did exercise leverage on Belgrade. However, within them, there was perhaps room for fine-tuning. One sanction was the exclusion of FRY from the OSCE, a rather double-edged weapon since it provided FRY with the pretext to refuse any OSCE mission. An alternative was to use the incentive of FRY's admission into the OSCE to gain other objectives, either a rather stronger OSCE presence in Kosovo[16] or a framework for a conflict resolution process according to OSCE principles.

Foreign human rights advocates began to urge sanctions more precisely targeted at members of the ruling elite, such as freezing personal foreign bank accounts and banning officials from travel in the EU.[17] When such measures were finally deployed against 300 FRY officials after the 1999 war, initial results seemed promising.[18] Even before Drenica, there was enough evidence against named individuals for them to face measures arising from their personal responsibility for torture or personal profiting from 'privatisation'. Pressing specific individual cases could have been used to strengthen the general case about the criminal nature of the regime.

Where should International Funding for 'Confidence Building' and 'Democratic Development' be Directed?

A strategy of progressively strengthening Kosovo's self-determination would have given rise to a list of suggestions for improving Kosovo's social and economic infrastructure. It was only towards the end of 1997 that anybody[19] considered a scheme to offer a guaranteed price for crops, encouraging agricultural revival as well as relying on local produce to be available to distribute for humanitarian assistance. In general, the 'conflict management' thinking gaining ground in the West looked not only at macro-solutions but micro-possibilities, offering an opportunity for subtle and detailed proposals from Kosovo Albanians. The Riinvest report showed how foreign governmental support could be channelled into programmes of micro-enterprise that would strengthen Kosovo socially and economically and that would not contradict self-determination. Doubtless, if this report had borne fruit, it would have been replicated in other spheres. Unfortunately, the report did not appear until the end of 1998.

International 'goodwill' can be divisive and even manipulative. The West was interested either in influencing LDK policy, or in promoting more 'flexible' alternatives outside the LDK. However, before UÇK, so solid was the national consensus that nobody outside the LDK leadership could influence when to bend and when to be firm.

INTERNATIONAL SOLIDARITY TAKES TIME

An international campaign by an oppressed people cannot confine its efforts to governments or the bodies that pass resolutions. Rather they need friends who will pressure governments, who will keep the issue alive when media attention flags or is lacking, who will criticise, who will use international resolutions to bring more support and who will commit their own resources in cooperation with a movement in struggle.

The worldwide campaign against apartheid in South Africa provides many lessons and an inspiring example of what can be achieved. However, the image of its ultimate success is a misleading point of reference. That struggle built up over 40 years, counting on the support of virtually the whole African continent. It inspired powerful literature and films. It went through a number of phases, throwing up leaders who became household names internationally. Each phase was thoroughly strategised: Where were the international props of the apartheid regime? Where were resources for support? Which constituencies could be mobilised for what purposes and how? Where should international goodwill be channelled? How could the movement be protected against the divisive effects of 'aid' from foreign governments and foundations?

For relatively small populations, such as Kosovo's 2 million, hopes must be modest, recognising the strategic limits about what can be accomplished within what time frame. It takes years to build up a solidarity campaign. The Albanian-American lobby, as we have seen, was influential in Washington and the diaspora as a whole mounted demonstrations and contributed to Kosovo's economy. But asylum-seekers and refugees from Kosovo also had to contend with their existential problems. Bi-lateral links between trade unions and, latterly, women's groups were an important support for counterparts inside Kosovo, but by 1998, there was still only a handful of town/village twinning projects. As for literature in English, Ishmail Kadare's only work of fiction set in modern Kosovo is not readily available in English and Alice Mead's youth novel *Adem's Cross* did not become widely available until 1998.[20]

INTERNATIONAL SUPPORT FOR PEACEBUILDING

A number of development agencies and the international development departments of some governments (for instance in Scandinavia) had a particular interest in a civil society approach to promoting peaceful coexistence in Kosovo. The broad framework is of processes of peacemaking and confidence building at the base, rather than efforts to engineer an ultimate 'constitutional settlement'. The hope is that activities 'from below' can perhaps unblock progress at other levels and at least help to sustain it. Two complementary goals in this approach would be:
  – to develop each community in a way that enhances its peaceful development;
  – to identify common interests between the communities and build on them.

Not only would civil society initiatives respond to a variety of human needs and desires, they would also aim to empower people to meet their needs and desires, and foster a climate conducive to peaceful coexistence. Even if inter-ethnic work was not possible, development of a civil society among just one community could improve the conditions for future efforts and contribute in the long term to what John Paul Lederach has called 'an infrastructure for peace-building'.[21]

As always, there could be pitfalls in this approach, in Kosovo especially if it was guided by outsiders without an appreciation of the severity of the ethnic divide, under pressure to show results rather than to progress in small steps, or evading issues of 'justice'.[22] Somehow, too, specific complaints needed to be taken seriously without feeding a self-perpetuating sense of grievance and victimhood within a particular community. However, with 'good practice', there was clearly plenty of scope for peacebuilding in

Kosovo, integrating international concerns with aspects of – or tendencies within – the nonviolent struggle.

The development of civil society initiatives in Kosovo after 1994 was greatly aided by the activities of the Open Society Foundation (OSF/Soros), where Shkëlzen Maliqi worked. OSF's existence in FRY (the Kosovo office began as a branch of OSF in FRY) was a matter of struggle, OSF vigorously defending itself in the media by referring to the quantities of humanitarian aid it brought in. On this precarious basis both the OSF and international agencies expanded their work in the post-Dayton period. In Kosovo, both the OSF and international agencies tended to back sources of energy in the Albanian community outside the LDK. For the OSF this was less because of anti-LDK prejudice than because of the party's inertia,[23] but most foreign governments were too wary of the parallel school structures – as a symbol of the state-in-embryo – to recognise that they were the best means of reaching the majority of the population.

A severe problem was the vacuum of Serbian voluntary organisations independent of the local authorities. Secular Serbian life in Kosovo revolved around the state and administration, and it was hard to find socially engaged NGOs of Kosovo Serbs, although a few Serbs did participate in mixed NGOs and in the late 1990s there were elements of the Orthodox Church showing increased independence.

Internationals wishing to support social development in Kosovo were in a strong position to negotiate inter-ethnic cooperation. The most spectacular example was the autumn 1996 and spring 1997 polio immunisation campaigns, remarkably bringing together international agencies with state and parallel health structures.[24] The World Health Organisation (WHO) and UN Children's Fund (UNICEF) joined the Mother Theresa Association and the state system in a campaign aiming to immunise all children in Kosovo and in some municipalities in Serbia where there had been recent polio cases. The ethnic balance of the teams was drawn up to reflect the ethnic structure of the population where they would be working. The whole of Kosovo was covered by 1,290 teams. For the first time in five or six years, Serbian health managers were contacting their dismissed Albanian colleagues.

Serbia accepted that immunisation documents should be issued in the mother tongue of the children and eventually withdrew a demand for them to bear the official seal of Serbia or FRY. The first phase of the Kosovo programme was drawing up a registry of children born since 1990. A 'social mobilisation' phase aimed to show the need for vaccination, with posters and other propaganda material, including a clip broadcast by Albanian satellite TV. As well as organising meetings with teachers, the Mother Theresa Association asked mosques and Catholic churches in the week before immunisation to dedicate their Friday prayers and Sunday masses to this theme. Police promised no intervention and kept their word. Eventually, 224,252 children were vaccinated in the first round, 231,313 in the second.[25]

An experience of cooperation such as this offered hope for a 'normalisation' of Kosovo not based on ethnic domination. It was a mobilisation based around human need, a step towards social reconnection and building a measure of confidence. There were other projects to improve the health situation in Kosovo crossing ethnic divides. For instance, Oxfam's programme for improving water supplies, launched in 1995, worked in mixed villages not just to secure the regime's permission but also as a demonstration that both communities had certain interests in common. Belatedly, in 1999, some international agencies began to look at possibilities for Peace through Health work in Kosovo, based on experience in Bosnia-Herzegovina. The main idea is that health issues represent an important common interest between hostile communities living side by side and that, at least formally, medical professionals have a shared set of ethics. Even if practical examples are isolated, perhaps there are enough to suggest that a determination to mount similar 'problem-solving' campaigns could have built up a stronger resistance to war.

In the period after Dayton, the number of international agency offices in Prishtina began to multiply, reaching about 15 in January 1998, and with them more funds became available. When a movement of social struggle attracts such well-meaning interest, it has the job of educating it – not relying on the outsider's definition of needs or sensitivities in the situation. There were people willing to inform outside agencies, including the Mother Theresa Association and other groups described in Chapter 6. However, the LDK itself, the party that claimed to govern and lead, did little to harness such goodwill to the needs of the whole of Kosovo, rural as well as urban, manual workers as well as intellectuals. Yet this clearly would have strengthened the community and given people a stake in building on the present rather than risking everything through an armed struggle that was coming ever nearer.

THE CRISIS ERUPTS

If the new assertiveness shown by the students at the end of the 1997 demonstrated possibilities for 'active nonviolence', the public showing of the Kosova Liberation Army (UÇK) on 28 November 1997 came as a warning that the time for any form of nonviolent protest was running out. On 8 December, Adem Demaçi called on the UÇK to observe a three-month ceasefire to give politicians a last chance to reach a peaceful settlement[26] while Rugova continued to turn a Nelson's eye. The squabbling between Prishtina politicians intensified, without significant fruit. Demaçi's PPK had tried to launch an all-party Democratic Forum in November, but failed to secure the participation of the LDK itself and its satellite parties. Then, when Rugova announced dates for the presidential and parliamentary elections – 22 March 1998 – the PPK showed its own disarray by declaring the candidacy of its leader, Demaçi, only to have him say the day after that he would not stand.[27] If Rugova's party political opposition lacked a basis for action, the LDK itself had nothing new to offer. In February, the third LDK Electoral Congress saw a mismanaged rebellion by vice-president Hydajet Hyseni as Rugova moved to strengthen further his personal control.[28]

With Germany, Sweden and Switzerland considering that Kosovo was sufficiently 'normalised' for them to send back refugees, and with the incapacity of any political leadership – LDK-aligned or alternative – UÇK started to behave as if its time had come. From November 1997 to February 1998, it began to declare certain parts of Drenica, central Kosovo, under its control. This was largely a piece of theatre. UÇK ambushes made it unsafe for police to patrol – especially after dark – and the UÇK would set up roadside checkpoints. By mid-January 1998, UÇK claimed to have killed 21 people, ten Serb police and other officials and eleven Kosovo Albanians.[29]

In January 1998, the Serbian authorities began to build up forces in Kosovo ready to respond. This was well known at the time – to every journalist covering Kosovo and to every diplomat in Belgrade, including to the UN Human Rights monitoring office in Belgrade. When a visitor to that office asked in February 1998 what it was doing about the upcoming police action, the reply was that the High Commissioner had issued a call to both sides for restraint, but could not criticise a state for re-asserting its authority over a portion of its territory. The idea of preventive deployment – sending observers to

Drenica before the offensive – was simply off the agenda, excluded by the logic of most foreign governments: if Kosovo was part of FRY, then Belgrade had the right to put down illegal armed groups with force. Both US Secretary of State Madeleine Albright and US special envoy Robert Gelbard went further, even referring to the UÇK as a 'terrorist group'.[30] In Vojvodina, political leaders were supporting army reservists refusing to be stationed in or near Kosovo,[31] yet internationally the regime and its Special Forces had been given a green light for the 'policing' action it was about to take.

Not only was the Serbian offensive expected, but past police operations indicated that there would be atrocities against unarmed civilians. There could be no surprise either in the Kosovo Albanian reaction to such atrocities. Predictably, Serbian repression proved to be the best recruiter for the UÇK. Whatever people had felt before about the UÇK, now its numbers swelled. From around 350 in January 1998,[32] suddenly there were thousands. After the event, as the cameras entered Drenica, giving a glimpse behind those all-too-penetrable walls that had failed to protect, came storms of international protest.

The Drenica offensive was directed against the whole Albanian population. Ignoring calls from Prishtina urging them to stay in their homes, thousands of villagers left their homes in flight in a pattern familiar in the Balkans for more than a century – just as the police intended. A subsequent offensive was launched in Deçan and then other areas where there was any kind of UÇK presence.

The first of the Drenica massacres took place in the villages of Likoshane and Qirez 28 February–1 March 1998.[33] Police vehicles surrounded Likoshane, a helicopter circled overhead. Instead of fleeing, the men in the Ahmeti family stayed inside their house, feeling they had nothing to hide. After four hours, an armoured car crashed through the gate of the family compound, uniformed men entered the house and ordered everybody outside to lie on the ground, beating the men with rifle butts and kicking them. Ten Ahmeti men and a guest from another village were executed. Their neighbours, an old man recently deported from Germany and his son, were also killed – the only 'weapons' they had were a hunting rifle and an axe. In Qirez, two armoured vehicles battered their way into the courtyard of the Nebiu family. They shot the father in the leg, then killed his heavily pregnant daughter-in-law and one of his sons. They took another son to the police station for interrogation and returned his corpse the next day.[34] Outside another compound, four sons were executed. Five others were killed in Qirez that day, two of them last seen in police custody.

While the actions were triggered by clashes between the police and the UÇK in which four police officers were killed, the Albanian deaths occurred, according to Amnesty International, after UÇK withdrawal. No autopsies were allowed, contrary to FRY law, and there were reports that corpses bore signs of torture, including eyes gouged out. The shock wave was heightened because the Ahmeti family had been following the advice given by the CDHRF and others over the years, making no attempt at self-defence.

Massive protests followed in Prishtina and other Kosovo cities. The first, on Sunday, 1 March, was a women's initiative – some 2,000 women gathering outside the US Information Office. The next day saw the largest demonstration, perhaps 100,000. As well as dispersing crowds with tear gas and truncheons, the police beat various well-known figures, chased demonstrators, attacked women and children watching from the balconies of their flats and ransacked the offices of *Koha Ditore*. Rugova declared 3 March a day of national mourning, while – despite police roadblocks – an estimated 30,000 villagers made their way to Likoshane and Qirez to bury the 26 dead.

The massacre of a family as clearly following the nonviolent 'old way' as the Ahmetis signalled the end of the strategy of 'refusal to be provoked'. The next weekend a further massacre in Donji Prekaz, 10 kilometres from Likoshane, provided a different type of symbol. Adem Jashari – one of the brothers for whom the police had been searching in December 1991 (see Introduction) – was a known UÇK militant. In July 1997, he had been sentenced *in absentia* to 20 years' imprisonment, and in January 1998, with help from his 'friends in the woods' (UÇK), the Jashari household had beaten off a police attack. The March attack was different. Police armed with heavy weapons and operating in military formations surrounded the village and concentrated their fire on the Jasharis' quarter. Women, children and unarmed men retreated into the safest room, while men with weapons resisted the attack. From the compound where Adem Jashari lived, the only survivor was his eleven-year-old niece. After this incident, 56 bodies were buried – including some not identified and two from a separate incident in Llausha. Of the 41 Jashari family members identified, twelve were women and eleven children under the age of 16. Other corpses were believed to lie under the rubble of the family compound. The dead Adem Jashari became a more potent symbol in 1998 than the passive Rugova or the erratic Demaçi.[35]

On International Women's Day, 8 March, women returned to the US Information Office holding aloft blank white papers to symbolise the lack of rights in Kosovo. The Coordinating Committee for Political Parties was re-convened and set up a protest organising committee – boycotted by Demaçi and the PPK. This adopted the UPSUP demonstration scheduled for 13 March which became an impressive peaceful statement of resolve – maybe 50,000 people calling for an end to Serbian terror. On Sunday, 15 March, the Catholic diocese called for masses to be held throughout Kosovo, followed by demonstrations with people carrying candles and photos of the most famous Albanian Catholic, Mother Theresa. Some 15,000 took part in the rally in Prishtina.

The most visual demonstration took place on 16 March, a 'Bread for Drenica' march of women. Some 12,000 women carrying loaves of bread began an intended 50-kilometre march from Prishtina, heading for the besieged area of Drenica. Although the main demonstration was stopped after seven kilometres by police in Fushë Kosova/Kosovo Polje and turned back, a group of women is reported to have processed from Vushtrri to Drenica. On Wednesday, 17 March, police opened fire on a demonstration in Peja, killing one and injuring five protesters. This was the day for youth demonstrations, with protests by a reported 10,000 in Prishtina and in smaller numbers in all the municipalities of Kosovo.

Rugova decided to go ahead with the parallel elections on 22 March, postponing only those in Drenica – a show of strength discrediting those who called for a boycott, and demonstrating to the 200-strong foreign media corps in Kosovo that he was still the 'president'. In those constituencies where elections were held, the turn-out was 88.71 per cent, with Rugova himself receiving 99.29 per cent backing from voters.[36]

Demonstrations continued with women on 25 March asking for a 'peaceful divorce' from Serbia. On Thursday 9 April, a massive 'Give Peace a Chance' protest in Prishtina was attended by Rugova personally, initiating a plan for half-hour protests each midday in the *korzo* streets. These daily processions continued into June, usually without chanting or slogans, except on the large protests at weekends. Otherwise Rugova and the LDK seemed paralysed.

Meanwhile, at the international level, the warnings gave Milošević pause. In the next three months, the Contact Group[37] analysed what threats were available and Milošević estimated how few concessions he could make, while at the Security Council China and Russia continued to insist that Kosovo was an 'internal affair' (as are Tibet and Chechnya). Milošević had done just enough by 25 March – reducing the police attacks and agreeing a schedule for the re-opening of university buildings to Albanians – to prevent the Contact Group from imposing further sanctions. After five days of shuttle diplomacy by US Special Envoy Richard Holbrooke, Milošević agreed to meet Rugova in Belgrade on 15 May without foreign mediation. Holbrooke – and therefore Rugova – accepted this, a major concession made by Rugova without even consulting his advisory group: if he still retained the loyalty of the majority of the population of Kosovo, in terms of political initiative he was reduced to complete dependence on the 'international factor'.

In May, the Contact Group moved to impose an asset freeze and investment ban. At the end of May, however, the regime began a new offensive, prompting NATO defence ministers to order a study of options for military intervention and to authorise air exercises over Albania and Macedonia, Operation Determined Falcon. Milošević went to Moscow where on 16 June he agreed with President Yeltsin to allow unimpeded access to Kosovo by humanitarian organisations and the presence of the Kosovo Diplomatic Observer Mission, a 50-strong OSCE mission. Wanting a firmer grip on the local leadership, over the summer he finally eased out the Serbian university rector (a nationalist suspected of links with organised crime), and downgraded the local administration, causing the resignation of the long-standing Secretary for Information, Boško Drobnjak.

The UÇK grew in numbers by spreading in areas with few Serb residents – primarily the central plain around Drenica and Malisheva, and border areas with Albania, especially near Deçan. Some senior local LDK leaders swung to the UÇK or 'came out' such as Jakup Krasniqi – elected to the LDK presidency in February 1998 and who in June became UÇK's first authorised spokesperson in the field.[38] The political prisoners who dominated the CDHRF branches in the municipalities also tended to align with the UÇK.[39] Things seemed to be going UÇK's way in July when it claimed to 'control' half of Kosovo. The new saying was 'We are all UÇK'. While the UÇK's expansion met little Serbian resistance, there was reluctance from a number of Albanians now and later. What they feared transpired in July and August: the UÇK showed itself capable of provoking attack but not of protecting the population. Its failed attempt to take the town of Rahovec on 19–21 July marked a turning point, showing it had over-reached itself. Within a month, Serbian forces had retaken nearly all the territory claimed by UÇK. While nobody – including Rugova – now publicly questioned the need for some protective force, it was the UÇK's lack of defensive capacity – not any continued allegiance to nonviolence – that led some villages to ask the UÇK to leave and to hand in to the police weapons distributed by the UÇK.

Zoran Kusovac analysed that the UÇK:

... drew its cannon fodder mainly from peasants from the 'liberated' areas who had no alternative but to join armed men appearing in their territory; returning émigrés from German-speaking countries of Europe who spent a long time away from the reality of Kosovo; and overzealous village youths who often staged their own local operations long before any UÇK commander turned up.[40]

It lacked the backing, he went on, either of intellectuals or of the leaders of various large families. There were several grounds for suspicion – the 'Enverist'-flavoured ideology and the links of certain UÇK groups with gangsters in northern Albania, while the fact that so many of the UÇK's initial attacks were against Albanians – alleged collaborators – suggested that perhaps some personal scores were being settled.

The party political scene continued to be hopelessly divided. Rugova's opponents competed to become the 'voice of UÇK', a post finally awarded to Demaçi in August once he agreed to abandon all talk of his 'Balkania' federation. MTA, UPSUP and the local NGOs were now primarily oriented towards humanitarian assistance for displaced people. Meanwhile neither international diplomacy nor the growing presence of international monitors and journalists seemed able to brake the Serbian drive. From FRY, several hundred police reportedly refused to be posted to Kosovo and parents protested against the deployment of their sons in or near Kosovo. There were reports of the horrors in Kosovo in all FRY's independent media, the Humanitarian Law Centre and *Vreme* going into especially damning detail. Groups such as Women in Black and the student-led Anti-War Campaign demonstrated publicly against the war, but without illusions of stopping the slaughter.

In the course of 1998, according to the CDHRF Annual Report for 1998, the Serbian operations killed 1,934 Albanians – nearly a quarter of them unidentified. Few of these seem to have been members of the UÇK and of those who were, most were executed extra-judicially; 229 were women, 213 children and 395 elderly people. The numbers of houses shelled, burnt or looted was 41,538. As for refugees or people displaced inside Kosovo, at the height of displacement in September, Mercy Corps reported the figure of 411,769.[41]

I wrote an article for *Peace News* about my encounters with people who told me 'I would still like to follow the nonviolent way, *but* ...':

"... but how can we protest about the continued closure of our university buildings when children in Drenica are dying?" demanded the new university rector, echoed by students.

"... but we can no longer guarantee that students won't fight back", said the student leader ...

"... We used to go to villages after a police raid not only to document the violence but to urge the villagers to stay calm and not retaliate. Now we have run out of credits", said a human rights activist. "In Likoshane the Ahmeti family did not return fire. The men sat and waited: they were taken out, tortured and then executed." ...

For years the space for nonviolent action has been squeezed by Serbian repression ... Now [it] is limited by the population itself: they still expect to suffer and sacrifice, but not without retaliation.[42]

Rugova's policy had failed to avoid war. International diplomacy and threats had failed to prevent Kosovo becoming another Bosnia. And yet even as his forces scorched the earth of Kosovo, it could not be said that Milošević was succeeding. Serbs no longer had a crusading spirit towards Kosovo. Rather what the UÇK had revived was a Serbian resolve at least to teach the contemptible *Šiptari* a lesson.

OSCE – TOO LITTLE, TOO LATE

From August 1998 onwards, the OSCE was present in Kosovo with its Diplomatic Observer mission investigating incidents and escorting humanitarian organisations, including the Mother Theresa Association. The number of international agencies in Kosovo multiplied fivefold. And the Serbian offensive continued –

monitored but unabated – until finally on 24 September, NATO issued an ultimatum for Serbia to cease fire and withdraw forces or face air strikes. On 8 October, the UÇK announced a unilateral ceasefire, and a week later a marathon negotiating session between US envoy Holbrooke and Milošević concluded with an agreement for a ceasefire and the deployment of a 2,000-strong OSCE unarmed 'verification' mission (KVM).

As the Serbian special forces withdrew, there took place the most hopeful event of a dreadful year for Kosovo. Adem Demaçi, as Political Representative of UÇK, travelled to Deçan to greet the Orthodox Hieromonk Sava and assure him that 'there is no place for fear now that the police have gone'.[43] Father Sava and the Deçan monks were noted for condemnation of violence on both sides and for their willingness to shelter and give aid to Albanians as well as to Serbs during the hostilities. Sava and Demaçi had met at a 'Track Two' encounter in Thessaloniki, and now shook hands in front of the cameras, avowing to 'solve problems in a tolerant, peaceful and democratic way'.

There were few other signs of hope for KVM. This mission when it arrived was too late and too poorly prepared. The idea of an international civilian monitoring presence in Kosovo had been a consistent feature of international policy since 1992. However, if such a deployment is to make a significant contribution towards preventing war, the essential element is that it should be 'timely'. This mission was at least a year late and it was hastily assembled. Even upon its withdrawal after five months, it had reached only 67 per cent of its intended complement. In general, it was a victim not only of the OSCE's lack of funds and lack of infrastructure for mounting such operations but also of a more general lack of international preparedness for 'preventive' civilian deployment.

At the time, I made five specific criticisms of KVM:

- Lack of a coherent recruiting policy. Some countries have made an effort to recruit people with experience in peacebuilding or in nonviolence; more have concentrated on sending people with military experience; most were slow in developing criteria for who should go.
- Lack of training or relevant, evaluated experience. The training programme offered for the observers is far too brief, and the existing experience which those recruited bring with them – if

any – tends to be of Bosnia, where there has been a lack of public evaluation of international civil intervention.

- Its economic impact has not been considered. As well as the rent inflation caused by sending in 2,000 relatively highly paid international workers on a short-term mission, there are a number of problems around employment. Local staff generally have to speak English, Albanian and Serbian.[44] A proper code of practice would have reserved jobs for at least some Serbs on the condition that they learn Albanian.
- The Mission began without an understanding of what there was to build on and what needs to be built. Lacking analysis, its reports use the lazy journalistic division between 'moderates' and 'extremists' or 'militants'. It also lacks a vision of the potentials for peace that could be developed among both the Albanian and Serbian communities of Kosovo.
- Its policy framework is still one that excludes the option of freeing Kosovo from Belgrade, and therefore would not look at what kind of coexistence key Serbian bodies (such as the Orthodox Church) within Kosovo might accept and what guarantees they want.[45]

The KVM did manage to de-fuse certain explosive situations.[46] It can also claim some of the credit for securing the release of prisoners held by the UÇK. In general, however, it could not stem the rising tide towards war. Although the KVM reported expressions of trust from Albanian and Serb communities, neither side had any faith in the ceasefire, the UÇK using it to arm or to re-establish itself in villages even when it was not wanted.[47] In general, there was a cycle of provocation by the UÇK and over-reaction by the Serbian police. In such a context, what a year earlier might have been a gallant attempt at unarmed peacekeeping or peacemaking became another step towards NATO intervention.

On 20 March, the OSCE KVM withdrew. Perhaps if the OSCE had refused to withdraw its verifiers in March 1999 – or rather if the verifiers and other international agency staff had had a choice whether to stay or to leave – their presence would have forced NATO to pay more attention to the protection of civilian life. But by itself the KVM's own analysis was that an unarmed presence was not equipped to handle the growing violence. Armed groups on both sides could simply deny KVM access to certain sites and areas. The intent of FRY and Serbian forces 'to apply mass killings as an instrument of terror, coercion and punishment ... was already in evidence ...Arbitrary killing of civilians was both a tactic in the campaign to expel Kosovo Albanians and an objective in itself.'[48] The KVM's confirmation of the execution of 45 Albanians at Reçak on 15 January was followed by killings in Rogovo and Rakovina the same month, the shelling of villages in Vushtrri in 'winter exercises' in February and March and a combined police and military offensive in Kaçanik in February burning and destroying homes 'in order to clear the area of UÇK' – rehearsals for the ethnic cleansing to come.

NATO BOMBS FOR CREDIBILITY

Perhaps the key negotiations around Rambouillet in February 1999 were not those that took place between the conflicting parties but those among Kosovo Albanians. Agani and Christopher Hill, US Ambassador to Macedonia, were shuttling hither and thither from November until February when they began to get enough unity among the splintered Kosovo Albanians to bring them to the negotiating table. On 2 February 1999, Adem Demaçi – as political representative of the UÇK – explained his view that to go to Rambouillet was to capitulate, that he had advised the UÇK against it and that he personally would not go. However, the UÇK general staff overrode this. The Albanian delegation at Rambouillet were almost ready to unite – and eventually did unite – behind the position of replacing the KVM with a NATO peace-keeping force without giving up the demand for independence.

Visiting Kosovo in November and December 1998, I met no local person expecting the already bullet-riddled ceasefire to hold even until spring. The press on each side offered improbable explanations to exonerate its own side's attacks. The death toll rose – according to the CDHRF, 151 people were killed in Kosovo in January (at least 11 Serbs) and 59 in February (nine Serbs). The international media had a readymade narrative of Milošević as the school bully, the KVM 'school prefects' were powerless and now it seemed time for the headteacher to intervene.

The agreement signed by Kosovo Albanian delegates to Rambouillet was for NATO to send an international protection force, KFOR, for a three-year period of 'self-government' during which the OSCE would supervise the construction of joint Serbian-Albanian civilian institutions. Civil administration would be reconstructed primarily through the communes, with an elected Assembly for the whole territory. This Assembly would in turn elect a president and appoint a prime minister and judges, subject to provisions guaranteeing representation from ethnic groups. A disputes procedure and other safeguards were agreed if the Assembly majority pushed for decisions deemed against their vital interests by other 'national communities'. Anybody facing charges from the International Criminal Tribunal (ICTY) would be barred from office. FRY would retain various federal responsibilities. Citizens of Kosovo could participate in the political affairs of FRY and the Republic of Serbia, including elections and the Assembly, and could call upon the Republic for assistance with education and welfare programmes. Each 'national community' in Kosovo could form its own democratically elected institutions. The OSCE would reconstruct a 3,000-strong police force, organised at the communal level, and an interim police academy. The republic police in the transition would be withdrawn to approved sites and restricted to civil functions under OSCE control until they could be replaced by the new force. Special units, heavy weapons and all Yugoslav Army units, except frontier guards, would be withdrawn five days after the agreement was signed. The economy would function 'in accordance with free market principles', with federal taxes paid to FRY and other taxes to the communes of Kosovo. Finally, 'three years after the entry into the force of this Agreement, an international meeting shall be convened to determine a mechanism for a final settlement for Kosovo, on the basis of the will of the people, opinions of relevant authorities ...'[49] This is usually taken to mean that there would be a referendum on status after three years, although the precise mechanism is left open.

Rambouillet was the kind of deal towards which LDK policy had been steering. Albanian concessions were mainly symbolic – no recognition of the illegitimacy of the annulment of autonomy or of the legitimacy of the Republic of Kosova, together with a temporary acceptance that Kosovo was part of FRY. For Serbs, on the other hand, it represented defeat – a defeat brought on by their own maltreatment of Albanians. Any further attempts at revision or re-negotiation by Serbs were treated as mere time-wasting, as reports from inside Kosovo became more alarming.

One line of analysis is that Belgrade rejected the 'imposition' of Rambouillet as much as its core content (international protection, transitional administration). Nobody should have expected (and probably nobody did) that on the first occasion that Western powers opened the door to the idea that Kosovo's future might lie outside FRY, the Milošević regime would do the same. Even under the bombing, however, FRY would not accept Rambouillet without three further concessions. First, to put the international operation under the UN, making KFOR a UN force 'based on NATO' but with Russian participation and answerable to the Security Council, where Russia has a veto. Second, to deny KFOR access to FRY except Kosovo. And third, to remove the notion of a 'final settlement ' after three years. In a way, it suited the LDK and the UÇK leaderships not to be represented in negotiations where such concessions were needed to secure the withdrawal of Serbian forces.

Rambouillet was a diktat to Serbia. The time had come when – at last – Western leaders recognised Milošević as a criminal. He had exploited their differences and indecision throughout the decade, he had broken agreements, he had cheated his own people (who still elected him) and he had fomented war. In an area where NATO's writ was supposed to run, he was again preparing to carry out ethnic cleansing. Now the West wanted a showdown. NATO, not the OSCE, had won the institutional battle for responsibility for European security and its credibility was at stake if it did not stop the crime under preparation.

Kosovo Albanians expected 'protection' – the deployment of ground troops, the use of attack helicopters against tanks and other units, at least some tipping of the balance in favour of the UÇK forces. But NATO embarked on a campaign not to protect Kosovo, but rather to defeat and punish Serbia. What public support had built up for this war could quickly evaporate if ground troops were being killed and so the war was fought with minimal risk to 'our boys'. Their initial scenario seemed to be that once you stand up to the school bully, you discover that s/he is a coward and will back down. When this proved to be wrong, NATO's targeting strategy became increasingly permissive. Rather than engage with the units carrying out the ethnic cleansing, NATO bombed bridges nearer Hungary than Kosovo. Serbia's entire industrial infrastructure and even media-workers in Belgrade came to be designated as 'military targets'. NATO unity was brittle. Thus, when certain members suggested a 'bombing pause' to test new diplomatic possibilities, the USA and Britain brought them into line, fearing any loss of momentum.

Most Kosovo Albanians either fled or were expelled from their homes. By 10 June, the UN High Commission for Refugees recorded that there were 780,700 refugees from Kosovo divided between Bosnia, Montenegro, Macedonia (245,000) and Albania (444,200). A further 81,705 had been helped by the UNHCR to travel on to third countries and there were more than half a million displaced people in desperate conditions inside Kosovo. In Prishtina, Ibrahim Rugova was under house arrest, Veton Surroi was in hiding, while Adem Demaçi was arrested twice but apparently felt free to walk in the street. Many others who had decided to stay during the NATO campaign rethought their plans when they saw that NATO was not coming to protect them. One of these was Fehmi Agani, taken off a train when he was trying to leave and killed.

There was something casual about the way the ethnic cleansers went about their business. They did not need to kill – people were only too ready to flee – and yet kill they did, en masse, and rape and beat; they looted and torched, they threw animal or human corpses down wells to poison them. Did they really believe that this was reclaiming Kosovo for Serbia? Or rather were they just inflicting one final punishment on the Kosovo Albanians?

There was more unanimity among Kosovo Albanians about the need for NATO intervention than there ever had been about nonviolence, and there remains a genuine gratitude to NATO and to the international leaders who – Kosovo Albanians hope 'finally' – pushed Milošević out of Kosovo. Despite the problems of NATO strategy, the NATO bombings were the final vindication of the Kosovo Albanian reliance on the West.

At this point I have to acknowledge the dilemma of pacifists when a situation escalates this way. We work for the creation of a world order not based on military force, to see military alliances dissolved not expanded. Yet there are times when it is too late to speak of 'nonviolent alternatives'. The subsequent Finnish and Russian mediation can be taken perhaps to show that the US dominance of the process was mistaken, and the *macho* US/British style even more so. However, by the time of Rambouillet, there was no easy option and little desire from either NATO or from Kosovo Albanians to avoid a 'final' confrontation with the Belgrade regime.

While I will never advocate a military intervention, if there had been a sensible military proposal to protect the innocent I would have kept my own counsel. However, the strategy adopted by NATO was something else, strengthening the precedent for quick-fix international interventions. 'As a police force,' I wrote at the time:

Nato is not like the traditional British bobby, but is rather a 'Dirty Harry' type of cop, breaking the rules and ignoring agreed procedures. It is a police force that is concerned only with a few selected criminals and least of all with the criminals in its own ranks.[50]

I would now offer these seven points:

i) The bombings were an indictment of the previous Western policies towards the wars of succession in Yugoslavia as a whole and Kosovo in particular.

ii) A fraction of the resources consumed in the bombing campaign invested in a peace process even as late as 18 months earlier could have changed the course of events.

iii) The withdrawal of any international presence from Kosovo removed any restraint on Serb forces from engaging in ethnic cleansing and other war crimes.

iv) The NATO operation further weakened international procedures restraining the use of war as a means of settling disputes.

v) The NATO operation showed that ethnic conflict in Europe matters more than in Africa or Asia.

vi) NATO's targeting strategy treated all Serbs as combatants. The conduct of the operation was another demonstration of what has been dubbed the Clinton Doctrine, 'punishing the innocent in order to express indignation at the guilty'.[51]

vii) The operation set a pattern of punishing Serbs collectively that continued after the war, damaging any prospect for peaceful coexistence in Kosovo.

Even as Serbian security forces began to withdraw from Kosovo – before any Albanian act of vengeance – some 50,000 Serbs left their homes, recognising that it was now their turn to flee. More were to follow.

8
Reflections on Civil Resistance

THE BALANCE SHEET ON CIVIL RESISTANCE: THE KOSOVO PERSPECTIVE

Writing in 1997, Tim Judah suggested:

> Of all the leaders of former Yugoslavia, Rugova has perhaps played the shrewdest game … He has avoided giving the Serbs an excuse to use force to try to ethnically cleanse Kosovo. His policy is one of waiting until there are simply no more Serbs left in Kosovo or their numbers become so insignificant that somehow the province falls to his people like a ripe fruit. It is a long-term policy and, despite discontent aroused by the belief that so far it has achieved nothing, in fact it has achieved much. It has saved lives and, unlike the Krajina Serbs for example, kept Kosovo's Albanian population … in their homes.[1]

It was not quite as simple as a fruit ripening. Kosovo Albanians needed some mechanism to turn the opponents' loss into their 'gain'. Demographics and attrition were not enough. The main hope had been international intervention. Whilst civil resistance did not bring this about, it did ensure that intervention, when it came, was on their side. Any subsequent 'victory', however, came at a great cost, not just in lives but also in the hopes for inter-ethnic coexistence and the prospects for democracy in Kosovo. Meanwhile the ultimate constitutional status for Kosovo remains undecided. Partition may still be the price of independence.

Anthony Borden of IWPR, in Prishtina just after Rambouillet, interviewed two key negotiators, Veton Surroi and Fehmi Agani. He asked Surroi 'was the nonviolent approach championed by Ibrahim Rugova and the Democratic League of Kosova (LDK) a mistake?'

> Surroi: No, it was necessary. First, if we had gone to war in 1991–92, we would have seen a much bigger destruction. The

peace approach prevented this place from flaring up earlier when it was totally unprepared. Second, it prepared an atmosphere through which we will be opting for an evolutionary not a revolutionary change. Third, it prepared the world to deal with this issue. Ten years ago, nobody would have cared what kind of agreement was set up here as long as you could patch something up quite rapidly. Now, after the wars in Croatia and Bosnia, the world has understood a bit better the dynamic of ethnic conflict, the dynamic especially of this place and the former Yugoslavia in general. And now independence is seen as one of the future options – not only by isolated individuals but also within think tanks and certain foreign ministries.[2]

Agani's response to a similar question was:

Agani: The real defeat of Serbia was a political defeat, and this was achieved by the LDK. It was not enough, but the KLA [UÇK] emerged at a time when Serbia had already become a strange presence in Kosovo. The ground was prepared for them. ... So there is a link between the LDK and the KLA periods. Serbia has been reduced in Kosovo to the police and army and force. Politically, it has been totally isolated in Kosovo, and has no support in any stratum of Albanian society ...
IWPR: But young Albanians are radicalised. They say that the LDK failed ... Violence has been successful.
Agani: Yes, but the theory has to be tested. You have to compare the goals and what has been achieved. [In the year since Drenica] We have more than 2,000 killed, 5,000 injured and more than 50,000 refugees. For a period, we had 400,000 internally displaced. We have 40,000 houses burned. This is a big cost. And it has been mainly paid for by ordinary people: human rights organisations say that 95 per cent of the Albanians killed were civilians and only 5 per cent from the KLA.[3]

Both Agani and Surroi looked back on civil resistance as a phase, buying the time needed but not itself capable of bringing about the final blow to end rule from Belgrade. In extremely difficult conditions, civil resistance managed to postpone war, to maintain the integrity of the Albanian community in Kosovo and its way of life, to counter Serbian pressure on Albanians to leave and to enlist international sympathy.

Most observers probably share James Pettifer's view that 'it can be stated with certainty that Nato would not have intervened in Yugoslavia without the emergence of the KLA.'[4] This statement, however, could boil down to say that NATO would not have intervened without the Serbian atrocities of 1998 and January 1999 and these would not have occurred without the UÇK. Such a pretext was needed in order to exceed Čubrilović's recommendations for creating 'a suitable psychosis' to force emigration, or to surpass the practices of the Ranković era and indeed the period of 1990–97.

More important are the questions, first whether an alternative *international* strategy would have yielded better results – such as less death and destruction, better prospects for future peaceful coexistence in a self-governing Kosovo – and second whether improvements in the Kosovo Albanian strategy could have brought about either changes in the international response or changes in the Serbian regime/society. These questions have to remain open. My own perspective before 28 November 1997 (the UÇK funeral appearance), was optimistic that a more active nonviolent strategy with a stronger constructive programme could have made a significantly greater international impact. As for changes inside Serbia, Kosovo Albanians could not have had an enormous impact even if they had tried – the point was to be open, periodically testing to see if a different moment had arrived, multiplying contacts and keeping existing channels functioning until there was a more favourable conjuncture.

The regime's course in Kosovo before the arrival of the UÇK seemed to be mapped by inertia. The regime, as much as the LDK, seemed to be incapable of initiative. It was as if two chess players were each waiting for their opponent to make a losing move – or for the flag on the opponent's clock to fall. In many ways, once it became clear how unrealistic the programme was for re-Serbianising Kosovo – with even refugees refusing to be re-settled there – it rather suited Milošević to have the conflict simmering. It justified his large police force; it was permanently available if he needed a 'crisis' to distract attention from problems elsewhere or if he had a 'grievance' to invoke. However, there was no doubt that the Kosovo Albanians had a stronger will to Kosovo than Milošević himself – for them it was their home, for him it was a situation and a symbol he could use.

Time was strengthening the Kosovo Albanians' international position because they were educating international opinion.

Domestically however, time was running out in the absence of a development programme within Kosovo and without an influential movement in Serbia whose vision of democracy extended to Kosovo.

To summarise the balance from a Kosovo Albanian point of view then, in terms of civil resistance to occupation, the Kosovo Albanian movement was a success that needed something more to bring decisive international intervention. As a movement for independence, too, the verdict is similarly positive despite the uncertainties and remaining negotiations. As a movement for democracy and pluralism with inter-ethnic coexistence, the balance judged from the perspective of 1989 must be one of disappointment. The poison of war is strong – revenge and the bullying disguised as revenge, the gangsterism, the distortion of perceptions, the corrosion of values and the making of politics by intimidation rather than discussion and negotiation. But war alone is not the explanation. There is also the resentment left by nine years of Serbian repression and humiliation – which for many seemed the continuation of a century-long story – unbalanced by any other experience of Serbs. The minority who used to work for self-organisation, for democracy, pluralism and coexistence set a path of hope in adverse conditions. Now, with the Serbian regime out of Kosovo, they continue to create new opportunities.

THE BALANCE SHEET ON CIVIL RESISTANCE: THE INTERNATIONAL DEBATE

Every experience of civil resistance feeds into an international debate about its potential as a non-military strategy for resisting authoritarian regimes. Kosovo is of particular interest, testing what is possible for a nonviolent movement resisting a regime which was – both on its own behalf and along with its allies and its agents – associated with policies of ethnic cleansing.

A group of the more sceptical researchers (Schmid et al.) studying civil resistance against Communist regimes identified ten conditions that 'can be taken as sufficient conditions for social defence [defence by civil resistance] to be realistic and practicable'.[5] A summary of these follows together with my brief notes in italics on their applicability in Kosovo.

1. The presence of a social carrier acquainted with the basic principles of nonviolent resistance and prepared to apply them.
   Perhaps the nearest to this initially would be the 'Kosova Alternative' circle.
2. A degree of independence in terms of the skills and resources necessary for a defence effort.
   Present.
3. The capacity to communicate a) within its own ranks, b) with third parties, c) with the aggressor's social base.
   a) Present. b) Present. c) Technically present, but limited by the regime's control of most Serbian media.
4. A tradition of free democratic activity with an informed and politically conscious population.
   Such a tradition was absent.
5. A social system which is perceived as more legitimate than that imported by the attacker.
   More than this, there was a general will among Albanians to be free of Serbia.
6. An ability on the part of defenders to maintain (or obtain) social cohesion.
   More than this, there was social solidarity.
7. Dependence of the aggressor on the defender's (or an ally's) economic, social or administrative system.
   Absent.
8. Human contact between resisters and aggressors.
   Limited.
9. Widespread acceptance by a) public opinion, b) foreign governments or c) the attacker of the legitimate status of the defenders.
   a) Present. b) Not widespread, although the widespread concern about human rights violations threw doubt upon the conduct of the aggressor. c) Absent initially.
10. The chief adversary – or those in a position of influence – must be rational and not permanently fanatical or crazy.

Schmid further comments: 'If ideology or madness supersedes every other consideration with the adversary and he is going to extremes without regards to consequences and costs, only armed force is likely to stop him.'[6] Evidently Serbian attitudes to Kosovo, Milošević's own 'borderline personality' and the nature of the regime were all factors militating against the success of civil resistance in Kosovo.

Items 3 (communications) and 7 (the regime's dependence) are held to be 'crucial', Items 9 (international acceptance of legitimacy) and 10 (regime psycho-factors) are important to make resistance viable. Schmid also tentatively suggested that Items 3 (communication), 6 (social cohesion), 7 (any dependency of the aggressor) and 9 (the defence's legitimacy) might have a 'multiplicatory impact'.

This list was derived from a questionnaire to researchers on nonviolent social defence who operate from various – sometimes conflicting – premises. Therefore it 'could not be based on a mature theory of social defence', but rather should be seen more 'as a checklist of factors worth looking for, ... useful in determining potential limits and possibilities'.[7] As such, it would indicate that there was little basis for civil resistance in Kosovo. The achievements of the actual resistance therefore raise questions about the framework implicit in the list.

Two essential points are that the potential for civil resistance has to be judged in relation to a time span and in relation to what other options exist. Additionally, there is an interplay between the strengths and weaknesses, so that the strength of the Albanian will to be free of Serbia and of their remarkable social solidarity compensated for and provided the time to address weaknesses.

Any strategy has to be based on an assessment of the objectives and capacities of the aggressor and the resister. The resister should tailor strategy according to his/her strengths and weaknesses, with some timeframe for overcoming certain remediable weaknesses. If in Year 1, there is little knowledge of the methods and strategic principles of civil resistance, this should be less the case in Year 2 and not the case at all in Year 8. The absence of a 'tradition of free democratic activity' calls for an explicit organisational philosophy promoting values of decentralised initiative within an overall consensus. A movement lacking internal means of communication can develop them.

In general, civil resistance is likely to be a slow-working strategy. In this, it is essential to have a realistic time frame. 'Lack of persistence, a major cause of failure in nonviolent conflict', comment Ackerman and Kruegler, 'is often the product of a short-term perspective.'[8] The Kosovo leadership always counselled patience, but popular acceptance of its strategy rested on illusions about the timeframe and the likelihood of Western intervention. Kosovo Albanians were deceived by images of the 'people's power' events of 1989 and by the speed with which four of the republics of Yugoslavia were granted independence. Their optimism was confirmed by Rugova's reception in Washington in 1990 and later by the Bush-Clinton promise of 1992–93. The teachers – who played a central role in maintaining parallel institutions – did not have a perspective that went beyond two or three years. It was largely the warning of war represented by the situation in Bosnia and the belief that international support was coming that ensured that the population kept its patience.

In addition to the factor of time, the existence of a military option complicates strategic calculations. It introduces several chains of effects – as a threat behind the apparent civil resistance, as a pretext or even genuine reason for repression and not least as a reason why some people lose patience with nonviolence. When Kosovo Albanians saw no option for military resistance, they charted a course between subjugation and destruction, which defeated Serbia politically and ultimately enabled the regime's military defeat. Even treating this as one phase in a struggle – prior to the UÇK's triggering of more overt Serbian aggression and then the military intervention of NATO – it was a considerable achievement.

If they had not expected results more quickly, perhaps the Kosovo Albanians would have been more hesitant about entering this kind of struggle. Had they believed there was a military option – for instance if their territorial defence had not been abolished and weapons caches removed – then perhaps at the beginning of 1990 the LDK might have supported the armed uprising some of its founders wanted, or perhaps later they would have been lured into opening a second front during the war with Croatia or even in Bosnia. However, choosing a military struggle in the early 1990s would have alienated international support even more than the goal of independence – probably with catastrophic results.

Therefore they overcame their scepticism about an unfamiliar form of resistance and for eight years almost the entire population followed a strategy of civil resistance – albeit an inadequate and underdeveloped strategy. The military option provided by the UÇK altered the whole character of the situation because the regime then had a pretext for the mass deployment of security forces, but the movement had already achieved its decisive success: international support.

An alternative to the outlook of identifying optimal conditions for civil resistance would be to say that in most situations there is some potential, although it may take time and determination to optimise this. At times when armed struggle could be catastrophic, even if the potential for civil resistance is also limited, it is better suited to preserving the life of the population. The point is then to assess what type of strategy can achieve what kind of goals within what time span.

Some writers on civil resistance have dismissed civil resistance as ineffective against a 'genocidal'[9] opponent. The main experience of 'defeating' genocide in the twentieth century involved the mass bombing of civilian populations and gave impetus to the development and use of weapons of indiscriminate mass destruction – 'genocidal' weapons. It is therefore hard to speak at all of effective strategies against genocide other than prevention, that is other than combating preparations for it as soon as they manifest themselves, a combat that will usually be political, social and cultural rather than military.

The experience in Kosovo strengthens the argument that, even if civil resistance by the threatened population might not stop extreme criminality, war provides the conditions most conducive for such criminality to be carried out. For Serbs, Albanians were the most hated nationality in Yugoslavia, yet it was not until the arrival of the UÇK that the regime began to use methods familiar in Bosnia, and not until the OSCE's withdrawal of the KVM in March 1999, that the expulsion began of the vast majority of the Albanian population. In the first half of 1998, the CHDRF had a list of 416 killed – compared with a total of 209 in the previous nine years. In 1999, the death toll escalated further – in the five months after Serbian withdrawal, international forensic investigators had already found 2,108 bodies in mass graves.[10]

As Goebbels himself recognised during the Second World War:

[The Führer] is right in saying that the war has made possible for us the solution of a whole series of problems that could never have been solved in normal times. The Jews will certainly be the losers in this war come what may.[11]

VICTIM BEHAVIOUR AND NONVIOLENCE

Yesterday's victims have become today's oppressors. It is one of the most familiar patterns of human history. In former Yugoslavia, nationalist groups have competed with each other to appropriate the status of 'victim' for their particular nation. The dominant ethnic groups – the Serbs and Croats – and the militarily weaker Bosnians and Kosovo Albanians play the same game, building up their own sense of nationhood and righteousness while in fact excluding the point of view of the Other. The crumbling of the Yugoslav myth of 'Brotherhood and Unity' has left the field open for policies of naked ethnic domination.

Nonviolence is sometimes assumed to be able to break the cycle that turns victims into oppressors, yet one of its characteristic dynamics – moral or political *ju-jitsu* – has also been interpreted as accentuating the victim attitude. In general there is a suspicion that nonviolence rather than expressing and 'cleansing' resentment and hatred, allows it to fester.

In one of the first studies of nonviolent civil resistance, Richard Gregg proposed the concept of 'moral *ju-jitsu*' to describe how 'the nonviolence and good will of the victim act like the lack of physical opposition by the user of physical ju-jitsu to cause the attacker to lose his moral balance.'[12] Gene Sharp, taking a more hard-nosed approach, later developed this notion by bringing into focus the political consequences of violence, speaking of 'political *ju-jitsu*':

> Nonviolent action involves opposing the opponent's power, including his police and military capacity, not with the weapons chosen by him, but by quite different means ... Repression by the opponent is used against his own power position in a kind of political *ju-jitsu*, and the very sources of his power thus reduced or removed, with the result that his political and military position is seriously weakened or destroyed.[13]

At a superficial level, one might see a correspondence between the application of political *ju-jitsu* and the attitude 'The worse they look, the better for us'. There is, however, a distinction between either moral or political *ju-jitsu* and 'playing the victim'. Most street beggars can be said to be 'playing the victim'[14] – somehow trying to touch the pity of passers-by to help them or their dependants survive, enduring their fate. Maybe a few people give out of human solidarity, others out of shame or superstition. An oppressed group taking nonviolent action, however, does not have the beggars' fatalism. Instead there is an assertion of dignity, of humanity, a demand to be heard or to be allowed to practise certain rights. A fully thought-out tactical application of political *ju-jitsu* does not project 'pity me' but rather aims to reduce the 'social distance' between the defender and any constituency it is aimed at influencing, projecting 'identify with my humanity'. While victim behaviour exaggerates the power of the oppressor and underestimates one's own capacities, political *ju-jitsu* turns the oppressor's force against him (or her).

The issue of victim behaviour has exercised feminist writers on nonviolence.

> One of the greatest problems facing victims is to become visible to their oppressors, to make them hear the sound their fist makes striking vulnerable flesh, smell the fear they inspire, feel the pain for the reality it is, and to do this without encouraging sadistic instincts.[15]

Women's everyday oppression is often invisible. Thus, the argument runs, their suffering lacks purchase on male consciences. This does not, however, speak against the use of nonviolence as a form of *ju-jitsu*, but rather parallels the experience of slaves, colonised peoples or other groups expected to be submissive or victims. The answer is at least twofold: one in terms of organisation, the other in terms of self-assertion.

Kosovo Albanians had lived with police harassment for years, in the 1920s and 1930s, in the Ranković era and after 1981. Every family has its stories to tell of police maltreatment. The change brought by the nonviolent movement was the idea that it was worth trying to do something about this. Hence a monitoring body – the CDHRF – was established, organisers visited the scenes of incidents, the *For Democracy, Against Violence* petition organisers committed themselves to mark each death caused by police and various bodies began to prepare a stream of detailed reports to international bodies. This level of organisation underpinned the new Kosovo Albanian self-assertiveness of the 1990–92 period, the time when they felt they were taking charge of their own destiny.

After 1992, however, in the period when there were no public demonstrations, no 'homages' in the streets or factories, daily experience was of avoidance of conflict and fear. Police were no longer repressing demonstrations, but they were repeatedly disrupting daily life. Theirs was a strategy of intimidation, meted out randomly, and usually with no more provocation than being an Albanian in Kosovo trying to survive. The normal way of life was to try to avoid this violence. The CDHRF and other groups documented what they could, aiming to restrain this violence and to use it to shame the regime especially in the court of international opinion. But at the level of daily experience, the 'victim' identity again took hold.

Within the population at large, there was little challenge to 'victim' thinking. Most Kosovo Albanians blamed 'the Serbs' for every power cut even at a time when Serbs in cities in FRY were also suffering power cuts. Unless they saw somebody doing it, many regarded any suggestion for activity as 'impossible' because of 'the Serbs' – without even putting this to any kind of test. This ruling passivity was not confined to Rugova – indeed some of Rugova's opponents used him as an additional scapegoat for their own inactivity.

Writing in 1993, Gani Bobi[16] discussed the explosive situation in which Albanian anger and hatred were being suppressed. 'The peaceful orientation of the Albanians and endurance (*durimi*) all the way to self-sacrifice', he wrote, had as its main motive 'the fear of the consequences of an open confrontation with a large and destructive power.' It would not be very difficult to guess 'what might happen one day when the Albanians become more frightened of living under the occupier than of dying fighting it'.

That is the situation at the end of 1999. The post-war atmosphere in Kosovo is one where Serbs are held collectively and indiscriminately guilty for everything that has happened, both in 1998–99 and earlier. Intimidation is organised, by young thugs, by gangster elements, by people pretending to be UÇK and by some who did fight as UÇK (although the UÇK leadership condemns intimidation). The result is that it is now unsafe for Serbs to venture unprotected outside the enclaves where those remaining – perhaps 100,000, nearly half the pre-war Serbian population – are concentrated.

The Kosovo Albanian population in the mid-1990s was organised, but no longer sufficiently assertive. In their different ways, both the 'active nonviolence' of UPSUP and the armed struggle of the UÇK were making the switch from enduring the occupation to fighting it, 'casting fear aside'.[17] UPSUP's nonviolence did this in a more far-reaching way. This was real political *ju-jitsu*, replying to the Serbian slogan 'Don't even give them pencils' with 'Education is a right for everybody' – a clear message that they would be neither victims nor executioners.

The UÇK attitude was far from passive – spokespeople repeatedly stressing that one had to work for independence. Nevertheless they did not break so decisively with victim behaviour, but rather played the role of 'underdogs'. A few years earlier, they might have been dismissed internationally as 'typical Balkan rebels'. Their early strategy provoked violence – in the form of police reprisals against a population that was usually defenceless – thereby increasing the number of the population who saw the 'need' for armed defence. This is a common guerrilla strategy and, had it not been for the years of nonviolence, hardly any government would even have blinked at their slaughter/'pacification'. The UÇK were not championed by the international media as much as fascinating the journalists, each responding to the challenge to throw more light on 'the army of the shadows'.[18] Having played the role of underdog, some former UÇK members are only too ready to play the master.

Another limit on any assertive impact of the UÇK in Kosovo Albanian society at large is the disparity between public reporting and the reality. Ethnic loyalty in the face of a horrific Serbian offensive meant that both the CDHRF and KIC, rather than informing readers that certain people had been killed in shoot-outs with police, continued to project all Kosovo Albanians as victims. Unless it was to say that someone was killed in 'unclear circumstances', they did not discriminate between unarmed people killed and those whom the UÇK honoured as martyrs and heroes.

Neither did the UÇK make use of any trial as a platform. Perhaps none of the 17 alleged 'terrorists' sentenced to a total of 186 years imprisonment in December 1997 was a member of the UÇK. The evidence was based mainly on torture and the key defendant, Nait Hasani, sentenced to 20 years, declared 'I maintain that the peaceful approach in pursuit of Kosova's independence is still the best.'[19] However, also due to be on trial with them was Adrian Krasniqi, killed in a botched UÇK attack on a police station and declared the UÇK's first martyr.[20] I question if his presence would have changed either the conduct of the defendants or the tone of the CDHRF/KIC reporting.

Whatever cathartic effects have been claimed for violence, in the case of the UÇK it is hard to see that it was changing the victim attitude, 'setting afoot the new man', as Frantz Fanon claimed for the war of liberation in Algeria. 'At the level of individuals,' wrote Fanon, 'violence is a cleansing force. It frees the native from his inferiority complex and from his despair and inaction; it makes him fearless and restores his self-respect.'[21] At the same time, Fanon wrote of the toll their actions took on liberation fighters, including one who had attacks of vertigo after he made friends with citizens of the former colonial power and began to wonder whether a bomb he had placed had killed people like them. 'We are for ever pursued by our actions', wrote Fanon, 'but can we escape becoming dizzy? And who can affirm that vertigo does not haunt the whole of existence?'

This inspired one of the classic essays of nonviolence, Barbara Deming's 'Revolution and Equilibrium',[22] in which she argues that wherever Fanon makes a claim for the liberating effects of violence one can substitute a phrase about bold nonviolent action.[23] The 'equilibrium' she refers to is the balance between self-assertion and respect for others, intrinsic to her approach to nonviolence but lacking in violence. Deming gets to the heart of an assertively nonviolent attitude that breaks the victim pattern:

> If nonviolent action is boldly taken, it does allow people to speak out of their deepest feelings; and if it is boldly taken, it does allow them to feel that they are standing up to others like human beings. It may not permit them to act out their hatred for others by taking revenge; but it allows – it requires – them to act all the truth they feel about what the other has done, is doing to them, and to act out their determination to change this state of things. In this very process, one's hatred of the other can be forgotten, because it is beside the point; the point is to change one's life. The point is not to give some vent to the emotions that have been destroying one; the point is so to act that one can master them now.[24]

LEADER SYNDROMES

Many people associate nonviolent movements with the leadership of Gandhi or Martin Luther King – personalities to whom it is fitting to apply the overused term 'charisma'. Such a leader inspires people to go beyond their limits. Also in both cases, they used their leadership at times to restrain their movements. Neither of them descended from heaven but rather they built themselves or were built up as leaders – Gandhi in India especially after his return from South Africa, and King who found himself as the voice of the Montgomery Bus Boycott. They were in the heroic mould; personal courage prepared them for assassination. Rugova – contrary to popular belief – was not a founder of the LDK, nor even apparently the first person offered the post of LDK president. Rather he came to the helm as someone who had shown integrity as president of the

Writers' Association and through lack of an alternative around whom there could be unity. His build-up came subsequently. He was not in the heroic mould. Maliqi's view in 1996 was that 'he precisely is the man who was best suited for this situation of neither war nor peace, the politics of non-doing.'[25] This was not a hostile remark, but rather an appreciation of the qualities of prudence and patience that Rugova displayed. However, apart from his Friday press conferences, Rugova seemed increasingly remote from his own population, without this in any way affecting their faith in him. Somehow the more Rugova refused to answer his critics, the more presidential his aura became. Criticisms of him invariably seemed to rebound against their authors. Such a style of leadership was as alien to the young journalists on *Koha Ditore* as to the Western journalists who turned to them for local analysis.

Reliance on a few leaders is a weakness, according to Boserup and Mack:

> An ideology, which instead of the excellence of leaders and individuals, emphasises the people as a whole and its unity as the true basis of strength seems much more likely to be able to resist the occupant's efforts at disruption ... It is not heroism *per se* which is needed, but flexibility by the leadership, in adapting to those forms of resistance which the population can sustain and is willing to sustain under the given conditions.[26]

To this should be added the need for a structure that can combine maintaining unity with encouraging diversity, both of initiative and at times in terms of who bears the brunt of a strategy.

In the case of Kosovo, it is natural to write about the leader, Rugova, what he could or should have done at different points. He personally was a symbol. The power to take key strategic decisions was increasingly concentrated in a small circle around him. Nevertheless, the history of the leadership of civil resistance in Kosovo is not just his personal history, but shifts with time. Leadership may reside with a person, a decision-making structure, an organisation and/or it can be diffuse, encouraging self-organised activity initiated locally. Various tasks involved in leadership are divided – perhaps between different levels of leadership or different types of bodies. Any new structures for decision-making or initiative have to negotiate their place with what existed in society. In Kosovo, recent traditions offered three models of organisation: the authoritarian and nepotistic LCY; the patriarchal extended family, conformity to the 'social circle' and residual 'customary law' (including Councils of Elders/Neighbours); and the conspiratorial 'cell' structure of the Enverist groups of the 1980s. In 1989, two other models from Eastern Europe were also popular: 'civil society' movements and independent trade unions.

At the beginning of the nonviolent struggle, there seemed to be a convergence of organised workers, students and intellectuals. The need for restraint – persuading people not to join the street protests in January 1990 or to lynch Serbs for the 'poisoning' of March 1990 – was imposed not through authority structures, but through debate between peers, the LDK's involvement being belated. Then diverse initiatives were pursued rather spontaneously – the petition *For Democracy, Against Violence*, the variety of 'semi-resistance' protests, the 'homages' and the campaign for reconciliation of blood feuds. These drew on and in turn enhanced the unity of the people.

As Kosovo's autonomy was annulled, the former parliamentarians bestowed legitimacy upon a fairly representative leadership, presided over by the rather consensual figure of Ibrahim Rugova who in turn headed the dominant new organisation, the LDK. Self-organisation at the level of teachers and parents in the schools, human rights monitors in the CDHRF, or medics through the MTA brought into existence other essential structures, while the solidarity funds of the unions and of the LDK itself became a major source of humanitarian assistance. Self-restraint and refusal to be provoked emerged as a social consensus that was supported by the activity of CDHRF and LDK activists going to the scenes of incidents.

Increasingly, however, especially after the 1992 elections, President Rugova and the LDK projected themselves as the authentic voice of Kosovo Albanians. The Republic of Kosova became responsible for organising a voluntary taxation system (on an all-party basis), for paying teachers' wages, and for distributing some humanitarian assistance. As far as Kosovo's constitutional status or any future negotiations were concerned, this legitimacy was essential. It had been clearly established through the 1991 referendum and 1992 elections, and was scrupulously recognised by minority figures – such as Maliqi, Gazmend Pula and Surroi – who took a more flexible approach to negotiations. Those rare attempts by Serbian parties to co-opt 'flexible' – as distinct from either 'loyal' or 'separatist' – Kosovo Albanians were generally met by a firm principled insistence that the legitimate voices of the Kosovo Albanian had to be heard.

The massive education protests in October 1992 were primarily organised by the education unions, with LDK backing. Afterwards, they agreed that little would be gained at too great a cost by organising similar general demonstrations at this time, and the LDK began to put a general bar on demonstrations as 'provocations'. At the time, this seemed a wise decision, although it carried the danger that the people would be de-mobilised for too long. Also in 1993 Maliqi and Surroi found themselves politically adrift. It was becoming clear that the LDK – and even more the attitudes dominant in *Bujku* and traditional Albanian forms of social pressure – restricted initiative and established a conformity that became more than a matter of maintaining nonviolent discipline. In 1992, Fehmi Agani was not alone in asking: 'How long can the political leaders, the patriarchs and the hoxhas channel the discontent?'[27] However, it became increasingly clear that Kosovo's established leaders were no longer 'channelling', rather their attitude was one of extreme passivity, waiting for something to happen on the international stage, while taking a posture of *laissez-faire* on improving daily life in Kosovo. The refusal to convene the parliament, the failure to open a Belgrade office and the lack of a development programme justify references to this not as a period of stability but rather of stagnation. In retrospect, one might even suspect that there was an almost deliberate attempt to create conditions for the arrival of a liberation army.

However, another form of leadership began to emerge. Leaving aside the rather sterile political debate with its repeated (although legitimate) calls for a more collegiate style of leadership, the new initiatives were coming from diverse sources. They came above all from people – especially women's groups – looking to start NGOs dealing with the everyday issues of life in Kosovo, from the kind of discussions encouraged by *Koha* and for the type of activities that the Open Society Fund was willing to fund. These were not concerned with posing an alternative platform – only *Koha* operated as an explicit challenge to the established leadership – but rather with generating energy for change and a different and more diffuse form of social leadership within every community. The student leadership was rather different, even before it was sucked into the explicit politics of boycotting the elections. It saw itself as the democratically elected and representative head of a constituency within Kosovo, entitled not only to defy Rugova in the name of that constituency but also to lay down a strict discipline for demonstrations. Perhaps, I thought, they could learn from Poland where from the mid-1980s on the small group actions of Wolnosc i Pokoj and the Orange Alternative galvanised a situation where Solidarnosc had lost momentum. This was not for them.[28]

By the time of the public appearance of the UÇK at the end of 1997, there were many reasons to regard the LDK as a fossil and it seemed incapable of any new initiative. Yet it continued to command the allegiance of the population, as did Ibrahim Rugova personally.

Contemporary Western social movements – be they feminist, ecological or anti-militarist – tend to be sceptical of anyone aspiring to personal leadership. Instead they prefer either a collective style of decision-making or a diffuse coordination where each group takes its own initiatives, sometimes within only the loosest guidelines. My view, stemming no doubt from such predispositions, was that persistence in the struggle in Kosovo would have been better sustained less through obedience, conformity and faith than by (i) a more collective style of decision-making combined with (ii) greater self-organisation through diffuse leadership operating within (iii) clear strategic themes and guidelines. However, leadership is one of the most culturally specific forms of social organisation, and I am acutely aware that I write from outside that culture.

Western commentators typically found Rugova an 'unlikely' leader figure. Repeatedly they wrote him off in 1998 and again during 1999 – a year that one might have expected to prove disastrous for his career. He had a period under house arrest, was filmed on TV smiling with Milošević while Kosovo was being ethnically cleansed, later seemed undecided whether to live in Italy or Kosovo and on his return to Kosovo behaved more like a constitutional monarch than a practical politician. Yet even at the end of 1999 opinion polls still showed him to be by far the most popular and trusted figure among Kosovo Albanians.

In May 1998, the *Guardian*'s Jonathan Steele attended the funeral in the Peja municipality of the first local LDK branch leader to be killed in the Serbian offensive. Steele was scandalised that not only was there no LDK central representative present, there was not even a message from a leadership that seemed completely bankrupt. Its hardest worker, Fehmi Agani, admitted that they had nothing to say to the villages. That evening Steele and I were finding it hard to imagine another social struggle where a local leader could be killed without a representative of the national leadership making a day trip to attend the funeral. Yet discussing this with Kosovo Albanians, they found nothing surprising about this behaviour, and not just because it was what they had come to expect of the LDK. It was as if once the national consensus had been established – something that took place in the period when urban activists went to villages after incidents and when Çetta led the blood feud campaign – it should hold until the time arrived to change. Inactivity, relying on the solidity of local structures and family discipline, therefore became the appropriate response to a challenge. Facing a new situation, the LDK was paralysed.

GOALS AND TRANSITIONS

Gene Sharp and others have argued that nonviolent methods offer a 'functional alternative to war', an alternative to military methods of settling disputes. This pragmatic advocacy of nonviolence is addressed to those who share general values of justice and democracy but do not embrace any philosophy of nonviolence. Most of the effective campaigns of civil resistance, they point out, have been mounted by populations without a philosophical commitment to nonviolence but rather using it as the best strategy for their circumstances and purposes. The civil resistance in Kosovo is clearly such a pragmatic case. It is a misnomer to call a strategy 'pacifist' that repeatedly called for international military intervention. Nonviolence in Kosovo was a *strategic* commitment.

For nonviolence to be a 'functional alternative to war', however, it is not enough to consider methods alone but also goals. Some goals suggest and even demand the appropriate means. In particular, pluralism and democracy as ends dovetail with means based on the practice of pluralism and democracy. Other goals can themselves be a recipe for war if pursued uncompromisingly whether or not there is any intention of escalating towards violence. Certainly the LDK could have had a stronger peace policy – less focused on independence as a goal and more open to other options, alongside a strategy more communicative with Serbs and putting more effort into confidence building. But was independence for Kosovo itself a 'war option'?

Rugova and Agani tried to pursue independence in a way that offered an alternative to war – both by means based on refraining from violence and by 'softening' the goal of independence. Having recognised (at least in formal terms) the rights of Serbs and other ethnic groups within an independent Kosovo, they offered additional reassurances to Serbia itself and internationally by envisaging Kosovo as a neutral and demilitarised state with open borders towards its neighbours. Later, Rugova went further by calling for an international protectorate as a transition to independence, and Agani, the chief negotiator, was always clear that while Kosovo had the right to independence, negotiations might yield something different and still be acceptable. They would have agreed the text of Rambouillet at any time in the previous eight years – ceasefire, international protection, transitional administration. That the failure of Rambouillet heralded war was not the result of their negotiating stance, nor of the belated Western acceptance of the idea of an open transition. Rather this was the point to which the situation had been brought.

When civil resistance still prevailed, there were two particular problems with the goal of independence. The first problem is that, while Kosovo Albanian civil resistance was able to 'defeat' Milošević politically, it was not able to determine the form that defeat would take – it needed allies either within FRY or internationally to influence that. It is not far-fetched to suggest that if Serbia had to 'lose' Kosovo – officially as well as in practice – it suited Milošević's domestic political strategy that he should be seen as fighting for it, losing in battle as had Tsar Lazar, rather than meekly surrendering.[29] Milošević's rule has brought Serbia a string of military defeats without yet weakening his hold on power. Perhaps a military operation could gain a favourable partition of Kosovo.

The second was that the over-emphasis on final status and underemphasis on steps towards self-determination contributed to the ossification of the movement under the leadership of the LDK. It was not only the divisive and provocative impact of the UÇK that rendered Kosovo Albanians rudderless at the start of 1999. The movement had needed more awareness that it was gaining control of the situation, that how self-determination would be implemented was in their hands. Writing in 1993, Dušan Janjić of the Forum for Ethnic Relations in Belgrade warned: 'The absence of interim or transitional objectives ... involves maximum mobilization of the masses for demands which are difficult to obtain. That results in the exhaustion of the masses and narrowing of the political span for dialogue.'[30] In fact, the degree of mobilisation in the 1991–92 period was not sustained. Whether or not they were exhausted, 'the masses' were demobilised to an extent that they opened the door for the UÇK.

To create a 'functional alternative to war', both in terms of means and goals, required a reformulation of demands in order to link the ultimate goal with a set of subsidiary objectives, so marking progress and bringing the goal more within reach. As an ultimate goal, the negative 'End Belgrade's rule of Kosovo' was clearly more acceptable internationally than an independence that most people interpreted as 'Albanian rule of Kosovo'. 'Self-determination' – without fixing on a precise form (independence, confederation or 'autonomy plus') – offered a more open process towards change, more easily concretised in various areas of life and carrying with it the onus to build confidence with other ethnic groups in Kosovo. If the Kosovo Albanian leadership were less suspicious than the Belgrade regime of a step-by-step approach, they nevertheless generated few intermediate demands – such as 'international observer presence', 'withdraw special police', 're-open the schools', 'reinstate dismissed workers' or 'negotiate for an open transition' – and focused more on the issue of the status of Kosovo.

The two most recent books in English on the strategy of nonviolent struggle – Ackerman and Kruegler's *Strategic Nonviolent Conflict* and Burrowes' *The Strategy of Nonviolent Defense* – each offers five criteria for the 'functional objectives' (Ackerman and Kruegler)/'list of demands' (Burrowes). Ackerman and Kruegler:

i)   They should be concrete and specific enough to be achievable within a reasonable timeframe.
ii) They should readily suggest the use of a diverse array of nonviolent sanctions.
iii) They should be seen to preserve the vital (as opposed to marginal) interests of the nonviolent protagonists, and, ideally, be of more compelling interest for them than for the adversary.
iv) The goals must attract the widest possible support within the societies affected by the conflict.
v)   Objectives should resonate with the values or interests of external parties, in order to attract their support and potential assistance.[31]

Burrowes:

i)   The demands must be concrete, easily understood and 'within the power of the opponent to yield'.

ii)   They should accurately reflect the needs of the people engaged in the defence effort in order to mobilise widespread support for the struggle.

iii) They should include an explicit commitment to the needs of the opponent.

iv)   They may expose moral weak points in the position of the opponent elite.

v)   They should constitute the substance of the political purpose.[32]

These sets of criteria illuminate several differences between the 'technique-based' and the 'values-based' poles of opinion among advocates of nonviolence. Ackerman and Kruegler (technique pole) are frank: 'Simply put, this book is about who wins based on who makes best use of the resources and options at hand.'[33] To the extent that Burrowes (values pole) sees a need for nonviolent coercion, it is in order to secure 'the participation of the opponent elite in a problem-solving process'.[34] The most emphatic difference in these sets is Burrowes' prioritising the 'explicit commitment to the needs of the opponent', the most specifically Gandhian and nonviolent characteristic of all the criteria, the one most demanding of an oppressed population and yet the one that most decisively steers the conflict away from war.

CIVIL RESISTANCE AND CONFLICT RESOLUTION

A central insight of Gandhian nonviolence has been that 'the means determine the ends'. Consequently many proponents of nonviolence concentrate on means, on process. Whereas violence is most effective in seeking to *impose* a settlement,[35] nonviolence can be proposed as a method that aims to *construct* an alternative to the status quo. It can do this through its ability to involve a wide range of the population, through its own programme of constructive work and to its commitment to respecting the needs and rights of the adversary.

Among proponents of nonviolence, however, there is a tension – sometimes even an opposition – between nonviolence/civil resistance as a technique of conflict aiming to win (as expressed by Ackerman and Kruegler and as is common in the 'functional alternative' school) and those who work for conflict resolution, who seek 'win-win' solutions. Gandhi tried to develop a way of combining these approaches. He rejected the term 'passive resistance' upon finding that it 'was too narrowly construed, that it was supposed to be a weapon of the weak, that it could be characterized by hatred, and that it could finally manifest itself as violence'.[36] In his view, the passive resister struggles *against* the opponent, seeks a victory *over* the opponent and sees the end result as a change of relations which will benefit one side and *discredit* the other. Contrary to this, Gandhi posed his idealised notion of *Satyagraha* – 'unflinching adherence to Truth'. *Satya* – ultimate Truth – is many-sided and unknowable. Therefore, while the *Satyagrahi* [practitioner of *Satyagraha*] acts on Truth by refusing cooperation with evil, the other side of that is that s/he is open to learning from the Truth held by the Other and therefore has a commitment to dialogue. For Gandhi, then, conflict resolution/transformation went hand in hand with resistance, non-cooperation with the mutual search for Truth; the solution is not victory for one side but instead tries to include the opponent.[37]

To ask an oppressed people to 'reach out' to their oppressors as human beings is not likely to convince those contemplating or embarked upon armed struggle to adopt a strategy of civil resistance. Nor does it appeal to an occupied nation to ask the population to engage in dialogue with conquerors who have no right to be there. Thus, advocates of 'pragmatic' nonviolence have tended to downplay this aspect of Gandhi's thinking. However, the aftermath of the 1989 'revolutions' in Eastern Europe and various other transitions – from dictatorship in Latin America or from *apartheid* in South Africa – have forced attention more on the vacuum left after the tyrant has been removed, on the conflicts that surface once the repression is ended and on the need to strengthen a social tissue conducive to peaceful cohabitation.

Moreover, the ethnic conflicts that erupted after the Cold War brought an enormous expansion in international interest in conflict resolution, many of whose insights actually tally with Gandhi's apparently more idealistic thinking. In the 1990s, reports such as then UN Secretary General Boutros Boutros-Ghali's *Agenda for Peace*[38] popularised a fuller notion of international conflict intervention than the traditional negotiations and 'good offices'. To the tripartite division of peacekeeping, peacemaking and peacebuilding proposed in earlier years by Johan Galtung,[39] the 1990s added 'peace enforcement' – UN-authorised military intervention. However, many

– including Boutros-Ghali and Kofi Annan (his successor as UN Secretary General and previously Head of Peacekeeping) also saw an essential role for 'civil society', non-governmental organisations (NGOs).[40] Peacemaking cannot be restricted to treating the overt expression of the conflict but has to address its social roots and propose programmes to tackle them. Moreover, it cannot be confined to the leaders of the conflicting parties but rather has to engage other circles in their society, ultimately extending down to grass-roots groups and potential civil leadership, such as among the youth. The recognition that a real resolution of conflict entails transforming relationships of domination and injustice brought a vogue – a considered vogue, not a mindless following of fashion – favouring the term 'conflict transformation' rather than 'conflict resolution'. What many trainers of local groups interested in peace-building also discovered – not only in the Balkans – was that the first need was for a sense of empowerment, the feeling that people can do something to shape the societies in which they live and can change the course of the conflict in which they are caught up.

In short, there is a strong overlap between a local peacebuilding agenda and the agenda of a movement for civil resistance that incorporates a commitment to dialogue with the Other and to trying to find a mutually acceptable solution. The 'local capacities' referred to in peacebuilding reports are likely to be selfsame groups a civil resistance perspective would suggest were constructing the 'great chain of nonviolence'. At the level of overall leadership, this is bound to introduce a number of tensions within a movement that require clarity, especially of strategy and expectations, so that the leadership will not be vulnerable to the drumbeat of war-minded critics. In particular, it is essential to distinguish between negotiations and dialogue in a broader sense.

Negotiations in a narrow sense take place between representatives acting on behalf of constituencies and interests, and are bound by what can be accepted (or what they judge can be accepted) by their community. Any agreement reached tends to reflect the balance of power at work in the situation. Dialogue on the other hand is oriented towards understanding different viewpoints and exploring the boundaries of what is possible: it has the freedom to put to one side political 'realism' and so widen the realm of what can be considered. Impressions gained from dialogue meetings can be fed back into the community and can sometimes be a useful corrective to stereotyped images of the Other. At the same time, the contact can help to prepare the ground for negotiation and play a trust-building role between potential negotiators, recognising that in addition to high level negotiations such as Rambouillet and Dayton, there are many low-level negotiations such as about the use of certain facilities in a community.

Foreign states are often interested in promoting a leadership they find more 'acceptable'. While an inclusive conflict process might seek out 'unheard voices' and encourage them to 'say an unsayable' truth, that is the way for exploratory dialogue – not for negotiation. It is the population not the international third party that has to choose negotiators. It might have been feasible to broker an agreement between Milan Panić and, say, Gazmend Pula of the Kosovo Helsinki Committee, a frequent participant in Track Two events, but neither of them could have carried popular support.

As we saw in Chapter 7, organisers of Track Two dialogue meetings were rather late in coming into action on Kosovo as were intergovernmental efforts at 'third party' involvement after the end of the CSCE mission. However, even since the establishment of the UN Mission of Implementation in Kosovo (UNMIK), bodies such as the US Institute for Peace have played a useful role in creating an environment for fruitful discussion.[41]

In Chapter 7, I argued that the nonviolent movement in Kosovo should have engaged more with the new international thinking about preventive strategies of conflict intervention, making detailed suggestions to channel that international interest. However, any form of conflict intervention by an international third party is complicated by a host of issues. In addition to the general questions of 'good practice' addressed for many years by international 'development' organisations, there are the complications of conflict between a variety of possible roles and forms of action – the impartial arbitrator, the non-partisan facilitator, the human rights monitor answerable to higher international standards, the neutral peacekeeper (doggedly standing between two sides no matter whether one, the other, or both are committing atrocities), the expert consultant, the trainer or the psycho-social counsellor. Few of those roles combine easily. Those primarily involved in mediation are often accused of ignoring issues of power and injustice, hence of siding with the status quo or the powers-that-be and therefore against movements struggling against oppression and injustice.[42]

The path of confidence building is full of potholes, especially faced with a regime with the record of manipulation, brinkmanship and bad faith of the Milošević regime. Therefore conflict intervention needs a shrewd analysis of the power-political realities in the situation. Unfortunately, some practitioners 'seek the best' in an interlocutor to the point of wilful naïvety. As a negative example, I would argue that while the Transnational Foundation for Peace and Future Research has made numerous potentially useful suggestions regarding Kosovo, these have been vitiated by its determination to present the best that can be said about the regime along with the maximum that can be said about the international 'unfairness' to it.[43] Of course, the media script for Kosovo was dangerously simplistic, but its basic truth was this: 'The vast majority of the population of Kosovo are oppressed by the criminal regime of Milošević.' Not one word of that sentence can be denied. Of course, there should be a search for other starting points from which to resolve a problem and an effort to include a variety of perceptions, but these should not distract from this immediate experience of a population's everyday life.

While I am convinced that 'conflict resolution' (and even more 'conflict transformation') approaches have an important contribution to make in many situations, and I hope sometimes a decisive contribution, there are no panaceas in conflict. In particular, approaches based on dialogue and on the mutual search to satisfy human needs have to be accompanied by forms of pressure on power-holders, and – just as family counsellors sometimes recommend separation rather than continued cohabitation – so in the case of conflicts within states, there are times for a peaceful divorce.

EARLY WARNING, CIVIL RESISTANCE AND SMALL NATIONS

Civil resistance has a special appeal to 'small nations', partly because they lack other means to pursue their aspirations. As Ackerman and Kruegler have put it:

> The sheer cost of losing an ethnic conflict is so high that many leaders will be loath to escalate fights beyond their capacity to control costs for their own people. They may want to garner for their struggle the advantages of legitimacy and international support that sometimes comes with adopting a nonviolent approach.[44]

The Unrepresented Nations and Peoples Organisation (UNPO) recognised this in their 1997 conference on 'Nonviolence and Conflict: Conditions for Effective Peaceful Change'.[45]

The war in Kosovo stands as an indictment of international confusion on the right to self-determination and of the inadequacy of international preventive mechanisms, an indictment of international policy forged through media manipulation, and on media values that determine that, as Belgrade Women in Black put it when journalists were falling over each other in pursuit of the 'shadowy' UÇK, 'Nonviolence is not News'.

One of those moved by the disintegration of Yugoslavia to reflect on the difficult question of whether outside governments should encourage or restrain the break-up of states is Michael Ignatieff.

In retrospect, Western governments should have informed the nationalist leaderships of the Balkans in the late 1980s that a peaceful dissolution of the Yugoslav federation was possible, but that any attempt to transfer populations or alter republic boundaries by force would be met with economic and military sanctions, including the use of selective air strikes ... The correct moment to shift Western policy is obvious only in hindsight.[46]

This emphasis on action at a 'correct moment' that can only be discerned in hindsight offers no policy guidelines but leaves interstate action hostage to the caprices of international media attention, domestic influences (including elections and sexual scandals) and other forms of opportunism. Moreover, the early military threat – this Ignatieff suggests for the late 1980s, early in the nationalist mobilisation, when the only accusations of 'forced emigration' were being made not against but by Serbs – runs against the instinct to make a graduated response of threats or sanctions in proportion to the offence perceived. Dismayed that the graduated military response in Bosnia prolonged the war, helping the victims to survive without combating the main aggressor, Ignatieff damns half-measures and draws the conclusion either to stay out or to up the military ante.

An alternative in 1990 would have been for the CSCE (as it then was) to have been charged with setting up a framework for negotiating the future of Yugoslavia, including its possible peaceful dissolution. This could have been accompanied both by the deployment of international observers to the various flashpoints in

212 Civil Resistance in Kosovo

Yugoslavia and a warning of 'firm action' (meaning a range of non-military sanctions) against those who tried to transfer population or change borders by force. In turn, this would have meshed with a proposal elaborated during the war in Croatia by intellectuals from every republic, initiated by the Zagreb philosopher and UJDI leader Žarko Puhovski: they proposed an internationally monitored ceasefire and a three-year suspension of federal institutions during which Yugoslavia's future could be negotiated.[47]

Continuing his reflections, Ignatieff suggests that the acid test for whether a right to secession is backed internationally is 'if minority and majority have slaughtered each other in the recent past', provided that the territory claimed is 'defensible and economically viable' and the seceding party guarantees minority rights. Writing at a time when nonviolence still held sway in Kosovo, Ignatieff – later a vocal supporter of the NATO bombing – does not touch on the issue of Kosovo's self-determination. Presumably in view of the history since 1912 Kosovo would have satisfied his criteria of 'a history of bad blood – of real and recurrent killing', but there is a real danger that a criterion requiring 'slaughter' to justify international action militates against responding to civil resistance with effective preventive action. It could be a recipe for those who wish to provoke war.

In deriving his conditions from *realpolitik* rather than international standards or international law, Ignatieff further penalises those who refuse to take up arms with his criteria of 'defensibility': Kosovo sought independence not on the basis of being 'defensible' but of being non-aggressive – that is, demilitarised, neutral and with open borders. Similarly his economic criterion needs to take account of the fact that many areas that claim self-determination complain that for years their economy has been distorted by exploitation or central government policy.[48] While Kosovo's natural resources should make it economically viable in the medium term, it will take some years to rectify its mal-development.

The lack of consistency in international response has encouraged political opportunism and military adventurism, especially but not only on the parts of Milošević and Tudjmann and their sidekicks. The alternative is not to base politics in the shifting sands of *realpolitik* and diplomatic improvisation, but to clarify principles and processes, to offer frameworks. If we are in a Hobbesian world of the war of all against all, the response is not ad-hockery and making early and powerful military threats – which presumably if unsuccessful can only escalate to yet more powerful weapons – but to establish and insist on standards. Prevention is not a matter of prescience but of devising guidelines and preparing tools appropriate to types of situation that are predictable.

Prevention, along with fascination about a remarkable movement of civil resistance, was my entry point for involvement in the Kosovo issue. Why was the war most warned about not prevented? Part of the answer is greater clarity in interstate standards and procedures over self-determination. In the absence of a UN Commission on Self-Determination, the proper interstate framework for managing international-social conflict in Europe should be a fully resourced OSCE, with strengthened capacities for mounting major preventive missions (the type it was incapable of sending to Kosovo in 1998), for assessing claims for self-determination according to principles not conjunctural interests and for monitoring the protection of minorities.

Another partial answer is an enhanced international capacity for preventive civilian deployment, playing a range of peacebuilding roles – from human rights advocates to civil society capacitators. Those who in the 1990s prioritised funding for the military alliance NATO over funding for the civilian OSCE created a situation that left them short of non-military means when they, belatedly, wanted them (in October 1998). At the end of 1999, there are 325 international agencies registered in Kosovo, around 48,000 international soldiers and 4,700 international civilian police – a formidable international presence among a population of around 2 million. A fraction of this commitment at an earlier point – at the time of Dayton the deployment of even 200 international civilian staff with a human rights monitoring and peacebuilding brief – would have made a dramatic difference. The *humanitarian* presence increased after Dayton and even more after Drenica, but the idea that an intergovernmental body – presumably the OSCE – should try to coordinate a design for 'an infrastructure for peacebuilding' and negotiate its implementation was simply not present.

The war in Croatia – where the presence of 'ice-cream men' (the white-suited EC Monitoring mission) sometimes provided the occasion for hostilities – should have ended any illusion that there is something automatically preventive or inhibiting about an international civilian presence. Internationals can also make useful hostages. The modes for preventive civilian deployment need as much sophistication and theorising as other forms of conflict intervention.[49] They need 'framework principles',[50] they need an appropriate concept, clarity of purpose and role together with the skills, cultural understanding and, above all, relationships of trust with local bodies.

The anguish over Bosnia in the 1990s has reshaped NATO thinking and capacity; it also converted voices for peace and disarmament into hawks for military intervention. The anguish there should be over Kosovo – a more protracted if less bloody experience – should cause people to reflect on the failure of prevention, the failure to esteem and reward those who rejected the war option.

Appendix I: Tables

Table 1: Kosovo Census Data: 1948, 1953, 1961, 1971, 1981, 1991

	1948		1953		1961		1971		1981		1991	
	Pop	%	Pop	%	Pop	%	Pop	%	Pop	%	Pop	%
Albanians	498,242	68.5	524,559	64.9	646,805	67.1	916,168	73.7	1,226,736	77.4	1,607,690*	82.2
Serbs	171,911	23.6	189,869	23.5	227,016	23.6	228,264	18.4	209,498	13.2	195,301	10.0
Montenegrins	28,050	3.9	31,343	3.9	37,588	3.9	31,555	2.5	27,028	1.7	20,045	1.0
Muslims (Slav)	9,679	1.3	6,241	0.8	8,026	0.8	26,357	2.1	58,562	3.7	57,408	2.9
Gypsies	11,230	1.5	11,904	1.5	3,202	0.3	14,593	1.2	34,126	2.2	42,806	2.2
Turks	1,315	0.2	34,583	4.3	25,784	2.7	12,244	1.0	12,513	0.8	10,838	0.6
Croats	5,290	0.7	6,201	0.8	7,251	0.8	8,264	0.7	8,717	0.6	8,161	0.4
Others	2,103	0.3	3,441	0.4	8,316	0.9	6,248	0.5	7,260	0.4	12,498	0.6
Total	727,820		808,141		963,988		1,243,693		1,584,440		1,954,747	

* Estimate of Kosovo Albanians by Federal Institute for Statistics based on data on natural augmentation and migrations since 1981.
(Where columns of percentages do not add up to 100% this is a result of rounding figures to the first decimal point.)

Table 2: The economic and social gap between Kosovo and Yugoslavia

	Year	Kosovo	Yugoslavia
Population	1987	1,802,000	22,499,000
Family size	1953	6.24	4.29
	1981	6.92	3.62
Live births per 1,000 inhabitants	1955	43.6	26.9
	1987	29.9	15.3
Infant deaths per 1,000 live births	1955	164.0	112.8
	1987	55.2	26.2
Deaths per 1,000 inhabitants	1955	18.2	11.4
	1987	5.3	9.2
Natural population increase per 1,000	1955	25.4	15.5
	1987	24.7	6.1
Life expectancy: men	1954	48.64	56.92
women		45.29	59.33
men	1987	67.66	68.06
women		71.48	73.23
% of economy based in agriculture	1948	80.9	67.2
	1981	24.6*	19.9
% of people unemployed	1988	36.3	14.2

Per capita income in Kosovo relative to Yugoslav national average:
    48% in 1954
    33% in 1975
    28% in 1980

Adapted from J. Reineck, *The Past as Refuge: Gender, Migration and Ideology among Kosovo Albanians* (PhD dissertation, Berkeley: University of California, 1991), p. 34, n. 8.

* In 1981, although only 24.6% of the economy was agriculturally based, approximately 50% of the population still lived in rural areas.

Appendix II: Notes on Terms, Pronunciation and Glossary

This book normally uses the term 'Kosovo' – still the standard international term for the area known to Albanians as Kosova and referred to by Serbian officials as Kosovo and Metohija (Kosmet for short). Where naming Kosovo Albanian organisations, or speaking of the self-declared Republic of Kosova, I use the term Kosova, while quotations follow the usage in the original. For me the term Kosovar signifies a citizen of Kosovo of whatever nationality. I therefore normally use the term 'Kosovo Albanian' or 'Kosovo Serb'. When this is too cumbersome and the context is clear, you will find the occasional 'Kosovar'. In quotations, 'Kosovar' invariably refers to Kosovo Albanian. Most place names in Kosovo are usually rendered in an Albanian spelling.

The Kingdom of the Serbs, Croats and Slovenes became Yugoslavia in 1929. However, for the sake of simplicity, I use the name 'Yugoslavia' to refer to the state created after the First World War and recreated after the Second World War. The current rump-Yugoslavia, the Federal Republic of Yugoslavia, is referred to as FRY. The term 'Serbs' is often used to cover both 'Serbs' and 'Montenegrins' as has been customary in talking about migration to and from Kosovo. Without apology to Greek sensitivities, I refer to the former Yugoslav Republic of Macedonia as Macedonia. The League of Communists of Yugoslavia (Communist Party up to 1952) is referred to as both the LCY and the Party.

PRONUNCIATION GUIDE

Albanian

c   'ts' as in cats
ç   'ch' as in church
dh   'th' as in this
ë   'uh' as in French *deux*

217

gj   'dg' as in drudge
j   'y' as in 'you'
q   'tj' as in fortune
th   'th' as in thin
x   'dz' as in adze
xh   'j' as in job
y   'ü' as in German *über*

Serbian

c   'ts' as in cats
č   'ch' as in church
ć   'tj' as in fortune
dj   'dg' as in drudge
dž   'j' as in job
j   'y' as in you
lj   'lli' as in million
nj   'n' as in canyon
š   'sh' as in she
ž   'zh' as in pleasure

GLOSSARY

[A] = Albanian   [S] = Serbian

besa	sworn oath, or in specific contexts, truce [A]
burrnia	manliness, or strength of character [A]
četa	band of fighters [S]
četnik	a member of such a band
Četnik	specifically used of Draža Mihailović's forces in Second World War [S]
durim	endurance [A]
fis	kin, clan [A]
Gheg	dialect used in (or inhabitant of) northern Albania and Kosovo [A]
gjakmarrja	blood feud [A]
hoxha	Muslim religious teacher [A]
kaçak	originally outlaw or bandit; after 1912, Albanian guerrillas [A]

kanuni	code of customary law [A]
korzo	evening promenade [A]
Metohija	monastic lands [S], hence the official name for Kosovo was Kosovo and Metohija (Kosmet) from 1945 to 1968
narod	nation, people [S]
narodnost	nationality [S]
ndëri	honour [A]
pleqëria	council of elders [A]
rreth	social circle [A]
rilindja	awakening, renaissance (also newspaper and publishing house) [A]
Shqiptar	Albanian [A] (*Šiptar* said by Serbs is viewed as a pejorative)
Tosk	dialect used in (or inhabitant of) southern half of Albania [A]
Vidovdan	St Vitus' Day, 28 June – Serb national day, anniversary of 1389 Battle [S]
Zajedno	Together, Serbian opposition coalition 1996–97.

Appendix III: Leading Characters

AGANI, Fehmi	Sacked university lecturer. LDK vice-president and chief negotiator. Delegate at Rambouillet. Assassinated April 1999.
AHMETI, Sevdie	Sacked from national library. One time coordinator of CDHRF. Founder of the Centre for Protection of Women and Children.
ARTEMIJE, Bishop	Head of Orthodox Church in Kosovo.
BERISHA, Sali	President of Albania 1992–97.
BROVINA, Flora	Sacked doctor. Founder League of Albanian Women, currently serving 12 year sentence in prison in Serbia.
BUKOSHI, Bujar	Prime-minister-in-exile Republic of Kosova. Delegate at Rambouillet.
ÇETTA, Anton	Leader of Campaign to Reconcile Blood Feuds.
ĆOSIĆ, Dobrica	Member of LCY Central Committee dismissed for 'nationalism' in 1968. Prominent member of SANU. President of FRY 1992–93.
ČUBRILOVIĆ, Vaso	Author of *The Expulsion of the Albanians*, 1937.
DEMAÇI, Adem	Former political prisoner. Chair of CDHRF 1991–97. Leader of PPK 1997–98. Political Representative of UÇK August 1998 – February 1999.
DJINDJIĆ, Zoran	Serbian oppositionist. Co-leader of *Zajedno* 1996–97.
DOBRUNA, Vjosa	Sacked doctor. One-time president PPK Women's Forum. Founder of the Centre for Protection of Women and Children.
DRAŠKOVIĆ, Vuk	Serbian oppositionist. Co-leader of *Zajedno* 1996–97.
DUGOLLI, Bujar	President of UPSUP 1997–98.

GJERGJ, Don Lush	Catholic priest. Co-leader of Campaign to Reconcile Blood Feuds. President of Mother Theresa Association.
GORANI, Hajrullah	President of BSPK (independent trade union federation).
HOXHA, Enver	President of Albania 1944–85.
HOXHA, Fadil	Partisan. Leading Kosovo Communist. Vice-president of Yugoslavia 1978.
HYSENI, Agim	Teachers' union leader.
HYSENI, Hydajet	Former political prisoner. Vice-president LDK 1995–98. Delegate at Rambouillet.
ISHMAJLI, Rexhep	Sacked university lecturer. Board member of the LDK at various times.
JASHARI, Adem	From Prekaz, killed in March 1998. Symbolic figure for the UÇK.
JASHARI, Kaqusha	Sacked Communist provincial leader. Later leader of faction of Social Democratic Party.
KADARE, Ishmail	Leading Albanian novelist.
KANDIĆ, Nataša	Director, Humanitarian Law Centre, Belgrade.
KELMENDI, Nekibe	Lawyer. Sometime board member of CDHRF. Secretary General of the LDK 1998.
KOSUMI, Bajram	Former political prisoner. Sometime leader of PPK.
KRASNIQI, Jakup	Former political prisoner. Schoolteacher. Local LDK leader in Gllogovc. First spokesperson for the UÇK inside Kosovo. Delegate at Rambouillet.
KURTI, Albin	Vice-president and international spokesperson for UPSUP. Currently serving 15-year prison sentence in Serbia.
MALIQI, Shkëlzen	Sacked university lecturer. Active in UJDI. Co-founder of Social Democratic Party (leader 1991–93). Programme Director of Open Society Fund/Soros 1994–99.
MILOŠEVIĆ, Slobodan	President first of Serbia, then of FRY.
MORANI, Rrahman	Imposed Kosovo Communist leader. Former Interior Minister.
PANIĆ, Milan	Belgrade-born Californian pharmaceuticals magnate. FRY prime minister 1992.

PESIĆ, Vesna	Serbian oppositionist. Co-founder of Centre for Anti-War Action. Co-leader of *Zajedno* coalition 1996–97.
PULA, Gazmend	Sacked university lecturer. Chair of Kosova Helsinki Committee.
PULA-BEQIRI, Lulieta	Leader of faction of Social Democratic Party, 1993–
RANKOVIĆ, Aleksandar	Partisan. Yugoslav Minister of the Interior from 1944. Vice-president from 1963. Purged 1966. Died 1983.
ROGOVA, Igballe	Sacked radio presenter. Co-founder Motrat Qiriazi.
RUGOVA, Ibrahim	President of the Writers' Association. President of the LDK. President of the Republic of Kosova.
QOSJA, Rexhep	Founder and president of the Forum of Albanian Intellectuals.
SARAÇINI-KELMENDI, Afërdita	Sacked radio journalist. Founder of Women's Media Project and Radio 21.
SAVA, Father	Deçan 'cyber-monk' and Serbian voice for peace in Kosovo.
SHALA, Blerim	Leader in Youth Parliament. Editor of *Zëri*. Delegate at Rambouillet.
SKENDERBEG, Gjergj Kastrioti	Fifteenth century Albanian leader.
STATOVCI, Ejup	University Rector 1991–98.
SURROI, Veton	Founder Prishtina UJDI. Leader in Youth Parliament. Founder and publisher of *Koha* and *Koha Ditore*. Delegate at Rambouillet.
TAHIRI, Edita	President LDK Women's Forum. Various times vice-president of the LDK.
THAÇI, Hashim	Student pro-rector 1992. Founder and leader of the UÇK. Delegate at Rambouillet where agreed as prime minister of Republic of Kosova.
TRAJKOVIĆ, Momčilo	Kosovo Serb politician.
VLLASI, Azem	Sacked Kosovo Communist provincial leader.
ZAJOVIĆ, Staša	Co-founder, Women in Black, Belgrade.

Notes and References

INTRODUCTION

1. All quotations from my first visit to Kosovo are from *Peace News*, February 1992.
2. Jacques Semelin, *Unarmed Against Hitler: Civilian Resistance in Europe, 1939–49* (Praeger, 1993), p. 27.
3. Author's interview, Jakup Krasniqi, October 1999. This seems to have been one of several meetings around Kosovo in 1993.

CHAPTER 1: WHEN A DAM BREAKS

1. More like 'the cesspool of unfinished business' in Mark Thompson's phrase, *A Paper House: The Ending of Yugoslavia* (Hutchinson Radius/Vintage, 1992), p. 131.
2. A concept suggested by James C. Scott, *Domination and the Arts of Resistance: Hidden Transcripts* (Yale University Press, 1990). I say 'selected' as there was no new transparency but rather a change in what people concealed.
3. The population estimates (and categories) of the Ottoman, Austro-Hungarian and Serbian authorities vary enormously, normally estimating the Albanian or Albanophone population at between 65 and 80 per cent, and the Serbian or Serbo-Croatian speaking population at between 20 and 35 per cent.
4. Edith Durham, *High Albania* (1909, reprinted by Virago 1985), extract 'In the Debatable Lands' in Robert Elsie (ed.), *Kosovo: In the heart of the powder keg* (Columbia University Press, 1997), p. 326.
5. A Serbian schoolteacher quoted by Noel Malcolm, *Kosovo: A Short History* (Macmillan/New York University Press, 1998), p. 228.
6. Malcolm's rough estimates (there are higher) are 50,000 Muslim arrivals and from 1878 to 1912 60,000 departing Serbs, pp. 229–30.
7. Tucović advocated a Balkan federation of equal states, including an Albania unified with Kosovo. An Albanian translation of his *Serbia and Albania* was published in Prishtina in the new political climate in 1968.
8. Leo Freundlich, 'Albania's Golgotha: Indictment of the exterminators of the Albanian people' (1913), translated by Robert Elsie in Elsie (ed.), *Kosovo: In the heart of the powder keg*, p. 334. Others made the same point. Leon Trotsky, a newspaper correspondent in the region, at first heard that 'thugs and robbers' in the army were to blame for the Serbian atrocities. Later, however, he learnt that Belgrade saw them as 'necessities of state'. *The War Correspondence of Leon Trotsky: The Balkan Wars*

1912–1913 (Pathfinder, 1991), pp. 120 and 267. In 1914 a Carnegie commission reached a similar conclusion:

> Houses and whole villages reduced to ashes, unarmed and innocent populations massacred ... such were the means which were employed and are still being employed by the Serb-Montenegrin soldiery, with a view to the entire transformation of the ethnic character of regions inhabited exclusively by Albanians.

The Other Balkan Wars: A 1913 Carnegie Endowment Inquiry in Retrospect With a New Introduction and Reflections on the Present Conflict by George Kennan (Carnegie Endowment, 1993), p. 151.

9. Kjell Magnusson, 'The Serbian Reaction: Kosovo and Ethnic Mobilization Among Serbs', in *Nordic Journal of Soviet and East European Studies*, Vol. 4:3 (1987), p. 24.
10. The 1921 census recorded the population of Kosovo as 436,929, of whom 64.1 per cent had Albanian as their mother tongue (generally accepted to be an under-estimate).
11. From *četa*, meaning armed band.
12. Malcolm, *Kosovo: A Short History*, p. 282: 'just over 13,000 families, perhaps 70,000 people altogether'. Miranda Vickers, *Between Serb and Albanian: A History of Kosovo* (Christopher Hurst/Columbia University Press,1998), p. 105: '10,877 families in the two waves of settlement 1922–29 and 1933–38'. For the incoming settlers 330 settlements and villages were built with 12,689 houses, 46 schools and 32 churches. Hivzi Islami, 'Demographic Reality of Kosovo' in Dušan Janjić and Shkëlzen Maliqi (eds), *Conflict or Dialogue: Serbian-Albanian relations and integration of the Balkans* (Subotica, 1994), p. 44, cites Milan Obradović: 'over 11,000 Serbian families with about 54,000 members and 12,000 individual colonists'.
13. Gjon Bisaku, Shtjefën Kurti and Luigi Gashi, 'The Situation of the Albanian Minority in Yugoslavia: Memorandum presented to the League of Nations (1930)' in Elsie (ed.), *Kosovo: In the heart of the powder keg*, pp. 361–94.
14. Some Albanians suggest half a million. Michel Roux, *Les Albanais en Yougoslavie: minorité nationale, territoire et développement* (Maison des Sciences de l'Homme, 1992), p. 223, estimates 77,000 for Muslim emigration from Kosovo. Malcolm, *Kosovo: A Short History*, p. 286, faults this for relying on the 1921 census; he suggests between 90,000 and 150,000.
15. All quotations taken from Vaso Čubrilović, 'The Expulsion of the Albanians: Memorandum presented in Belgrade on 7 March 1937', retranslated by Robert Elsie in Elsie (ed.), *Kosovo: In the heart of the powder keg*, pp. 400–24. Čubrilović became a senior figure in the Serbian Academy of Arts and Sciences (SANU).
16. Malcolm, *Kosovo: A Short History*, p. 294.
17. Giovanni Lorenzoni, quoted in Tommaso Di Franceso and Giacomo Scotti, 'Sixty Years of Ethnic Cleansing', *Le Monde Diplomatique*, May 1999.

18. Malcolm, *Kosovo: A Short History*, pp. 305 and 313. Dušan Bataković, 'The Serbian-Albanian conflict: an historical perspective', Ger Duijzings, Dušan Janjić and Shkëlzen Maliqi (eds), *Kosovo-Kosova: Confrontation or Coexistence* (University of Nijmegen Peace Research Centre, 1997), p. 7, suggests a figure of 100,000 for the whole war.

19. Some Serbs attribute this rise to immigration from Albania – in the late 1980s, some claimed that 260,000 Albanians settled in Yugoslavia in the period 1941–48. Malcolm, *Kosovo: A Short History*, p. 313, dismisses this claim as 'pure fantasy', stating that only 'a few thousand people' moved from Albania to Kosovo. Islami, 'Demographic Reality of Kosovo', p. 43, reports that the 1981 census showed that only 3,311 Kosovo residents had originally come from abroad, of these 1,543 from Albania. Vickers, *Between Serb and Albanian*, p. 123, reports that Italians projected resettling 'up to 72,000 Albanians', which may explain Bataković's use ('The Serbian Albanian Conflict', p. 7) of the figure of 75,000 Albanian settlers. C. von Kohl and W. Libal, *Kosovo: Gordischer Knoten des Balkan* (Vienna: Europaverlag, 1992), p. 35, report a figure from the Yugoslav Ministry of the Interior in 1989 of 15,000 settlers. By the late 1980s, Serb suspicion of the manipulation of post-war history under Tito permitted them to believe nationalist propaganda claims that would otherwise have been incredible.

20. The number of 'Turks' registered in Kosovo jumped from 1,315 in the 1948 census to 34,343 in 1953. In the 1950s, around 200,000 people emigrated from Yugoslavia to Turkey – Malcolm, *Kosovo: A Short History*, p. 323; Vickers, *Between Serb and Albanian*, p. 157.

21. Magaš, *The Destruction of Yugoslavia* (London: Verso, 1993), p. 46 n. 54, reports that at the height of the campaign in 1956 some 30,000 people were 'manhandled' and 100 killed. For the whole course of the repression, Islami, 'Demographic Reality of Kosovo', p. 46, reports 'over 50,000 tortured' and 1,909 killed.

22. Malcolm, *Kosovo: A Short History*, p. 320, reports that in 1956 Udba officers in Kosovo were 58 per cent Serb and 28 per cent Montenegrin, only 13 per cent Albanian.

23. Von Kohl and Libal, *Kosovo*, pp. 67–70, quoting from reports to the Holy Synod by Bishop Pavle (later Patriarch Pavle) of the Raška-Prizren diocese in 1959, 1961, 1967 and 1977, and his predecessor in 1954.

24. Quoted by Malcolm, *Kosovo: A Short History*, p. 324.

25. As Duijzings commented:

> On the basis of the census results, 'ethnic keys' were established, pertaining particularly to the regional and local levels of administration [of Yugoslavia]. By means of these ethnic keys, jobs, houses, (key) positions in administration, scholarships etc. were proportionally divided among the different nations and nationalities. Although the system was designed to guarantee a fair distribution of resources and to reduce old ethnic tensions, in many places it was counterproductive. I think in poor, underdeveloped and ethnically mixed regions in the south, it stimulated or at least kept alive ethnic rivalry.

The consequence was the creation (or continuation) of a political arena in which ethnic affiliation was of primary importance. Ger Duijzings, 'Egyptians in Kosovo and Macedonia', E. Hardten, A. Stanislavljević and D. Tsakiris (eds), *Der Balkan in Europa* (Frankfurt, 1996), p. 114.

26. There were later various accounts of nepotism – a product of Albanian kinship systems – within the Kosovo LCY. Magnusson, *The Serbian Reaction*, p. 12, n. 38.
27. Quoted by Magnusson, ibid., p. 5.
28. Magaš, *The Destruction*, pp. 193–4.
29. In 1968 it became legal in Kosovo (but not in Macedonia) to raise the flag of Albania (the Skenderbeg double-headed eagle, plus Communist star).
30. Srdjan Bogosavljević, 'A Statistical Picture of Serbian-Albanian Relationships' in Janjić and Maliqi (eds), *Conflict or Dialogue*, p. 23. Bogosavljević gives the figure of 70,000 for 'net migration'. He notes information based on censuses 'fail to reflect all migration modalities' and 'information is lost on people who move several times' or who die between censuses.
31. Malcolm, *Kosovo: A Short History*, p. 330, citing Hivzi Islami, 'Demografski problemi Kosova i njihovo tumačenje', in S. Gaber and T. Kuzmanić (eds), *Zbornik Kosovo – Srbija – Jugoslavija* (Ljubljana, 1989), reports that 111,828 Serbs had moved to Serbia from Bosnia and 110,704 from Croatia. One might add that, whereas the Serbian population of Kosovo in 1981 was 209,000, there were 1,321,000 Serbs in Bosnia and 532,000 in Croatia.
32. The job to ethnicity ration in 1968 was Serbs 1:4, Montenegrins 1:3, Turks 1:7, Albanians 1:17 – Malcolm, *Kosovo: A Short History*, p. 326 – and in 1980 Serbs 1:5, Albanians 1:11. Eggert Hardten, 'Administrative Units and Municipal Reforms in Kosovo', in Duijzings et al. (eds), *Kosovo-Kosova*, p. 161. Von Kohl and Libal, *Kosovo*, p. 53, note that in 1985 when Albanians constituted 77.5 per cent of the population, of 600 persons holding jobs in Kosovo, 109 were Albanians, 228 were Serbs and 258 Montenegrins.
33. In 1971, the University of Prishtina set a quota allowing twice as many Albanian as Serbian students to enrol, although Serbian high school graduates in Kosovo outnumbered Albanians. The quota was 2,250 Albanian and 1,105 Serb students when there were 2,873 Albanian high school graduates and 3,985 Serbian and Montenegrin. Hardten, Administrative Units, p. 170, n. 15. In mitigation, the university could plead that no other Yugoslav university offered Albanian-language teaching, that there remained generations of unemployed high-school graduates in Kosovo still seeking further education – or that in 1968–69 it admitted 657 Albanians as against 799 Serbs and Montenegrins and only one Albanian medical student. Sami Repishti, 'Human Rights and the Albanian Nationality in Yugoslavia', in Oskar Gruenwald and Karen Rosenblum-Cale (eds), *Human Rights in Yugoslavia* (Irvington, 1986), p. 248.
34. Hardten, Administrative Units, p. 170 n. 15.
35. 41 per cent gave 'indirect pressure' from Albanians as a reason for migration, and 21 per cent 'direct pressure', ranging from verbal abuse

(8.5 per cent) to material damage (7.5 per cent) and personal injury (5 per cent). Malcolm, *Kosovo: A Short History*, p.331.

36. One of the SANU researchers, while re-affirming that this discrimination pointed to the creation of an ethnically 'pure' Kosovo, complained that:

> the problem was media-developed as an ethnic conflict, essentially eternal and beyond resolution ... The political misuse and abuse of facts on migration contributed to either the excessive growth of passions (among the nationalist opposition) or to doubt or outright rejection of these facts (especially by a part of the civil opposition).

Marina Blagojević,'The Other Side of the Truth: Migrations of Serbs from Kosovo', in Duijzings et al. (eds), *Kosovo-Kosova*, pp. 74, 76, 78.

37. Srdja Popović, 'A Pattern of Domination', *Balkan War Report,* April/May 1993, pp. 6–7.

38. Magaš, *The Destruction*, p. 62.

39. From 1981–87, there were five confirmed inter-ethnic murders in Kosovo, two by Albanians, three by Serbs. Darko Hudelist, 'The Kosovo Autumn of 1987', *Start* (Zagreb), 31 October 1987, quoted by Arshi Pipa, 'The Political Situation of the Albanians in Yugoslavia, with particular attention to the Kosovo Problem: A Critical Approach', *East European Quarterly*, XXIII, No. 2, June 1989, p. 180, n. 23. Also Azem Vllasi in *Vreme NDA*, 25 September 1995.

From 1979–87, only 31 rapes or attempted rapes of Serbian women by Albanian men were reported in Kosovo, and in 1988–89 none at all, von Kohl and Libal, *Kosovo*, p. 70. They also report that, while in inner Serbia there were 2.43 reported rapes or attempted rapes for every 10,000 men, the rate in Kosovo was 0.96, and mostly within the same nationality. The figures Hudelist obtained from the Ministry of the Interior were, between 1982 and 1986, 16 Serbian/Montenegrin women were raped by Albanians and there were 19 attempted rapes.

40. L. Silber and A. Little, *Yugoslavia: The Death of a Nation* (Harmondsworth: Penguin, 1995, 1996, 1997), p. 36, n. 8. Later there were to be charges that Ranković's associates were active in the nationalist agitation in Kosovo, especially in the group *Božur*, and that the authors of Belgrade press stories 'exposing Albanian nationalism and irredentism' were often former police with access to secret files. Magaš, *The Destruction*, p. 109.

41. See Julie A. Mertus, *Kosovo: How Myths and Truths started a War* (Berkeley: University of California, 1999), pp. 100–14. While recounting details of the investigation, her main concern is to show the impact of this story.

42. Malcolm, *Kosovo: A Short History*, pp. 329 and 339. On the rape of nuns, the leading nun – the Mother Superior at Peć – told an international delegation to Kosovo in 1991 that she knew of no cases of nuns being raped, von Kohl and Libal, *Kosovo*, p. 70.

43. Silber and Little, *Yugoslavia*, p. 35.

44. Magnusson, *The Serbian Reaction*, pp. 14–15.

45. Magaš, *The Destruction*, p. 49–52.

46. Kosta Mihailović and Vasilije Krestić, *Memorandum of the Serbian Academy of Sciences and Arts: Answers to Criticisms* (Belgrade, 1995).

47. Silber and Little, *Yugoslavia*, pp. 37–8. Šolević is not himself a Kosovo Serb but is from Niš.
48. See Mertus, *Kosovo*, pp. 145–64, for a full discussion. Silber and Little, *Yugoslavia*, p. 41, report 10,000 attended the funeral of the only Serb killed. The bereaved father pleaded for them to stop abusing his son's death. Kelmendi's act was treated as part of a conspiracy and eight Kosovo Albanian recruits were sentenced to between two years and 20 years in prison.
49. Ivan Colović, 'Nacionalismos en los estadios de Yugoslavia', in Santiago Sergurola (ed.), *Fútbol y Pasiones Políticas* (Editorial Debate, 1999), pp. 143–4.
50. Vladeta Jerotić in *Theoria* (1988, nos 3–4, p. 120), quote by Muhammedin Kullashi, 'The production of hatred in Kosova (1981–91)', in Duijzings et al. (eds), *Kosovo-Kosova*, p. 68.
51. Michel Roux, *Les Albanais*, p. 381.
52. Muhamedin Kullashi, 'The production of hatred in Kosova (1981–91)', in Duijzings et al. (eds), *Kosovo-Kosova*, p. 58.
53. Renata Salecl, 'The Crisis of Identity and the Struggle for New Hegemony in the Former Yugoslavia', in Ernesto Laclau (ed.), *The Making of Political Identities* (Verso, 1994), p. 213.
54. Quoted by Dušan Janjić in 'National Movements and Conflicts of Serbs and Albanians', in Janjić and Maliqi (eds), *Conflict or Dialogue*, p. 129.
55. Tim Judah, *The Serbs: History, Myth and the Destruction of Yugoslavia* (Yale University Press, 1997), p. 77.
56. Quoted by Judah, ibid., p. 66. In contrast, 'the Islamised Albanians are the rudest people and much more apt to violence and oppression than the Ottomans', quoted by Ali Jakupi, *Two Albanian States and National Unification* (Institute of Economics, Prishtina, 1997), p. 119.
57. *Vreme NDA*, 4 July 1994.
58. Misha Glenny, *The Fall of Yugoslavia* (Penguin, second edition 1993), p. 35.
59. RFE/RL, *Radio Free Europe Research*, Vol. 14, No. 29, 21 July 1989, pp. 7–9.
60. RFE/RL, *Radio Free Europe Research*, Vol. 14, No. 29, 21 July 1989, pp. 7–9.
61. Quoted in Brian Hall, *The Impossible Country: A Journey through the Last Days of Yugoslavia* (Penguin, 1994), p. 248.

CHAPTER 2: THE ALBANIANS IN KOSOVO

1. Under the *devsirme* system, every few years officials would tour villages and forcibly recruit teenage boys, perhaps one from every 40 households. Taken to Turkey, they would be taught Turkish and trained as soldiers or servants in the imperial administration. N. Malcolm, *Kosovo: A Short History* (Macmillan/New York University Press, 1998), pp. 95–7.
2. Ali Jakupi, *Two Albanian States and National Unification* (Institute of Economics, Prishtina, 1997), p. 152.
3. Malcolm, *Kosovo: A Short History*, p. 258.
4. Motes calls this 'the first aerial bombardment of civilians'. Mary Motes, *Kosova-Kosovo: Prelude to War, 1966–98* (Redland Press, 1999) p. 14.

5. Quoted in Malcolm, *Kosovo: A Short History*, p. 260. Motes, *Kosova-Kosovo*, p. 14, notes that the king of Montenegro had instructed his subjects not to aid the Great Retreat.

6. The account of the *Kaçak* Movement is based on Malcolm, *Kosovo: A Short History*, pp. 272–8 and Vickers, *Between Serb and Albanian*, pp. 99–102.

7. 'So as not to offend the patriarchal mores of her people', Shota Bejta dressed as a man and assumed a male name, Qerim. Vickers, *Between Serb and Albanian*, p.100.

8. Malcolm, *Kosovo: A Short History*, pp. 269–72.

9. Shkëlzen Maliqi, 'The Albanian Movement in Kosova', in David A. Dyker and Ivan Vejvoda (eds), *Yugoslavia and After: A Study in Fragmentation, Despair and Rebirth* (Longman, 1996), p. 139.

10. Malcolm, *Kosovo: A Short History*, p. 296. The most notorious Albanian body was an SS Division known as 'Skenderbeg', set up towards the end of the war in Kosovo in 1944, responsible for rounding up 281 Jews for deportation in May 1944. It was, however, relatively short-lived and strategically 'insignificant' – Malcolm, ibid., pp. 309–10.

11. Vickers, *Between Serb and Albanian*, p. 122.

12. In April 1941, of the Communist Party's 270 members in Kosovo, a mere 20 were Albanian (Malcolm, ibid., p. 300); by 1942, of 343 members, 52 were Albanians, including 17 returnees from Albania (B. Magaš, *The Destruction of Yugoslavia* (London: Verso, 1993), p. 45, n. 35).

13. Quoted by Sami Repishti, 'Human Rights and the Albanian Nationality in Yugoslavia', in Oskar Gruenwald and Karen Rosenblum-Cale (eds), *Human Rights in Yugoslavia* (Irvington, 1986), p. 248.

14. Repishti, ibid., p. 237.

15. Vickers, *Between Serb and Albanian*, p. 142.

16. Vickers, ibid., p. 143.

17. Malcolm, *Kosovo: A Short History*, p. 312, considers 'exaggerated' the claim of more than 40,000 war dead in Kosovo. Among those executed – 'victims of internal division and the intransigence of the Communists' – were the father and grandfather of Ibrahim Rugova, three weeks old when they were arrested. Ibrahim Rugova, *La Question du Kosovo – entretiens avec Marie-Françoise Allain et Xavier Galmiche* (Fayard, 1994), p. 188.

18. K. Magnusson, 'The Serbian Reaction: Kosovo and Ethnic Mobilization Among Serbs', in *Nordic Journal of Soviet and East European Studies*, Vol 4: 3 (1987), p. 18.

19. Janet Reineck, *The Past as Refuge: Gender, migration, and ideology among the Kosova Albanians* (PhD dissertation, University of California, 1991), p. 13.

20. H.T. Norris, 'Kosova, and the Kosovans: past, present future as seen through Serb, Albanian and Muslim eyes', in G.W. Carter and H.T. Norris (eds), *The changing shape of the Balkans* (University College of London, 1996), p. 17.

21. Norris, ibid., p. 23. There are still Sufi communities in Kosovo today, notably the Bektashi sect.

22. Leonard Fox, 'Introduction' in *Kanuni i Lekë Dukagjinit/The Code of Lekë Dukagjini*, Albanian text collected and arranged by Shtjefën Gjeçov, translated with an introduction by Leonard Fox (Gjonlekaj, New York, 1989), p. xvii.

23. Reineck, *The Past as Refuge*, p. 193.

24. Ishmail Kadare, *Doruntine* (1979). English translation by Jon Rothschild, (Saqi, 1988). The novel is itself inspired by a song in the oral tradition.

25. A 1970 study in the Dukagjin area reported Albanian *zadrugas* with up to 120 members. Vera St. Erlich, 'The Last Big Zadrugas: Albanian extended families in the Kosovo region', in R.F. Byrnes (ed.), *The Zadruga: Essays by Philip E. Mosley and Essays in His Honor* (Notre Dame, Indiana, 1976), p. 245.

26. Reineck, *The Past as Refuge*, p. 56.

27. Gjon Bisaku et al., in R. Elsie (ed.), *Kosovo: In the heart of the powder keg* (Columbia University Press, 1997), pp. 393–4.

28. 'Between Prejudice and Desire', *Let's Invest in Today's Girls – Tomorrow's Women*, Women's Media Project, Prishtina, July 1997, pp. 12–13.

29. Reineck, *The Past as Refuge*, p. 165.

30. Reineck cites figures that 29 per cent of girls who began primary school in 1975 did not reach secondary school, while in 1987 only 50 per cent of the 16,000 girls who finished primary school entered high school – Reineck, *The Past as Refuge*, p. 168.

31. H. Islami, 'Demographic Reality of Kosovo' in Dušan Janjić and Shkëlzen Maliqi (eds), *Conflict or Dialogue: Serbian-Albanian relations and integration of the Balkans* (Subotica, 1994), pp. 36–7, gives figures from the 1981 census: whereas women with secondary school education on average gave birth to 2.24 children, the average for illiterate women was 7.04 children. The overall average for Albanian women in Kosovo was 6.66 children.

32. In 1971, 72.6 per cent of Kosovo migrant workers left their nuclear families behind, compared with 14 per cent of Slovenians. Reineck, *The Past as Refuge*, p. 128.

33. Reineck, ibid., pp. 135–63.

34. *Borba* reported in 1961 that Albania had smuggled 675 agents into Kosovo in the period 1948–60, of whom 115 had been tried in Yugoslav courts. Miranda Vickers, *The Status of Kosovo in Socialist Yugoslavia* (University of Bradford Studies on South Eastern Europe, 1994), p. 18.

35. In 1953 Serbs and Montenegrins were 27 per cent of the population of Kosovo, but comprised 50 per cent of the membership of the Kosovo LCY and held 68 per cent of 'administrative and leading' positions – Malcolm, *Kosovo: A Short History*, p. 323.

36. Repishti, 'Human Rights', p. 242.

37. *Borba*, 21 September 1966, quoted by Repishti, ibid., p. 244.

38. Malcolm, *Kosovo: A Short History*, pp. 321–2.

39. *The Times*, 22 September 1966, quoted by Repishti, 'Human Rights', p. 244.

40. Repishti, ibid., p. 245.

41. Repishti, ibid., p. 247. In contrasting their punishment with Belgrade students who revolted earlier in 1968, Repishti overlooks the fact that

Belgrade students were heavily beaten and some jailed. Or that some Kosovo students had guns. Motes, *Kosova-Kosova*, p. 106.

42. One feature of the rising expectations of Kosovo Albanians in the 1960s was the belief that once their numbers crossed the threshold of 70 per cent of the population, they would gain a republic. Motes, ibid., p. 101.
43. Quoted by T. Judah, *The Serbs: History, Myth and the Destruction of Yugoslavia* (Yale University Press, 1997), p. 151.
44. Rugova, *La Question*, p. 130.
45. Magaš, *The Destruction*, p. 36.
46. 12,226 Kosovo Albanians were members of the LCY in 1953, 27,623 in 1968. Vickers, *Between Serb and Albanian*, p. 319, eventually rising to around 100,000, Mehmet Kraja, *Koha Summary*, 3 May 1995.
47. 'Of these, 89 received prison sentences ranging from one to 15 years and another 503 were charged with making public nationalist statements.' Repishti, 'Human Rights', p. 255.
48. See 'Interview: One Man Accused of being a Ringleader', in J. Mertus, *Kosovo: How Myths and Trusts Started a War* (Berkeley: University of California Press, 1999), pp. 75–86.
49. Repishti, 'Human Rights', p. 256.
50. Vickers, *Between Serb and Albanian*, p. 193.
51. Hugh Poulton, *The Balkans: Minorities and States in Conflict* (Minority Rights Group, London 1991), p. 60.
52. Repishti, 'Human Rights', p. 263.
53. Repishti, ibid., pp. 266–7 – an exception was one group of eleven who had stopped a police van and stolen its firearms.
54. Magaš, *The Destruction*, pp. 6–7.
55. Magaš, ibid., pp. 12–13.
56. Plus '2,358 pamphlets distributed, and 688 authors unmasked', von Kohl and Libal, *Kosovo*, p. 75.
57. See the interviews in Mertus, *Kosovo*.
58. Translated by Robert Elsie in Elsie (ed.), *Kosovo: In the heart of the powder keg*, pp. 105–192.
59. In Brussels in October 1981 and in Stuttgart in January 1982. In reply there were armed attacks in 1982 against the Yugoslavia club in Brussels and the Embassy. Arshi Pipa, 'The Political Situation of the Albanians in Yugoslavia, with particular attention to the Kosovo problem: A Critical Approach', *East European Quarterly*, xxxiii, No. 2, June 1989.
60. By March 1982 some 600 were reported as expelled from the Party (Magaš, p. 9), rising to 1,500 by May 1986 (Magnusson, p. 11) only a few them leaders. Through 'differentiation', a total of 176 school-teachers by 1986 (Magnusson, ibid., p. 11) and 19 university teachers had lost their jobs by 1989.
61. M. Thompson, *A Paper House: The Ending of Yugoslavia* (London: Hutchinson Radius/Vintage, 1992), p. 128. From 1981 until September 1988, official sources recorded that 1,750 ethnic Albanians were convicted of political crimes in regular courts, while over 7,000 were summarily jailed for minor political offences. The military in the same period claimed to discover 241 illegal groups composed of 1,600 ethnic Albanians – Amnesty International EUR/48/08/89.

62. Rugova, *La Question*, p. 118; Zoran Kusovac, 'Another Balkans Bloodbath – Part Two', *Jane's Intelligence Review*, March 1998, p. 9.
63. Vickers, *Between Serb and Albanian*, reports accusations against BK, Zogists and Marxist-Leninist extremists, while Azem Vllasi later blamed the *Sigurimi* (Albanian secret service), Mertus, *Kosovo*, p. 39.
64. Vickers, ibid., p. 207.
65. Pipa, 'The Political Situation', p. 174.
66. Magnusson, *The Serbian Reaction*, p. 18.
67. Marco Dogo, 'National Truths and Disinformation in Albanian-Kosovar Historiography', in Duijzings et al. (eds), *Kosovo-Kosova: Confrontation or Coexistence* (University of Nijmegen Peace Research Centre, 1997) p. 42.
68. Reineck, *The Past as Refuge*, p. 193.

CHAPTER 3: THE TURN TO NONVIOLENCE

1. John Hodgson, 'Kosovo-Anatomy of a Conflict', Visiting Lecture, University of Bradford, 1992.
2. Each constituent unit of socialist Yugoslavia had a Socialist Alliance consisting of associations of youth, workers, etc., meeting at every level through to the federal level. Theoretically this was a channel, alongside the LCY, in which the self-managing 'masses' could involve themselves.
3. Shkëlzen Maliqi, 'Self-Understanding of the Albanians in Nonviolence', in D. Janjić and S. Maliqi (eds), *Conflict or Dialogue: Serbian-Albanian relations and integration of the Balkans* (Subotica, 1994), pp. 240–1, also in Shkëlzen Maliqi, *Kosova – Separate Worlds: reflections and analyses* (MM/Dukagjini, 1998).
4. B. Magaš, *The Destruction of Yugoslavia* (London: Verso, 1993), p. 209.
5. Shkëlzen Maliqi, 'The Albanian Intifada' in Magaš, ibid., pp. 180–1. Maliqi includes the demands in full.
6. Magaš, ibid., p. 231.
7. Maliqi in Magaš, ibid., p. 181.
8. An editor of *Mladina* (Ljubljana), quoted by M. Thompson, *A Paper House: The Ending of Yugoslavia* (London: Hutchinson Radius/Vintage, 1992), p. 138.
9. Magaš, *The Destruction*, p. 188.
10. Maliqi in Magaš, ibid., p. 183.
11. L. Silber and A. Little, *Yugoslavia: the Death of a Nation* (Harmondsworth: Penguin, 1995, 1996, 1997), p. 66. It affronted Serbs that anyone other than they might be the Jews of Yugoslavia.
12. Magaš, *The Destruction*, p. 210.
13. Magaš, ibid., p. 231.
14. *AIM*, 24 May 1997.
15. Mehmet Kraja, *Koha Summary*, 26 April 1995.
16. Amnesty International, *Yugoslavia: Police violence in Kosovo province – the victims*, September 1994, EUR 70/16/94, p. 4.
17. Magaš, *The Destruction*, p. 233.

18. Interview with Rexhep Ishmajli in *Serbie Kosovo: Forces démocratiques et Résistances civiles* (Mouvement pour une Alternative Nonviolente, Paris 1997), p. 88.
19. Mehmet Kraja, *Koha Summary*, 26 April 1995.
20. Magaš, *The Destruction*, pp. 246–7.
21. See Andrew Rigby, *Living the Intifada* (Zed, 1991).
22. Magaš, *The Destruction*, p. 253.
23. Maliqi, *Kosova: Separate Worlds*, p. 29.
24. Ibrahim Rugova, *La Question du Kosovo: Entretiens réalisés par Marie-Françoise Alain et Xavier Galmiche* (Paris: Fayard, 1994), p. 86, mentions Dobrica Ćosić as one of the main accusers.
25. Rugova, ibid., p. 163.
26. Mehmet Kraja, *Koha Summary*, 3 May 1995.
27. Magaš, *The Destruction*, p. 250.
28. Magaš, ibid., p. 251.
29. Names listed by *CDHRF Bulletin*, October–December 1997.
30. Maliqi, *Kosova: Separate Worlds*, p. 231 (interview with Momčilo Petrović).
31. Mehmet Kraja, *Koha Summary*, 3 May 1995.
32. What was called 'Marxist-Leninism' in Kosovo would not be recognised as such elsewhere. More, it was an identification with Albania.
33. Magaš, *The Destruction*, p. 250.
34. Ilaz Bylykbashi, 555 ... *Kronikë 1981–1995* (Rilindja, 1996), pp. 138–40.
35. CDHRF Memorandum to the Forty-Fourth Session of the UN Committee on Human Rights in New York, April 1992.
36. Cited in Rugova, *La Question*, p. 72, from *Borba*, 28–29 September 1991.
37. This incident was the subject of a Granada TV 'World in Action' documentary, reported in *Kosova Communication* 244, 5 December 1995. Mertus, *Kosovo*, pp. 187–98, reviews a variety of explanations.
38. *Vjesnik*, 4 April 1990, cited by Mertus, *Kosovo*, p. 189.
39. D. Janjić, 'National Movements and Conflicts of Serbs and Albanians', in D. Janjić and S. Maliqi (eds), *Conflict or Dialogue: Serbian Albanian relations and integration of the Balkans* (Subotica, 1994), p. 156.
40. Pax Christi International, *Kosovo: The Conflict Between Serbs and Albanians* (Pax Christi International, 1995), p. 16; H. Poulton, *The Balkans: Minorities and States in Conflict* (London: Minority Rights Group, 1991), p. 68.
41. Shkëlzen Maliqi, 'The Politics of Resistance', *Helsinki Citizens Assembly Newsletter*, Fall 1992, p. 5.
42. Rugova, *La Question*, pp. 134–5.
43. The account here is based on two interviews with Anton Çetta by members of the Mouvement pour une Alternative Nonviolente and the Movimento Nonviolento, and my own interview with Lala Vula-Meredith, May 1999. 'Intervention de M Anton Çetta, le 17 août 1993 a Prishtina', in *La résistance civile au Kosovo: Rapport de mission de la délégation du MAN* (Mouvement pour une Alternative Nonviolente, Paris 1994 – MAN 1994), pp. 49–61, and 'Anton Çetta: focolai di pace: intervista da parte di un delegation Italian (agosto 1994)', in *Kossovo: Conflitto e riconciliazione in un crocevia balcanico – Religioni e Società, 29*

settembre-dicembre 1997 (Rosenberg & Seiller), pp. 166–75. Bylykbashi photographed smaller meetings at the village level as well as the massive gathering at Verrat e Llukës, pp. 160–3, as did Vula-Meredith. Melissa Llewellyn-Davies made a documentary 'Forgiving the Blood', shown in the series 'Under the Sun' on BBC TV, 18 September 1992.

44. M. Thompson, *A Paper House: The Ending of Yugoslavia* (London: Hutchinson Radius/Vintage, 1992), p. 141.

45. Sami Repishti, 'Human Rights and the Albanian Nationality in Yugoslavia', in Oskar Gruenwald and Karen Rosenblum-Cale (eds), *Human Rights in Yugoslavia* (Irvington, 1986) p. 250.

46. Ishmail Kadare, *Broken April* (Saqi, 1990).

47. Mary C. Motes, 'The Blood Feud in Kosovo: Early Attempts at Eradication', published in translation in *Religioni e Società*, 29, p. 155.

48. Of the 511 blood feud killings from 1957–68, only one was committed by a secondary school graduate and more than 31 per cent of the perpetrators were illiterate.

49. Franz Muenzel, 'What Does International Public Law Have to Say About Kosovar Independence', (mimeo, no date), note 32.

50. *Amnesty International Report 1991*, p. 254.

51. Rugova, *La Question*, p. 132.

52. Mirie Rushani, 'La vendetta e il perdon, nella tradizione consuetudinaria albanese', *Religioni e Società 29*, p. 150.

53. Rushani, ibid., p. 152.

54. Zoran Kusovac, 'Another Balkans bloodbath? Part One', *Jane's Intelligence Review*, February 1998.

55. Former police inspector, Dragan Mladenović, talking to Belgrade's independent Radio-B92 about the connection between the Ministry of the Interior (MUP) and both organised and political crime. *AIM*, 27 July 1994.

56. Marcus Tanner – *Independent on Sunday*, 21 June 98 – says Rugova told him of an approach from Tudjmann. In *La Question*, p. 128, Rugova denies that Croatia offered arms. Other accounts suggest an offer to Bujar Bukoshi, prime-minister-in-exile.

57. The Yugoslav concept of General People's Defence did not treat territorial forces as a mere adjunct to the army. It was envisaged that in wartime they could play a variety of roles – both frontal and partisan, both lightly armed and with tanks and heavy artillery. Adam Roberts, *Nations in Arms: The Theory and Practice of Territorial Defence* (Chatto and Windus, 1976), Ch. 6.

58. Hajzer Hajzeraj was former Chief of Territorial Defence in Kosovo. At his trial in 1994, he was accused of being Minister of Defence and trying to build up a 40,000-strong defence structure. See Fabian Schmidt, 'Show Trials in Kosovo', *Transition*, 3 November 1995. In 1999, Hajzeraj told *Zëri* that such preparations had begun 'at the end of 1990' and that during 1991–93 he was Minister of Defence of Kosovo, authorised by Rugova and having had direct meetings with LDK vice-president, the late Fehmi Agani. *Zëri Digest* 1709, 2 October 1999.

59. James Pettifer, *The Times*, 9 December 1992; Aleksandar Vasović, 'Braced (and Armed) for Confrontation', *Balkan War Report*, January 1993.

60. Rugova, *La Question*, p. 119.
61. Rugova, ibid., p. 130.
62. Maliqi, *'Self-Understanding'*, p. 239.
63. Rugova, *La Question*, p. 192.
64. Shkëlzen Maliqi, 'Albanians Between East and West', pp. 118–20 in Duijzings et al. (eds), *Kosovo-Kosova*. Muslims and Catholics coexist within a number of Kosovo families.
65. *Index on Censorship*, Vol. 19, no. 8, September 1990, p. 13.
66. Thompson, *A Paper House*, p. 139.
67. J. Reineck, *The Past as Refuge: Gender, Migration and Ideology among Kosovo Albanians* (PhD dissertation, Berkeley: University of California, 1991), p. 202.
68. Rugova, *La Question*, p. 126, showing ignorance of Gandhi and Gandhi's own preference for the term *Satyagraha* (unflinching adherence to truth) to 'passive resistance'.
69. Maliqi, *Kosova: Separate Worlds*, pp. 101–4.
70. Mehmet Kraja, *Koha Summary*, 10 May 1995.
71. Maliqi – born 1947, the son of a prominent Communist (Kosovo Minister of the Interior from June 1981 to 1984) – was educated in Belgrade and participated in the 1968 Belgrade demonstrations, not in those in Kosovo in 1968 or 1981. Surroi – born 1961, the son of a Yugoslav ambassador – was educated in the USA, Bolivia and Mexico.

CHAPTER 4: TWO SOVEREIGNTIES

1. Dobrica Ćosić, Vuk Drašković and sections of the Orthodox Church could be taken as representative of heartfelt nationalism, Milošević of a power-political project, and Željko Ražnjatović (Arkan) of crime.
2. Nekibe Kelmendi, 'Kosova under the burden of discriminatory laws', http://www.kosova-state.org/English/Kosova_under_the_burden_of_the_s.html.
3. Reducing the *Albanian* birth rate.

    In tandem with the cult of blood and soil, the new Serbian nationalists also summoned to life the symbolic mediaeval figure of the *Mother Jugović* – the long-suffering brave, stoic mother of nine, offering her children up to death in defence of the fatherland ... Rada Trajković of the Association of Kosovo Serbs [has said]: 'For each soldier fallen in the war against Slovenia, Serbian women must give birth to 100 more sons.'

    Staša Zajović, 'Patriarchy, language and national myth', *Peace News*, March 1992. On Vidovdan 1993, local authorities awarded medals to Kosovo Serb mothers with four or more children. *Politika*, 30 June 1993, cited in *Kosova Communication* 119, 6 July 1993.
4. Kosova Information Center, *Serbian Colonization and Ethnic Cleansing of Kosova: Documents and Evidence* (Prishtina, 1993), p. 98 (translation amended).

5. *AIM*, 30 May 1994.
6. H. Poulton, *The Balkans: Minorities and States in Conflict* (London: Minority Rights Group, 1991), p. 70.
7. Ilaz Bylykbashi, *555 ... Kronkikë 1981–1995* (Rilindja, 1996), p. 104. Despite police roadblocks, tens of thousands attended the funeral.
8. *Amnesty International Report 1992*, p. 280. In February 1991 they were sentenced to between two and four and a half years of imprisonment but released on appeal. Amnesty then lost the trail of this particular case.
9. BSPK, *Report on the General Economic and Social Conditions Created after the Application of Repressive measures by the Serbian authorities on the Companies and Institutions of Kosova* (mimeo, Prishtina, August 1991) and BSPK, *National and Social Discrimination of the Albanian Workers in Kosova* (mimeo, no date), collected November 1997. From October 1993 onwards, most accounts used a figure in the range of 120,000–150,000.
10. Drita Mekuli, 'Kosova Health Service Under Emergency Management', *Kosova Watch*, Vol. 1, No. 1 (Kosova Helsinki Committee), p. 27.
11. More than 630 families were evicted in the period 1990–97, most of them in the early years – *CDHRF Bulletin*, Year VII No. 4, July–September 1997, p. 13.
12. B. Hall, *The Impossible Country: A Journey through the Last Days of Yugoslavia* (Harmondsworth: Penguin, 1994), p. 264.
13. Ibrahim Rexhepi, 'Seven-Year Long Strike: Unemployment as a Political Category', *AIM*, 28 October 1997, describes parallel processes in Ferizaj from January 1990 and Trepça from October 1990. Dismissal notices in the latter case were issued belatedly, after the abolition of the Kosovo labour court.
14. Adil Fetahu, 'Legal Basis for Undertaking Temporary Measures', *Bashkimi Sindikal*, February 1998 (but probably written in late 1992 or early 1993).
15. See Rexhepi, 'Seven-year Long Strike' and Humanitarian Law Centre, 'Spotlight Report No. 16', *Spotlight Report On Human Rights in Serbia and Montenegro* (1996) No. 16, p. 18.
16. I. Rexhepi, ibid.
17. B. Magaš, *The Destruction of Yugoslavia* (London: Verso, 1993), p. 233.
18. When I visited him in 1994, his (Albanian) former deputy, then Dean of Philosophy at the parallel university, arrived to return a book he had recently borrowed. Motes mentions another philosophy lecturer sacked for being an 'Albanian sympathiser'. M. Motes, *Kosova-Kosovo: Prelude to War 1966–1999* (Homestead, Fl: Redland Press, 1999), p. 262.
19. D. Janjić, 'National Movements and Conflicts of Serbs and Albanians', in D. Janjić and S. Maliqi (eds), *Conflict or Dialogue: Serbian-Albanian relations and integration of the Balkans* (Subotica, 1994), p. 153.
20. M. Thompson, *A Paper House: The Ending of Yugoslavia* (London: Hutchinson Radius/Vintage, 1992), p. 145.
21. Jane Kokan, 'Where even toddlers know hatred', *Index on Censorship*, Vol. 19, no. 8, September 1990, pp. 12–13.
22. Miranda Vickers, *Between Serb and Albanian: A History of Kosovo* (Christopher Hurst/Columbia University Press, 1998), pp. 250, 251 and 259. In January 1995, the Kosovo Serb daily *Jedinstvo* reported that 1,896 Kosovo Serbs had fought as paramilitaries in Croatia and Bosnia since

1991; 49 were killed, 182 wounded and three unaccounted for. *Jedinstvo* said this sent a message to Albanian separatists that they would be the first to defend Serbian territories. *Kosova Communication* 203, 16 January 1995.

23. This is the figure in Ibrahim Rugova, *La Question du Kosovo: Entretiens réalisés par Marie-François Allain et Xavier Galmiche* (Paris: Fayard, 1994), p. 115. According to Zoran Kusovac, 'Another Balkans Bloodbath – Part Two', *Jane's Intelligence Review*, March 1998, there was a regular presence of 13,000 policemen armed with paramilitary equipment, including armoured personnel carriers and armed helicopters, augmented by some 21,000 Kosovo Serbs as official police reservists issued with weapons. A further 25,000 police reinforcements could be transferred from Central Serbia within 72 hours.

24. Quoted by Denisa Kostovičová, *Parallel Worlds: Response of Kosovo Albanians to Loss of Autonomy in Serbia, 1986–1996* (Keele University European Research Centre), p. 61.

25. Adapted from an account by Belgrade feminist lepa mladjenović, 'Prishtina, September 1996', *Women for Peace* (Women in Black, Belgrade, 1997), p. 232.

26. CDHRF, 'Albanian Women as police and military victims of violence during 1993' (mimeo, no date, collected April 1994).

27. Between 20 May 1992 and 30 March 1993, FRY issued warrants against 30,000 Albanian or Muslim draft resisters/evaders – International Helsinki Federation for Human Rights, *From Autonomy to Human Rights: Human Rights in Kosovo 1989–1993* (Vienna, 1993), p.70. CDHRF reported 50 'forcibly conscripted', including being physically dragged from their homes, in 1993; 685 arrested or sentenced in 1994; 105 arrested, but with incomplete information suggesting that charges had been laid against 1,635 draft evaders, in 1995.

28. Amnesty International, *Yugoslavia: Ethnic Albanians – victims of torture and ill-treatment by police in Kosovo province* (AI Index: EIR 48/12/92). Human Rights Watch/Helsinki Watch, *Yugoslavia: Human Rights Abuse in Kosovo 1990–1992* and *Open Wounds: Human Rights Abuses in Kosovo*.

29. Rugova, *La Question*, p. 102.

30. See for instance, Gene Sharp, *Self-Reliant Defense: Without Bankruptcy or War* (Albert Einstein Institution, 1992).

31. Author's interview, Afërdita Saraçini-Kelmendi, November 1997.

32. *Amnesty International Report 1992*, p. 280.

33. Rugova, *La Question*, p. 172.

34. *Vreme NDA*, 1 June 1992. The Social Democratic Party gained one seat, occupied by Shkëlzen Maliqi. His personal defeat is a caution to outsiders impressed by his analysis. Despite the praise of many fellow-Albanians – including Rugova – Maliqi remained suspect among the population.

35. Slav Muslims and Turks had divided loyalties; there were other Muslim and Turkish parties participating in the Serbian elections. Kosovo had no regional Roma party, although ethnic Roma members of Milošević's SPS served in municipal bodies in Kosovo. Belgrade Helsinki Committee, *Report on National Minorities in Kosovo*, May 1998.

36. D. Kostovičová, *Parallel Worlds: Response of Kosovo Albanians to Loss of Autonomy in Serbia, 1986–1996* (Keele European Research Centre, 1997), p. 36, citing Fehmi Agani.
37. Bylykbashi, *555 ... Kronikë*, p. 147. Observers included a US Congressional delegation, a Danish Helsinki Committee and representatives of the Unrepresented Peoples Organisation. *Kosova Communication* 22, 28 May 1992, and *Kosova Communication* 24, 5 June 1992.
38. *Vreme NDA*, 1 June 1992.
39. MAN, 'Interview de Ibrahim Rugova et Rexhep Ishmajli, 16 août 1993', in *La résistance civile au Kosovo* (Paris: MAN, 1994), p. 41.
40. Other political prisoners, including Hydajet Hyseni, made similar remarks – see *Vreme*, 5 April 1993 – while J. Mertus, *Kosovo: How Myths and Truths Started a War* (Berkeley: University of California Press, 1999), pp. 82–3, records the testimony of a prisoner who spent the last five years of his sentence in Niš.

> When I entered prison in Niš, complete hatred existed between the Albanian and Serbian prisoners ... stimulated by the guards ...The attitude in the prison eventually changed. The conditions in the prison were very bad. We would have joint protests and hunger strikes. In a way, we were protected by the Serbian prisoners; some of them would take the blame for us [because the guards would punish them less]. The Albanian prisoners helped the Serbian prisoners too. We were the ones who were visited by the Red Cross. When the Red Cross came, we would pass messages for the Serbian prisoners ... Yesterday I was stopped in the street by a former prisoner, a Serb. He hugged me right there on the street. He said, I realize you are right, the policies against you are wrong.

41. Janjić, 'National Movements', p. 161.
42. Jacques Semelin, *Unarmed Against Hitler: Civilian Resistance in Europe, 1939–1943* (Praeger, 1993), pp. 48–54.
43. Author's interview, Rexhep Ishmajli, February 1993.
44. Shkëlzen Maliqi, *Kosova: Separate Worlds – Reflections and Analyses* (Prishtina: MM/Peja: Dukagjini, 1998), p. 250.
45. In the light of assertions by foreign analysts that the Albanian vote could 'undoubtedly have ousted Milošević', it should be noted that even all the votes cast in the Kosovo parallel elections of May 1992 – including the more than 100,000 cast in the diaspora – would not have bridged this gap.
46. Depos leader Vuk Drašković was no less nationalist than Milošević on the question of Kosovo.
47. Hugh Poulton and Miranda Vickers, 'The Kosovo Albanians', in Hugh Poulton and Suha Taji-Farouki (eds), *Muslim Identity and the Balkan State* (Hurst, 1997), p. 157.
48. *Balkan War Report*, December 1993, p. 4.
49. *Vreme NDA*, 8 November 1993.
50. Fehim Rexhepi, *AIM*, 7 September 1996.

51. Susan L. Woodward, *Balkan Tragedy: Chaos and Dissolution after the Cold War* (Brookings Institution, 1995), pp. 306, 500.
52. Sami Repishti, 'Albanian-American Community: Home-grown Lobbyists', *Balkan War Report*, April/May 1993, p. 18.
53. The Italian MEP Alexander Langer, who nominated Demaçi, had visited Kosovo in May in the company of Greens, feminists and pacifists from Belgrade and a group of Italians.
54. Author's interview, Boško Drobnjak, Secretary of Information for Kosovo-Metohija, April 1994.
55. Stefan Troebst, *Conflict in Kosovo: Failure of Prevention? An Analytical Documentation, 1992–1998* (European Centre for Minority Issues, 1998), p. 48.
56. Fabian Schmidt, 'Kosovo: The Time Bomb that has not gone off', *RFE/RL Research Report*, Vol. 2, no. 39, 1 October 1993, p. 23.
57. The London Conference on Former Yugoslavia of August 1992 transformed the European Community Conference on Former Yugoslavia into ICFY, with co-chairs from the UN and the EC. The Special Group on Kosovo was set up by the Working Group on Ethnic and National Communities and Minorities. Troebst, *Conflict in Kosovo*, p. 37.
58. Schmidt, 'Time Bomb', p. 24.
59. *Vreme NDA*, 19 February 1996.

CHAPTER 5: PARALLEL STRUCTURES

1. Quoted by Marie-Françoise Allain and Xavier Galmiche in Rugova, *La Question du Kosovo: Entretiens réalisés par Marie Françoise Allain et Xavier Galmiche* (Paris: Fayard, 1994).
2. Quoted by Peter Lippman, 'The Birth and Rebirth of Civil Society in Kosovo', *On the Record* (http://www.advocacynet.org).
3. Rugova, *La Question*, p. 139.
4. Quoted in Franklin DeVrieze, 'Stable and Explosive', *Helsinki Monitor*, 1995, No. 2, p. 43.
5. HLC, 'Spotlight Report No 16', p. 18.
6. CDHRF, 'Regarding the answer of the Serbian Government to Helsinki Watch's report on the violation of human rights', April 1992, para. 9.
7. CDHRF, 'Discrimination in Education', November 1991.
8. This petition is in *Kosova Watch*, Vol. 1, no. 1, January 1992, pp. 20–3.
9. HLC, *Education of Kosovo Albanians*, October 1997, p. 2.
10. HLC, 'Spotlight Report No. 16', p. 19.
11. HLC, *Education*, p. 4.
12. Reportedly, some 2,000 Turkish pupils attended parallel elementary schools, 400 secondary. International Crisis Group, *Kosovo Spring*, March 1998 (http://www.crisisweb.org/projects/sbalkans/reports).
13. The Serbian authorities sometimes granted public positions to Kosovo Gypsies, partly as a policy of 'divide and rule', partly pretending to an international audience that they were genuinely pursuing multi-ethnic policies.

14. Abdyl Ramaj, 'The Situation in Albanian Education in Kosova and Possibilities for its Temporary Normalization' (LDK, August 1997).
15. Author's interview with Abdyl Rama, November 1997.
16. Four schools succeeded in 1992–93, two in 1993–94 and two in 1996–97. HLC, *Education*, p. 5.
17. HLC, ibid., p. 3.
18. *Kosova Communication*, 6 September 1993. The killings of parents took place on 31 January 1992 in the village of Uça. Police went to the private premises of the parallel school and apparently arrested three pupils. They then opened fire on parents and others demanding their release, killing three parents. (Police claimed they fired in self-defence.) *Amnesty International Report 1993*, p. 314.
19. 507 in 1995, 211 in 1996, 295 in 1997, while there were 150 police interventions at schools in 1995 and 54 in 1996.
20. The precise figures were 12 per cent for Grades 1–4, 24 per cent for Grades 5–8, 25 per cent at secondary school. Author's interview, Bajram Shatri, Education Institute of Kosova, November 1997.
21. Gordana Igrić, 'Education is the Key in Serb-Kosovar Negotiations', *Transition*, 7 March 1997, p. 20.
22. Letter of 15 February 1995, in Hajrullah Koliqi, *The Survival of the University of Prishtina, 1991–96* (University of Prishtina, 1997), translation amended.
23. Koliqi, *The Survival*, p. 129 (plus one Serbian sympathiser).
24. Quoted in Pax Christi International, *Kosovo: The Conflict Between Serbs and Albanians* (Brussels: Pax Christi International, 1995), p. 28.
25. Marie-Françoise Allain and Xavier Galmiche in Rugova, *La Question*, p. 138. It is symptomatic that while Koliqi's history reports in detail on the sackings and the re-establishment of the formal university decision-making structures, he does not even mention the actual day of re-opening, let alone describe it.
26. Rector Ejup Statovci was arrested on 2 January for writing an appeal to world leaders and the Yugoslav Federal Authorities and sentenced to 60 days. After protest in Kosovo and internationally, he was released on 29 January. At this time the student 'pro-rector' appointed by the university authories was Hashim Thaçi, who later became a leader of UÇK.
27. Koliqi, *The Survival*, pp. 177, 180.
28. Quoted in Koliqi, ibid., p. 62.
29. By November 1997, 50 medical students had completed their practice in the clinic in Podujeva. Author's visit.
30. Koliqi, *The Survival*, p. 75, n. 103. Tirana University itself employed lecturers from Kosovo in subjects such as philosophy, jurisprudence and sociology where the Enverist legacy left it weak – Miranda Vickers and James Pettifer, *Albania: From Anarchy to a Balkan Identity* (Hurst, 1997), p. 155.
31. Koliqi, *The Survival*, p. 205, and p. 75, n. 103.
32. Koliqi, ibid., p. 52.
33. Interview, May 1998. Kelmendi succeeded Statovci in 1998.
34. Lino Veljak, 'Will the Logic of Violence or the Logic of Tolerance prevail?', *Women for Peace* (Women in Black, Belgrade, 1998), p. 129.

Masha Gessen, 'The Parallel University: a journey through Kosovo's secret classrooms', *Lingua Franca*, November/December 1994, p. 38, found only one Albanian critic of the parallel university's standards – a teacher of German who left feeling that the new German department was below standard and should be closed.

35. Teachers in the Medical Faculty worked without pay on the assumption that they could support themselves through private medical practice.

36. Some query the term 'voluntary' taxation. I know of no evidence of any form of pressure other than the force of opinion. People – especially businesses – expected to pay taxes to the Republic of Kosova (often in addition to the taxes collected by the Serbian authorities). Those with any doubts would probably still pay rather than face the disapproval of their social circle, especially as the form of collection was as personal as a visit from the finance council.

37. DM 1.6 million raised outside as against DM 5.5 million inside. *AIM*, 6 September 1994.

38. Author's interview, Podujeva Council of Finance members, November 1997.

39. Author's interview, Prishtina entrepreneur, November 1998.

40. Podujeva, a municipality with a particularly dense population, had 8,488 tax-paying families, while about 2,500 families were considered too poor.

41. Astrit Salihu, *Koha Summary*, 11 January 1995. Salihu, on the other hand, recommended a magazine *Zanore* (Vowel) whose existence would be threatened by this ban.

42. Confidential conversation, 1997.

43. The parallel school environment was clearly not conducive to learning 'the language of the oppressor', even if some might have considered it prudent in terms of pupil encounters with police or prefigurative in terms of inter-ethnic relations desired after independence with the Serbian minority in Kosovo and neighbours in Serbia.

44. Shkëlzen Maliqi, 'Reading, Writing and Repression', *Balkan War Report*, May 1996, pp. 44–5; *AIM*, 6 January 1996.

45. Gessen, 'The Parallel University', pp. 32, 34.

46. *Koha Summary*, 1 March 1995.

47. Avdyl Krasniqi in Rugova, *La Question*, pp. 70–4.

48. *Kosova Communication* 253, 16 February 1996.

49. *Kosova Communication* 157, 7 February 1994.

50. Hugh Poulton and Miranda Vickers, 'The Kosovo Albanians', in Hugh Poulton and Suha Taji-Farouki (eds), *Muslim Identity and the Balkan State* (Hurst, 1997), p. 191.

51. By the end of 1996, there were 75 outpatient clinics, treating an average of 2,711 patients per day. They were staffed by 329 doctors (GPs and specialists), 459 nurses and technical staff, and a varying number of medical students as interns. In 1996 humanitarian aid reached 62,340 families. Figures taken from a Mother Theresa Association handout, written by Jak Mita, no date, collected November 1997.

52. *Kosova Communication* 95, 8 April 1993, reported that three Equilibre staff were sentenced to 15 days imprisonment for trying to work in

Kosovo without permission. In 1993, French and Swiss NGO convoys to Kosovo were blocked.

53. There were 98 cases of typhoid in the first half of 1994. *AIM*, 13 November 1994.
54. Author's interview, Dr Vjosa Dobruna, April 1994.
55. *AIM*, 13 March 1994.
56. Press Now, *Dossier Kosovo* (Amsterdam, 1995).
57. *AIM*, 31 March 1994. Humanitarian Law Centre, 'Spotlight Report No. 6 – Kosovo Albanians I', *Spotlight on Human Rights in Serbia and Montenegro* (Belgrade, 1995), p. 54.
58. *Koha Summary*, 22 March 1995.
59. This was distinct from but a basic source for the separate bulletins produced by diaspora Kosova Information Centres, aligned with the government-in-exile.
60. Koliqi, *The Survival*, p. 60.
61. By July 1994, police had stopped 72 sports events in mid-competition. When Albanians organised an Athlete-of-the-Year ceremony on 28 December 1994, police raided the restaurant and arrested 25 of those present. One was Azis Salihu, a boxing bronze medallist in the Los Angeles Olympics (1984). He was tied to a radiator and beaten. Humanitarian Law Centre, 'Spotlight Report No. 16 – Kosovo Albanians II', *Spotlight on Human Rights in Serbia and Montenegro* (Belgrade, 1996), pp. 49–50.
62. Author's interview, Besim Hasani, chair Kosova Karate Association and Kosova Olympic Committee, November 1998.
63. In a 1996 tournament, a Kosovo karate team found itself due to play a team from FRY in the third round. The team from FRY decided to play (and duly won), but apparently their coaches were rebuked and sacked on their return to Belgrade, while in Prishtina the Serb police summoned the Kosovo organiser for 'informative talks'.
64. Economic data in the following section is drawn from the Riinvest report (http://www.kosova.com/RIINVEST); articles by Ibrahim Rexhepi in *Koha Summary*, 15 January 1997, 31 December 1996, 20 November 1996 and 1 March 1995; in *AIM*, 9 September 1997, 2 September 1997 and 22 July 1997; and in *Balkan War Report*, May 1996; articles in *Vreme NDA*, 22 March 1993, 7 March 1994, 20 June 1994; author's interviews, Naip Zeka, then LDK spokesperson, November 1997 and Zeki Bejtallahu, May 1999.
65. M. Vickers, *Between Serb and Albanian: A History of Kosovo* (Christopher Hurst/Columbia University Press, (1998), p. 249.
66. ICG, *Kosovo Spring*, 20 March 1998 (http://www/crisisweb.org/projects/sbalkans/reports).
67. J. Reineck, *The Past as Refuge: Gender, Migration and Ideology among Kosovo Albanians* (PhD Dissertation, Berkeley: University of California, 1991) p. 201.
68. *Vreme NDA*, 7 March 1994.
69. *Koha Summary*, 20 November 1996.
70. Considering the rise of gangsterism in neighbouring Serbia and Albania, the Kosovo Albanian community seems to have been comparatively free

of overt gangsterism in the early 1990s. After 1997 there were reports of gun-running and drug-smuggling. Rugova suggests that Serbs tried to implant gangsters but 'we put pressure on them, found their liaisons, and put a stop to it', Rugova, *La Question*, p. 140. In 1995 *Koha* investigated racketeering, exposing some loan 'enforcers' and some collaboration with police: 'it is not manifested in the harshest forms as in Belgrade.' *Koha Summary*, 22 March 1995.

71. Amnesty International, *Kosovo: the evidence* (AI-UK, September 1998), p. 37.
72. A. Rigby, *Living the Intifada* (London: Zed, 1991), pp. 124–5.
73. Rugova, *La Question*, pp. 175–6.
74. N. Malcolm, *Kosovo: A Short History* (London: Macmillan/New York University Press, 1998), p. 348.
75. Dušan Janjić, 'Towards Dialogue or Division?', *Balkan War Report*, May 1996.
76. Interview with Rexhep Qosja, in R. Elsie (ed.) *Kosovo: In the heart of the powder keg* (Boulder: East European Monographs, Columbia University Press, 1997), p. 499.
77. Denisa Kostovičová, 'Albanian School in Kosovo 1992–1998: "Liberty Imprisoned"', in Kyrill Drezov, Bulent Gokay, Denisa Kostovičová (eds), *Kosova: Myths, Conflict and War* (University of Keele European Research Centre, 1999), pp. 12–20.
78. *Vreme NDA*, 14 March 1994.
79. *Koha Summary*, 29 December 1994.
80. Shkëlzen Maliqi, *AIM*, 27 July 1994.
81. *Kosova Communication* 164, 29 March 1994.
82. Selatin Novosella interviewed in *Koha Summary*, 6 November 1996.

CHAPTER 6: POINTERS FOR AN ALTERNATIVE STRATEGY

1. As Gandhi's name has been taken in vain over Kosovo, it seems worth drawing some lessons from his example.
2. *AIM*, 1 April 1999.
3. *AIM*, 31 January 1996.
4. *Vreme NDA*, 14 May 1996.
5. Shkëlzen Maliqi, 'Broken April', *Balkan War Report*, May 1996.
6. George Lakey, *Strategy for a Living Revolution* (Grossman, New York, 1973), p. 103.
7. All quotes from *Kosova Communication* 277, 9 September 1996.
8. *AIM*, 27 December 1996.
9. *Koha Summary*, 27 November 1996.
10. *AIM*, 30 November 1996.
11. It concluded:

> And we were right, people of Serbia, when we did not accept to fight with you, as power-greedy red masters wished. And we are right today, us the Albanians, although with heavy police chains, when we are

directing a look of hope, offering a hand of a martyr to you, friendly people of Serbia.

AIM, 5 December 1996.
12. *AIM*, 14 January 1997.
13. Author's interview, Prishtina SPO activist, April 1994.
14. *AIM*, 22 December 1996.
15. Humanitarian Law Centre, *Spotlight Report* 26 (HLC, Belgrade, January 1997), p. 128.
16. *KIC Daily* 1034, 17 December 1996.
17. *AIM*, 30 November 1996.
18. *AIM*, 17 January 1997.
19. Ibid.
20. Author's interview, Hydajet Hyseni, then vice-president of LDK, November 1997.
21. For example, by 'Minister of Information' Xhafer Shatri, quoted by Tihomir Loza, 'Kosovo Albanians Closing the Ranks', p. 29, in *Transitions*, May 1997, p. 29.
22. Robert Burrowes, *The Strategy of Nonviolent Defense: a Gandhian Approach* (State University of New York, 1996), especially Ch. 8, pp. 125–34. Burrowes links power and will in the case of defence as any defeat of the defender's will is temporary and requires the continued presence of occupation forces unless the power to resist is also broken.
23. 'Relentless persistence' is the usual translation of *firmeza permanente*, a term used by nonviolent groups in Latin America in the 1980s.
24. Gene Sharp, *From Dictatorship to Democracy: A conceptual framework for liberation* (Albert Einstein Institution, 1994), p. 37.
25. J. Mertus, *Kosovo: How Myths and Truths Started a War* (Berkeley: University of California Press, 1999), Tables 11–13, reports on attitudinal surveys in the mid-1990s. Further reports are *AIM*, 8 March 1994 and *Vreme*, 2 August 1997, confirming the existence of 'profound rifts'.
26. I have developed this schematic for the Nonviolence and Social Empowerment programme of War Resisters' International. Howard Clark, 'More Power than we know', *Peace News*, March 1998.
27. The parliament elected in 1992 never met. The parliament elected in 1998 met on 15 July 1998. However, this was an opportunity missed. A hole-in-the-corner affair, it lasted an hour and seemed designed merely to silence those demanding its convening. It was not announced in advance, there was a complete absence of symbolism and it hurried through the formalities in order to finish just as the police arrived. *KIC Daily* 1492, 16 July 1998; *Koha Ditore*, 16 July 1998.
28. The model of small action groups is not just a Western phenomenon. In the 1980s small groups like the John Lennon Club in Prague or the Wolnosc i Pokoj (Freedom and Peace) network and Wroclaw's Orange Alternative in Poland injected surprise elements into anti-totalitarian movements. See Michael Randle, *People Power: The Building of a new European Home* (Hawthorn Press, 1991).
29. Bob Overy, *Gandhi as Organiser, 1915–1922* (Unpublished PhD thesis, University of Bradford, 1982), p. 358.

30. Overy, ibid., p. 336.
31. M.K. Gandhi, *The Collected Works of Mahatma Gandhi* (Publications Division, Ministry of Information and Broadcasting, New Delhi, 1961), Vol. 32, p. 342.
32. A. Rigby, *Living the Intifada* (London: Zed, 1991), pp. 124–5.
33. Author's interview, Zeki Bejtallahu, May 1998.
34. Privately, for instance with their neighbours, behaviour might be different.
35. Elise Boulding, *Building a Global Civic Culture* (Syracuse University Press, 1990), p. xxii.
36. M.K. Gandhi, *Constructive Programme: Its Meaning and Place* (Navajivan, 1941 edn.), p. 3. A crore is 10 million, a reminder that Kosovo, for Gandhi, would have been a local not a national struggle.
37. *AIM*, 16 June 1996.
38. Sharp, *From Dictatorship to Democracy*, p. 37.
39. Small groups in Belgrade – initially the Centre for Anti-War Action and continuously Women in Black – were active in supporting draft resistance and desertion from the beginning of the war in Slovenia. In 1998 two new groups grew out of the student movement, the Anti-War Campaign and *Otpor!* (Resist!).
40. Stipe Sikavica, 'The War Relocates to Serbia', *Helsinki Charter* (Bulletin of the Belgrade Helsinki Committee), July 1998.
41. Amnesty International, 'Federal Republic of Yugoslavia: The forgotten resisters – The plight of conscientious objectors to military service after the conflict in Kosovo' (AI Index: EUR/70/11199, October 1999), reports that there may be 'at least 23,000' men of military age from FRY who refused to participate and were now facing trial by military courts and lengthy terms of imprisonment.
42. This was a frequent occurrence at Blace on the Macedonian border. Nataša Kandić of Belgrade's Humanitarian Law Centre, interviewed in *Danas* (Zagreb), 3–4 July 1999, reported refugee groups sent from Mitrovica to Gjakova:

> Along the way they were met by various paramilitary units and police forces that robbed them. Police even refused to give them water. However, when the refugees came across the soldiers of the regular army, the young conscripts gave them water, food, milk for the babies. Witnesses talked of some soldiers who cried, who said that they were forced to be there, that they didn't know what was really happening, that they had witnessed terrible things, that they were sorry.

43. Discussing Israel-Palestine, Johan Galtung coined the term 'the great chain of nonviolence'. Johan Galtung, *Nonviolence and Israel/Palestine* (University of Hawaii Institute for Peace, 1989), Ch. 2.
44. See Rigby, *Living the Intifada*, Ch. 7. Having heard Zionists insulting Women in Black in Jerusalem and Serb nationalists insulting Women in Black in Belgrade, I see other parallels.
45. The @ indicated their openness on whether it was the Serbian Kosovo or the Albanian Kosova.

46. For instance, the Carnegie Endowment for International Peace, the Aspen Institute Berlin, the US-American Council on Foreign Relations' Center for Preventive Action, the Political Cultural Center 042 (the Netherlands), the Open Society Fund (Soros), the Hellenic Foundation for European and Foreign Policy, the Bertelsmann Science Foundation and Research Group on European Affairs, the Project on Ethnic Relations (backed by the US State Department), the Olof Palme Centre, the European Action Council for Peace in the Balkans and the International Helsinki Federation.

47. Even before the Pax Christi Link. In 1994, LDK Youth representatives made friends with youth representatives of the Civic Alliance in Belgrade at an international conference. On their return to Prishtina, the LDK youths were summoned by police for 'informative talks' at which the youth wing of the Civic Alliance, without consulting the senior leadership, took the unprecedented step of issuing a public protest. At another international conference, however, Kosovo Albanian youths signed a joint statement with others from former Yugoslavia and were severely censured on their return home not because of the content of the statement but for their public cooperation with 'Yugoslavs'.

48. Author's interview, Kjell Andersson, head ICRC Prishtina 1994–98, November 1997.

49. M. Vickers and J. Pettifer, *Albania: from Anarchy to a Balkan Identity* (London: Hurst, 1997), p. 163.

50. UPSUP was nominated by the winners from the previous year, Belgrade students.

51. The personal risk it would have involved was not the problem.

52. Without, however, being very specific. Magaš, p. 160, noted that 'for the first time women in Kosovo started to play a vital and indispensable role', while Lindholm wrote that 'women's groups have managed to bring the need for change of women's status in Albanian society to the political agenda'. Helena Lindholm, 'Nationalist movements: The Palestinian Intifada and Kosovo Compared', *Spectrum*, Vol. II (Schlaining, May 1991), p. 36.

53. Vjosa Dobruna, 'Women Living in Kosovo', Centre for Women's Studies, *Women and the Politics of Peace: Contributions to a Culture of Women's Resistance* (Zagreb, 1997), p. 118.

54. Information on Motrat Qiriazi taken from Igballe Rogova, 'Women are changing women', *Women for Peace* (Women in Black, Belgrade, 1995), pp. 241–5; publicity leaflet (http://www.igc.apc.org/balkans/quiriazi.html); Julie Mertus, 'Women in Kosovo: Contested Terrains – the role of national identity in shaping and challenging gender identity', in Sabrine P. Ramet (ed.), *Gender Politics in the Western Balkans* (Pennsylvania State University Press, 1999), pp. 171–86; and interview with Igballe Rogova by Peter Lippman, 'The Birth and Rebirth of Civil Society in Kosovo', *On the Record* (http://www.advocacynet.org).

55. Mertus, 'Women in Kosovo', p. 176.

56. Mertus, ibid., p. 177.

57. Author's interview, Sevdie Ahmeti, co-director, May 1998. After the massacres the Centre took the initiative in coordinating women's

demonstrations and then its work was dominated by field trips with the joint purpose of situation monitoring and organising humanitarian assistance.

58. Appeal quoted by Mertus, 'Women in Kosovo', p. 174.
59. *Kosova Communication* 262, 29 April 1996.
60. Quoted by Mertus, 'Women in Kosovo', p. 173.
61. Quoted in information received as member of BPT Coordinating Committee (CC), July 1997.
62. Information from personal visits and received as member of BPT CC.
63. For example, Living Waters workshops led by Merle Letkoff.
64. Author's interview with Adem Limani, November 1997.
65. Human Rights Watch, *Humanitarian Law Violations* (Human Rights Watch, 1998), p.55.
66. The basic information on UPSUP activity in autumn 1997 is taken from the following sources: conversations with students in November 1997, including several with Albin Kurti; UPSUP communiqués (http://www.alb-net.com); Balkan Peace Team, 'Student Protest in Prishtina' (BPT, October 1997), plus information received as a member of BPT CC; David Hartsough, 'Massive Nonviolent Protest in Kosova' (Peaceworkers, San Francisco, October 1997); CDHRF, 'Students' Protest: Report on Violence' (October 1987); Prishtina *KIC Daily* bulletins for this period; *AIM*, 2 September 1997, 3 October 1997 and 13 October 1997 and *Vreme NDA*, 2 October 1997.
67. Even though some student leaders were members of anti-Rugova parties.
68. *KIC Daily* 1242, 30 September 1997.
69. *KIC Daily* 1230, 12 September 1997.
70. The Main Principles and rules of Protesters in Nonviolent and Peaceful Protests of the University of Prishtina:

1) We are firmly determined for nonviolence in our thoughts, opinions, words and behaviour, even when provoked by police or when they use violence against us.
2) We are going to be open and honest towards everybody, without distinction.
3) The purpose of our protest is not political. Its intention is obvious: the unconditional release of premises, buildings and campus of the University.
4) We do not try to defeat our adversary, but we are demanding the respect of human rights and civil freedoms equally for all people.
5) We are not going to use violence against private and public property or against different ownership; we do not want to damage them.
6) We are not going to arm ourselves or use any kinds of arms.
7) Everybody who provokes the police will be considered a police informer.
8) If the police intervene brutally, this is not a sign that we ought to be violent as well.

9) We are not going either to call out slogans and whistle or to make other kinds of gesticulations, because we want to show our determination and will with our attitude.

10) If anyone – a protester or a supporter – uses violence against the police or somebody else, we shall do our utmost to prevent and stop their violence.

11) We have decided to stick to the instructions and orders of the Organizing Council for protests at the level of the University of Prishtina and of keepers and maintainers of order in the protests.

Organization Council, University of Prishtina Students Independent Union, 27 October 1997.

71. Author's interview, May 1998.

72. The workshop, planned by Kurti and David Hartsough, was scheduled for August in Tetova; I was to be a co-trainer. It was cancelled in July. Kurti soon afterwards became secretary to Adem Demaçi, the 'political representative of UÇK'. Kurti told me in November: 'You know I will never take up arms, and so I am trying to do what I can politically.' The Demaçi office played a role in securing the release of a number of hostages (Serbian and Albanian) while UÇK publicly declared the position that, of course, it would respect the Geneva Conventions. Kurti stayed in Prishtina during the NATO bombings and was arrested on 28 April 1999. On 14 March 2000, Albin Kurti was sentenced to 15 years in prison on charges of 'attempting to secede a part of Serbia'.

CHAPTER 7: WHEN THE WORLD TAKES NOTICE

1. International Alert, *Self-Determination: Statement and recommendations arising from the Martin Ennals Memorial Symposium on Self-Determination, Saskatoon, Canada* (London, 1993).

2. M.H. Halperin, D.J. Scheffer and P. Small, *Self-Determination in the New World Order* (Carnegie Endowment for International Peace, 1990).

3. N. Malcolm, *Kosovo: A Short History* (London: Macmillan/New York University Press, 1998), pp. 264–7, argues that Serbia's annexation of Kosovo was never legally ratified and that internationally Kosovo was subsequently recognised as part of Yugoslavia, not as part of Serbia.

4. Public International Law and Policy Group, *Intermediate Sovereignty as a Basis for Resolving the Kosovo Crisis* (International Crisis Group, November 1998), (http://www.crisisweb.org/projects/sbalkans/reports).

5. The Carrington Plan from September 1991 onwards was an attempted re-federation of Yugoslavia 'à la carte': each republic was asked how much sovereignty it desired and over what matters, and was offered a menu of choices for the kind of inter-republican relationships and institutions it would participate in. It was rather elaborate for negotiations during war and, unfortunately, Kosovo and Vojvodina – federal entities in the 1974 constitution – were not included. Kosovo was discussed in terms of some parallel with the Serbs who had declared their own republic in the Krajina.

6. Fabian Schmidt, 'Strategic Reconciliation in Kosovo', *Transition*, 25 August 1995, p. 18.
7. S. Troebst, *Conflict in Kosovo: Failure or Prevention? An Analytical Documentation 1992–1998* (Flensburg: European Centre for Minority Issues, 1998), p. 105.
8. European Action Council for Peace in the Balkans and Public International Law and Policy Group of the Carnegie Endowment for International Peace, *Kosovo: From crisis to permanent solution* (Amsterdam and Washington), 1 November 1997.
9. Mark Salter, 'Balkan Endgame: The Kosovo Conflict in a Southern Balkan Context', in Peter Cross (ed.), *Contributing to Preventive Action: Conflict Prevention Network Yearbook 1997/98* (Stiftung Wissenschaft und Politik, 1998), pp. 229–50.
10. Three evacuated university buildings became available to Albanians in May 1998, after some vandalism and all their equipment had been taken away. A further three faculties were handed back in February 1999.
11. Jan Øberg, 'Kosovo on the Agenda', *Balkan War Report*, May 1996, p. 33.
12. Zoran Lutovac of the University of Belgrade Institute for Social Sciences analysed twelve proposals: 'Respect for the Right to be Different', *AIM*, 19 April 1997, including 'maximalist' Serb and Albanian options. These were two variations on the former autonomy ('1974-minus' and '1974-plus'), Confederalisation (Demaçi's 'Balkania' was by no means the only proposal), Regionalisation (dividing FRY into 13 regions, including Kosovo and Metohija as two separate regions), a Unitarian state of FRY (advocated by Šešelj, direct rule from Belgrade), Independence, Unification with Albania, Partition (various proposals), International Protectorate (or transitional authority), Consociative democracy, Decentralisation mixed with regionalisation and consociation, Armed conflict and ethnic cleansing. Strangely, he omitted the idea of Cantonisation promoted by, among others, the Serb historian Dušan Batakovic which found favour in Orthodox Church circles. In an article after Drenica, Lutovac considered other models, including constitutional possibilities in practice in Southern Tyrol, the Åland Islands and Tatarstan – Zoran Lutovac, 'Models Suggested by the Contact Group to Resolve the Problem of Kosovo', *Review of International Affairs* (Belgrade), Vol. XLIX, 15 September 1998, pp. 7–10.
13. Schmidt, 'Strategic Reconciliation', p. 18.
14. *Balkan War Report*, April/May 1993, p. 18.
15. Not until after Drenica was there a publicly announced advisory group on negotiating strategy, the so-called G-15 which included a spectrum of non-UÇK points of view. In fact, the G-15 was never more than 13 as two of those invited – Adem Demaçi and Bujar Bukoshi – respectively refused or could not take part. Two others, Hydajet Hyseni and Bujar Dugolli of UPSUP, withdrew in protest at Rugova agreeing – without consulting the group – to meet Milošević in Belgrade without international mediation. The others were: Fehmi Agani (coordinator), Mahmut Bakalli, Rexhep Ishmajli, Bajram Kelmendi, Mark Krasniqi, Shkëlzen Maliqi, Pajazit Nushi, Blerim Shala, Esat Stavileci, Veton Surroi and Edita Tahiri.

16. The then German foreign minister Klaus Kinkel mentioned the idea of such a deal (*Koha Ditore*, 8 July 1998), rather belatedly – four months after the Drenica massacres. It is not clear whether any serious approach had been made earlier, including a proposed size for such a mission, nor whether Kosovo Albanian representatives had expressed any opinion on this.
17. See for instance ICG, *Kosovo Spring* or Human Rights Watch, *Humanitarian Law Violations in Kosovo* (October 1998).
18. Milenko Vasović, 'Travel Bans are more effective than Sanctions', *IWPR's Balkan Crisis Report*, 75, 14 September 1999.
19. The International Confederation of the Red Cross. Author's interview, Kjell Andersson, November 1997.
20. Ishmail Kadare's 'The Wedding Procession turned to Ice', translated by Robert Elsie, is included in R. Elsie (ed.), *Kosovo: in the heart of the powder keg* (Boulder: East European Monographs, Columbia University Press, 1997). Alice Mead, *Adem's Cross* (Laurel Leaf, 1998).
21. John Paul Lederach, *Building Peace: Sustainable Reconciliation in Divided Societies* (US Institute of Peace, 1997), pp. 112–23.
22. J. Mertus, *Kosovo: How Myths and Truths Started a War* (Berkeley: University of California Press, 1999), devotes a chapter to cautionary tales and recommendations to international NGOs, pp. 227–68.
23. It subsidised *Bujku* for a period.
24. *Koha Summary*, 27 November 1996.
25. It seems that some children were vaccinated more than once.
26. *KIC Daily* 1295, 8 December 1997.
27. *KIC Daily* 1323, 20 January 1998.
28. *KIC Daily* 1344, 26 February 1998; *Koha Ditore*, 26 February 1998.
29. OSCE-KVM, *Kosovo/Kosova – As Seen As Told: The human rights findings of the OSCE Kosovo Verification Mission* (December 1999), (http://www.osce.org/kosovo/reports/hr).
30. Gelbard warned in January that the USA was considering putting the UÇK on its list of 'terrorist organisations', (*RFE/RL Newsline*, Vol. 1, No. 191, 8 January 1998) and a similar attitude was reported throughout January and February. By the time he met UÇK leaders in June, however, the US attitude had changed so that, while the UÇK had carried out 'terrorist actions', it was not seen as a 'terrorist organisation', *New York Times*, 28 June 1998.
31. *KIC Daily* 1337, 4 February 1998.
32. Tim Judah suggests that the UÇK had 'barely 200 members' at the end of November 1997, 'The Growing Pains of the Kosova Liberation Army', K. Drezov, B. Gokay and D. Kostovičová (eds), *Kosovo: Myths, Conflict and War* (Keele European Research Centre, 1999), p. 21. Zoran Kusovac, 'Another Balkans Bloodbath – Part Two', *Jane's Intelligence Review*, March 1998, p. 16, infers from their pattern of operation that in February 1998 there were '120–150 men with some action experience, 40 of whom can lead a group, with a further 200 in the support structure as guides, providers of lodging, food suppliers and couriers.' In *Koha Ditore*, 8 July 1998, a UÇK commander Maloku spoke of the army growing from 150, including recruiting many Albanians with experience in the wars in

Bosnia and Croatia. Only 411 of the former UÇK combatants registered by the International Organization for Migration claimed 'to have been associated' with the UÇK before January 1998. International Organization for Migration, *Socio-Economic and Demographic Profiles of Former KLA Combatants Registered by IOM* (IOM Kosovo, 21 January 2000).

33. The accounts of the Likoshane, Qirez and Donji Prekaz massacres are based on the Humanitarian Law Centre, *Spotlight Report* No. 6 (Belgrade, May 1998), pp. 1–11, Human Rights Watch, *Humanitarian Law Violations in Kosovo*, pp. 19–32, and Amnesty International, *Kosovo: the Evidence*, pp. 41–4 and 77–84. These incorporate details from the CDHRF and are corroborated by numerous journalists' reports.

34. Moving on to another Nebiu house where there were only women and children – 23 of them – one police officer shouted 'mow them all down' but others argued against this.

35. At the time of writing, a painting of Jashari looks down from a building in the centre of Prishtina: he has the appearance of one of the *kaçaks* who drove the last Ottoman official out of Drenica a hundred years earlier or fought Yugoslav rule in the 1920s. In autumn 1999, youths claiming to be UÇK beat up a local LDK leader for allegedly maligning Jashari. Judah, on the other hand, depicts him as a 'local tough' and cites a local source that 'he liked to get drunk and go out and shoot Serbs', 'The Growing Pains', p. 24. Kusovac calls Jashari 'a hillbilly rogue and village bully', *Transitions*, May 1998, p. 32.

36. *KIC Daily* 1379, 22 March 1998 and *Eritrea* (Women's Media Project), No. 4. Of the 89 constituency MPs elected, 84 were LDK. This vote should have been a firm reminder to international correspondents that the circuit of commentators and analysts they tended to see in Prishtina were not representative of the whole population. *KIC* made great play of the fact that a relative of Adem Jashari voted in Prishtina for Ibrahim Rugova. At least up until the end of May, demonstrators saw no incompatibility between looking to the UÇK to defend villages while looking to Rugova to deliver international support.

37. The Contact Group on Bosnia-Herzegovina was founded in April 1994, consisting of Britain, France, Russia and the USA, and was expanded in May 1996 to include Germany and Italy.

38. Krasniqi had attended a UÇK meeting in 1993 where it was agreed he should work publicly. Author's interview, Jakup Krasniqi, October 1999.

39. Confidential source – former CDHRF worker in Prishtina.

40. Zoran Kusovac, 'Round Two: Serbian Security Forces', *Transitions*, September 1998, p. 22. The most thorough statistical profile of the UÇK is from the International Organization for Migration. Its Information Counselling and Referral Service tried to match the needs of former UÇK members with 'reintegration opportunities'. The IOM database on 25,723 former UÇK combatants shows that 98 per cent joined in 1998 and 1999 and 96.7 per cent were male. Ultimately 61.2 per cent were aged between 18 and 29. However, of those claiming an association with UÇK before 1998, the majority were in the 30-plus age range. A substantial proportion had probably lived abroad, 14.06 per cent

claiming to speak German, 12.81 per cent English. IOM Kosovo, *Socio-Economic and Demographic Profiles*.

41. *The Times*, 14 September 1998.
42. *Peace News*, June 1998.
43. *Koha Ditore*, 30 October 1998.
44. While the majority of adult Kosovo Albanians speak Serbian, only 5 per cent of Kosovo Serbs spoke Albanian. *Vreme*, 7 August 1998.
45. *Reconciliation International*, April 1999. A sixth would have been choosing a military head, especially one associated with counter-insurgency work in Central America.
46. *The Times*, 11 December 1998, reports on one such incident in Dragobilje near Rahovec.
47. In the municipality of Malisheva, the UÇK 'arrested' two LDK officials on 31 October 1998, releasing them four weeks later, *KIC Daily* 1599, 31 October 1998. Apparently they had appealed for the people to reject the UÇK and not repeat the mistake of the summer. In November, a family of some 30 people was ejected from one village for asking the UÇK not to come, author's interview, foreign NGO aid worker. A local journalist also told me about the UÇK 'eliminating' other opponents in the villages. Earlier in the year there had been agreements between Albanian and Serb leaders in mixed villages, although most seemed to break down. I wondered if it might be possible, with a strong international presence, to declare 'gun-free villages', but such an idea takes a long time to mature, needing courage and trust.
48. OSCE-KVM, *Kosovo/Kosova*.
49. 'Interim Agreement for Peace and Self-government in Kosovo', 23 February 1999.
50. *New Routes*, Vol. 4, No. 1, 1999.
51. Michael Mandelbaum, 'A Perfect Failure: Nato's War Against Yugoslavia', *Foreign Affairs*, September/October 1999.

CHAPTER 8: REFLECTIONS ON CIVIL RESISTANCE

1. T. Judah, *The Serbs: History, Myth and the Destruction of Yugoslavia* (Yale University Press, 1997), p. 307.
2. *IWPR Balkan Crisis Bulletin* 06, 13 March 1999.
3. *IWPR Balkan Crisis Bulletin* 32, 13 May 1999.
4. James Pettifer, 'The Kosovo Liberation Army – the Myth of Origin', in K. Drezov, B. Gokay and D. Kostovičová (eds), *Kosovo: Myths, Conflict and War* (Keele European Research Centre, 1999), p. 26.
5. Alex P. Schmid (in collaboration with Ellen Berends and Luuk Zonneveld), *Social Defence and Soviet Military Power: An Inquiry into the Relevance of an Alternative Defence Concept* (University of Leiden Centre for the Study of Conflict, 1985), pp. 2/–9.
6. Schmid, *Social Defence*, p. 29.
7. Schmid, ibid., p. 371–2.
8. Peter Ackerman and Christopher Kruegler, *Strategic Nonviolent Conflict: the Dynamics of People Power in the Twentieth Century* (Praeger, 1994),

p. 48. 'Lack of persistence' can be seen as a *cause* of failure, but also it is the most common *form* of failure; a reason for non-persistence may be that the strategy is inappropriate.

9. Although 'ethnic cleansing' is a euphemism, the alternative 'genocide' would not be strictly accurate, as the goal was not the elimination of a race but rather population transfer. In either case, the practice is horrific.

10. The final death toll cannot yet be estimated. Carla del Ponte, of the International Criminal Tribunal for former Yugoslavia (ICTY), reported on 10 November 1999 that ICTY had received reports of 11,334 bodies in 529 grave sites in Kosovo. Having examined approximately 195 (including the largest mass graves), they had found 2,108 corpses and evidence that some corpses might have been incinerated. *UNMIK Developments*, 10 November 1999.

11. Diary, 20 March 1943, quoted by Gene Sharp, 'The Lessons of Eichman', in Gene Sharp, *Social Power and Political Freedom* (Porter Sargent, 1980), p. 85.

12. Richard Gregg, *The Power of Nonviolence* (James Clarke, second revised edition, 1960), pp. 43–51.

13. Gene Sharp, *The Politics of Nonviolent Action* (Porter Sargent, 1973), p. 453.

14. Certain wisecracking New York beggars might be considered an exception.

15. Feminism and Nonviolence Study Group, *Piecing It Together: Feminism and Nonviolence* (Feminism and Nonviolence Study Group/War Resisters' International, 1983), p. 38.

16. Gani Bobi, 'In the maelstrom of the Living World of the Albanians', in D. Janjić and S. Maliqi (eds), *Conflict or Dialogue: Serbian-Albanian relations and integration of the Balkans, Studies and Essays* (European Civic Centre for Conflict Resolution, Subotica, 1994), pp. 226–36.

17. While I contrast activities carried out in the name of UPSUP and the UÇK, the reader should bear in mind that after Drenica perhaps 2,000 UPSUP members joined the UÇK, and the UPSUP president 1997–98, Bujar Dugolli, was made a minister in the UÇK-appointed 'provisional government' of 1999.

18. For instance, the first journalist to claim a scoop in talking with the UÇK – Chris Hedges, *New York Times*, 11 May 1997 – later wrote an exposé of assassinations within the UÇK, *New York Times*, 25 June 1999. James Pettifer has no doubt that:

> ... the mythical and secretive nature of the organisation assisted the KLA [UÇK] considerably in the early phases of its struggle. The quest of the media and diplomats to find 'the people who matter', and the impossibility of doing so, led to more and more interest in the movement, especially among newspaper editors.

Pettifer in Drevov et al. (eds), *Kosovo*, p. 28.

19. *KIC Daily* 1301, 16 December 1997.

20. Photos of Krasniqi and his AK47, apparently taken on separate occasions, appeared in the émigré magazine *Zëri i Kosova*. Reproduced in *Bota e Re*, November 1997.

21. Frantz Fanon, *The Wretched of the Earth*, translated by Constance Farrington (Penguin, 1967), p. 74.

22. Barbara Deming, 'On Revolution and Equilibrium', *Liberation*, February 1998; currently available as a pamphlet by the A.J. Muste Memorial Institute, 339 Lafayette Street, New York NY 10012, USA. Quotations taken from Barbara Deming, *Revolution and Equilibrium and other essays* (Grossman, 1971).

23. Deming's particular suggestion is 'radical and uncompromising action'. In the Kosovo context, 'radicalism' is used interchangeably with 'extremism' and is a term best avoided.

24. Deming, *On Revolution*, p. 217. Deming still used the term 'men' where 'people' would have been more accurate. 30 years later, in view of the intrusiveness of this word in the text of a feminist writer, I have taken the liberty of changing this.

25. S. Maliqi, *Kosova: Separate Worlds – Reflections and Analyses* (Prishtina: MM/Peja: Dukagjini, 1998), p. 239.

26. Anders Boserup and Andrew Mack, *War Without Weapons* (Frances Pinter, 1974), p. 163. Boserup and Mack went so far as to argue that unity is the 'centre of gravity' of the resistance, a view contested by Gene Keyes (who argues for 'morale') – in 'Strategic Nonviolent Defense: The Construct of an Option', *Journal of Strategic Studies* 4 (June 1981), p. 144 and by R. Burrowes, *The Strategy of Nonviolent Defense: A Grundhian Approach* (Syracuse: State University of New York Press, 1996), p. 168.

27. Quoted by Marie-Françoise Allain and Xavier Galmiche, 'Guerre sans armes au Kosovo: la tenace résistance d'un "peuple interdit"', *Le Monde Diplomatique*, May 1992.

28. Although *Bota e Re* and *Koha Ditore* both published an article from David Hartsough in spring 1998 arguing for nonviolence, including the formation of small action groups to plan particular campaigns, there was no take up on this suggestion – perhaps due to timing, perhaps due to a stronger cultural resistance.

29. In this sense, the current regime maintains the Titoite tradition that made capitulation or surrender an act of treason. Alternative Defence Commission, *Defence without the Bomb* (Taylor and Francis, 1983), p. 117.

30. D. Janjić, 'National movements and Conflicts of Serbs and Albanians', in D. Janjić and S, Maliqi (eds), *Conflict or Dialogue: Serbian Albanian relations and integration of the Balkans* (Subotica, 1994), p. 164.

31. P. Ackerman and C. Kruegler, *Strategic Nonviolent Conflict: The Dynamics of People Power in the Twentieth Century* (Westport: Praeger, 1994), p. 24.

32. For Burrowes, 'political purpose' has to be defined in terms of 'creating conditions that will satisfy human needs'. Burrowes, *The Strategy of Nonviolent Defense*, p. 208.

33. Ackerman and Kruegler, *Strategic Nonviolent Conflict*, p. xx.

34. Burrowes considers 'nonviolent coercion' as legitimate in securing such participation, but also suggests 'inducement' by addressing the opponent elite's 'unmet human needs'. *The Strategy of Nonviolent Defense*, Ch. 8.

35. This is not to ignore the side-effects of violence, especially war. Regardless of the level of destruction, waging a war has – either intentionally or unintentionally – a profound impact on the society where it is waged. A military struggle (conventional or guerrilla) requires certain structures – most obviously its need for established centralised chains of command and reliable supply lines – that tend to continue after the war. It also creates certain habits – above all the propensity to resort to violence to settle disputes and tendencies to exclude non-warriors from decision-making – that may insinuate themselves into the post-war society. For those who advocate nonviolence out of conviction, an important argument is that nonviolence provides a better basis for the future peaceful resolution of social conflicts, and that the habits and the structures they bring into being are more likely to shape society in a participatory and less authoritarian direction – indeed creating organs of participation and multiplying centres of initiative is part of the general strategy of nonviolent struggle.

36. M.K. Gandhi, *An Autobiography, or The Story of my Experiments with Truth* (Navajivan, 1927), p. 266. There remains a debate about how much the independence movement in India in practice met the demanding strictures of Gandhi's *Satyagraha*.

37. See for instance, Joan Bondurant, *Conquest of Violence: the Gandhian Philosophy of Conflict* (University of California, 1965); Raghavan Iyer, *The Moral and Political Thought of Mahatma Gandhi* (Oxford University Press, 1973); Thomas Weber, *Conflict Resolution and Gandhian Ethics* (Gandhi Peace Foundation, 1991).

38. Boutros Boutros-Ghali, *An Agenda for Peace: Preventive Diplomacy, Peacemaking and Peacekeeping* (United Nations, 1992).

39. Johan Galtung, 'Three approaches to peace: peacekeeping, peacemaking and peacebuilding', *Essays in Peace Research*, Vol. II (Christian Ejlers, 1976).

40. As one might expect from an assembly of states, the UN notion of an NGO tends to be bureaucratic, institutionalised and professionalised. This, however, is not the place for me to present a critique of how the UN and other inter-state bodies refashion notions from authentic independent civil society voices.

41. Towards the end of 1999, the US Institute for Peace has facilitated meetings between a spectrum of Albanian opinions and also between a spectrum of Kosovo Serbs, aiming to bring out the essentials in each community's view of what is necessary for peaceful coexistence.

42. See Committee for Conflict Transformation Support, 'Advocacy and Conflict Resolution: A Time to Take Sides?' (http://www.c-r.org/cr), Fall 1997.

43. In Pressinfo 45, the Transnational Foundation for Peace and Future Research wrote that FRY had 'tolerated' the parallel society. It is an odd definition of 'tolerate' that permits imprisoning so many schoolteachers, soccer coaches and the founders of a Chamber of Commerce.
    In Pressinfo 46, TFF said FRY 'allowed' the parallel parliament to meet. In fact police prevented the parliament meeting in 1992 and in 1998 a

one-hour session (held two hours ahead of schedule) finished just before the police arrived.

Pressinfo 57 analyses the Rambouillet agreement more harshly than most Serbian commentators. Two examples will suffice (text in quotation marks is from the Rambouillet document itself and text in italics is from TFF). a) *The Constitution and laws of Kosovo can not be modified by FRY or by Serbia while Kosovo citizens shall be elected to the Federal and Republican assemblies and governments and to its courts.* Clearly Kosovo Serbs and perhaps members of other ethnic groups would wish to sit in the FRY and Republican Assemblies, and also, Ch. I, Para. 7, 'to call upon appropriate institutions in the Republic of Serbia' on issues such as education and social benefits. b) *FRY is prevented from prosecuting crimes related to the conflict and holds that past political and resistance activities shall not be a bar to holding office in Kosovo.* The agreement stipulates that each party would grant a general amnesty for politically motivated crimes, except for serious violations of international humanitarian law (Art. II, Para. 12(b)); all candidates for public office should renounce violence; the only people barred would be those sentenced or charged by the ICTY in the Hague (Ch. I, Para. 9).

44. Ackerman and Kruegler, *Strategic Nonviolent Conflict*, p. xxii.
45. Held in Tallinn, Estonia, 21–23 July. Summary report available at http://www.unpo.org/press/0123nonv.htm
46. Michael Ignatieff, *Warrior's Honour: Ethnic War and the Modern Conscience* (Chatto and Windus, 1998), p. 101. While here I make specific criticisms of Ignatieff's conclusions, this does not detract from the importance of problems he raises or his sensibility in exploring them.
47. 'A Proposal to Stop the War in Yugoslavia', 19 December 1991, published in *Peace News*, January 1992.
48. Also, that a major objection to secession is if the area seceding contains valuable resources.
49. Alberto L'Abate made a proposal for Kosovo in the context of debates about a European Civil Peace Corps – 'Kosovo: A War Not Fought' (mimeo, May 1996) extracted as 'Civilian Peace Bodies in Kosovo', *Women for Peace* (Women in Black, Belgrade 1997), pp. 250–1. Also, Alberto l'Abate, *Prevenire la Guerra del Kossovo per evitare la destabilizzazione dei Balcani: Attività e Proposte della Diplomazia Non Ufficiale* (Edizioni la Meridiana, 1997). Preliminary general studies are Lisa Schirch, *Keeping the Peace: Exploring Civilian Alternatives in Conflict Prevention* (Life and Peace Institute, 1995), Jean-Marie Muller, *Principes et méthodes de l'intervention civile* (Desclée de Brouwer, 1997); while Thomas Weber, *Gandhi's Peace Army: The Shanti Sena and Unarmed Peacekeeping* (Syracuse University Press, 1996) is an excellent account of the Gandhian tradition, and Liam Mahony and Luis Enrique Eguren, *Unarmed Bodyguards: International Accompaniment for the Protection of Human Rights* (Kumarian, 1997) is an illuminating analysis of the work and impact of Peace Brigades International. In preparation is a valuable assessment of the Balkan Peace Team by Barbara Müller and Christian Büttner of the Institut für Friedensarbeit. John Paul Lederach, *Building Peace: Sustainable*

Reconciliation in Divided Societies (US Institute for Peace, 1997) offers a conceptual framework for peacebuilding.

50. Nick Lewer and Oliver Ramsbotham, *'Something Must Be Done': Towards an ethical framework for humanitarian intervention in international social conflict* (University of Bradford Peace Research Report No. 33, August 1993) suggests a range of questions that both non-governmental and government bodies should ask themselves about civilian intervention. They conclude with a set of 'ten framework principles', p. 98.

Select Bibliography

ENGLISH-LANGUAGE SERIALS

AIM (alternative information network of independent journalists – http://www.aimpress.ch)

CDHRF Weekly, Monthly and Quarterly Bulletins (Council for Defence of Human Rights and Freedoms, Prishtina)

Balkan War Report (Institute for War and Peace Reporting, London – formerly *Yugo-Fax*, 1991–97, merged into *Transitions)*

IWPR Balkan Crisis Bulletin (Institute for War and Peace Reporting, London,1999–)

KIC Daily (Kosova Information Centre, Prishtina)

Koha Ditore – Arta (English extracts from daily *Koha Ditore*, Prishtina, 1998–99)

Koha Summary (English extracts from *Koha weekly*, Prishtina,1994–97)

Kosova Communication (Bulletin of Ministry of Information of Republic of Kosova, London Kosova Information Centre, 1992–99)

Peace News (London)

Spotlight Reports (Humanitarian Law Centre, Belgrade)

Transition (Prague, merged into *Transitions)*

Transitions (Prague)

Vreme NDA (News Digest Agency from independent oppositionist Belgrade weekly, archive available on CD)

Zëri Digest (English extracts fom *Zëri* weekly, Prishtina)

Books on Kosovo or the Region

Banac, Ivo, *The National Question in Yugoslavia: Origins, History, Politics* (New York: Cornell University Press, 1984).

Bataković, D., *The Kosovo Chronicles* (Belgrade: Plato, 1992).

Bylybkbashi, I., *555 ... Kronikë (1981–1995)* (Prishtina: Rilindja, 1996).

Centre for Women's Studies, *Women and the Politics of peace: Contributions to a Culture of Women's Resistance* (Zagreb: Centre for Women's Studies, 1997).

Duijzings, G., Janjić, D. and Maliqi, S. (eds), *Kosovo-Kosova: Confrontation or Co-existence* (University of Nijmegen Peace Research Centre, 1997).

Dyker, D.A. and Vejvoda, I. (eds), *Yugolsavia and After: A Study in Fragmentation, Despair and Rebirth* (London/New York: Longman, 1996).

Drezov, K., Gokay, B. and Kostovičová, D. (eds), *Kosovo: Myths, Conflict and War* (Keele European Research Centre, 1999).

Elsie, R. (ed.) *Kosovo: In the heart of the powder keg* (Boulder: East European Monographs, Columbia University Press, 1997).

García Burillo, F. and Jiménez Morell, I., *Informe sobre el Conflicto y la Guerra de Kosovo* (Madrid: ediciones del oriente y del mediterráneo, 1999).

Glenny, M., *The Fall of Yugoslvia* (Harmondsworth: Penguin, 1992).

Gruenwald, O. and Rosenblum-Cale, K. (eds), *Human Rights in Yugoslavia* (New York: Irvington, 1986).

Hall, B., *The Impossible Country: A Journey through the Last Days of Yugoslavia* (Harmondsworth: Penguin, 1994).

Janjić, D. and Maliqi, S. (eds), *Conflict or Dialogue: Serbian-Albanian relations and integration of the Balkans, Studies and Essays* (European Civic Centre for Conflict Resolution, Subotica, 1994).

Judah, T., *The Serbs: History, Myth and the Destruction of Yugoslavia* (Yale University Press, 1997).

von Kohl, C. and Libal, W., *Kosovo: Gordischer Knoten des Balkan* (Vienna: Europaverlag, 1992, extract translated in Elsie, above).

Koliqi, H., *The Survival of the University of Prishtina (1991–1996)* (University of Prishtina, 1997).

Kostovičová, D., *Parallel Worlds: Response of Kosovo Albanians to Loss of Autonomy in Serbia, 1986–1996* (Keele European Research Centre, 1997).

International Crisis Group, *Kosovo Spring* (March 1998) (http://www.crisisweb.org./projects/sbalkans/reports)

— *Intermediate Sovereignty as a Basis for Resolving the Kosovo Crisis* (November 1998).

Magaš, B., *The Destruction of Yugoslavia* (London: Verso, 1993).

Malcolm, N., *Kosovo: A Short History* (London: Macmillan/New York University Press, 1998).

Maliqi, S., *Kosova: Separate Worlds – Reflections and Analyses* (Prishtina: MM/Peja: Dukagjini, 1998).

Mertus, J., *Kosovo: How Myths and Truths Started a War* (Berkeley: University of California Press, 1999).

Motes, M., *Kosova-Kosovo: Prelude to War, 1966–1999* (Homestead, Fl: Redland Press, 1999).

Mouvement pour une alternative non-violente, *La résistance civile au Kosovo* (Paris: MAN, 1994).

— *Serbie, Kosovo: Forces démocratiques et Résistances civiles* (Paris: MAN, 1997).

Pax Christi International, *Kosovo: The conflict Between Serbs and Albanians* (Brussels: Pax Christi International, 1995).

Pipa, A. and Repishti, S., *Studies on Kosova* (New York: Columbia University Press, 1984).

Poulton, H. *The Balkans: Minorities and States in Conflict* (London: Minority Rights Group, 1991).

Poulton, H. and Taji-Farkouki, Sha (eds), *Muslim Identity and the Balkan State* (London: Hurst, 1997).

Ramet, S. and Adamović, L. (eds), *Beyond Yugoslavia: Politics, Economics and Culture in a Shattered Community* (Boulder: Westview, 1995).

Ramet, S. (ed.), *Gender Politics in the Western Balkans: Women in Yugoslavia and the Yugoslav Successor States* (Pennsylvania State University Press, 1999).

Reineck, J. *The Past as Refuge: Gender, Migration and Ideology among Kosovo Albanians* (unpublished PhD dissertation, Berkeley: University of

California, 1991). (Available on order from http://www.umi.com/hp/ Support/DServices ref. 9228829).

Religioni e Società No 29: 'Kossovo, conflitto e riconciliazione in un crocevia balcanico' (Florence: Rosenberg and Sellier, settembre-dicembre 1997).

Riinvest, *Economic Activies and Democratic Development of Kosova* (Prishtina: Riinvest, 1998).

Rugova, I., *La Question du Kosovo: Entretiens réalisés par Marie-Françoise Allain et Xavier Galmiche* (Paris: Fayard, 1994).

Silber, L. and Little, A., *Yugoslavia: The Death of a Nation* (Harmondsworth: Penguin, 1995, 1996, 1997).

Taibo, C., *Para entender el conflicto de Kosova* (Madrid: Los Libros de Catarata, 1999).

Thompson, M., *A Paper House: The Ending of Yugoslavia* (London: Hutchinson Radius/Vintage, 1992).

Troebst, S., *Conflict in Kosovo: Failure of Prevention? An Analytical Docmentation, 1992–1998* (Flensburg: European Centre for Minority Issues, 1998).

Vickers, M., *Between Serb and Albanian: A History of Kosovo* (London: Christopher Hurst/New York: Columbia University Press, 1998).

Vickers, M. and Pettifer, J., *Albania: From Anarchy to a Balkan Identity* (London: Hurst, 1997).

Women in Black, *Women for Peace* (Belgrade: Year book, published in English, Serbian and Spanish editions, annually since 1994).

BOOKS ON CIVIL RESISTANCE/NONVIOLENT STRUGGLE

Ackerman, P. and Kruegler, C., *Strategic Nonviolent Conflict: The Dynamics of People Power in the Twentieth Century* (Westport: Praeger, 1994).

Bondurant, J., *The Conquest of Violence: The Gandhian Philosophy of Conflict* (Berkeley: University of California, 1965).

Boserup, A. and Mack, A., *War Without Weapons: Nonviolence in National Defence* (London: Frances Pinter, 1974/New York: Schocken, 1975).

Burrowes, R., *The Strategy of Nonviolent Defense: A Gandhian Approach* (Syracuse: State University of New York Press, 1996).

Gandhi, M.K., *Hind Swaraj or Indian Home Rule* (Ahmedabad: Navajivan, 1939).

— *Constructive Programme: Its Meaning and Place* (Ahmedabad: Navajivan, 1945).

Lakey, G., *A Strategy for Living Revolution* (Grossman, 1973) revised as *Powerful Peacemaking: A Strategy for Living Revolution* (Philadelphia: New Society Publishers, 1987).

de Ligt, B., *The Conquest of Violence* (London: George Routledge, 1937/Pluto, 1989).

Martin, B. et al., *Nonviolent Struggle and Social Defence* (London: War Resisters' International, 1991).

McAllister, P. (ed.), *Reweaving the Web of Life: Feminism and Nonviolence* (Philadelphia: New Society Publishers, 1982).

Overy, B., *Gandhi as Organiser* (unpublished PhD thesis, University of Bradford, 1982).

Randle, M., *People Power: The Building of a New European Home* (Stroud: Hawthorn Press, 1991).

— *Civil Resistance* (London: Fontana, 1994).

Rigby, A., *Living the Intifada* (London: Zed, 1991).

Roberts, A. (ed.), *The Strategy of Civilian Defence: Nonviolent Resistance to Aggression* (London: Faber & Faber, 1967).

Semelin, J., *Unarmed Against Hitler: Civilian Resistance in Europe, 1939–1943* (Westport: Praeger, 1993).

Sharp, G., *The Politics of Nonviolent Action*, 3 vols. (Boston: Porter Sargent, 1973).

— *Gandhi as a Political Strategist* (Boston: Porter Sargent, 1979).

— *Social Power and Political Freedom* (Boston: Porter Sargent, 1980).

— *Making Europe Unconquerable: The Potential of Civilian-Based Defence* (London: Taylor and Francis/Cambridge, Mass: Ballinger, 1985).

— *Civilian-Based Defence: A Post-military Weapons System* (Princeton University Press, 1990).

— *From Dictatorship to Democracy* (Cambridge, Mass: Albert Einstein Institution, 1994).

Index